Edinburgh's
Green Heritage

By Ian Nimmo

Discovering the Capital's parks, woodlands and wildlife

Edinburgh's green panorama . . . the views across the city from the indicator on the Braid Hills looking towards the extinct volcano of Arthur's Se

Explosion of colour . . . the 13,000 blooms in Saughton Park's Rose Garden is one of the sights of Edinburgh.

Precious green assets

EDINBURGH'S Council is responsible for the custodianship of 4,500 acres of the city's parks, open spaces and woodlands. They represent a resource that is central to the Edinburgh quality of life enjoyed by citizens and visitors alike.

We need only try to imagine Princes Street without the Gardens and treescape to remind ourselves of how vital are the natural elements that enhance our capital city. The Gardens, now home to the annual Bank of Scotland fireworks concert and the Hogmanay Festival, are just some of the multitude of green spaces that are an integral part of life in Edinburgh.

There have been many changes since the last written account of the then Edinburgh Corporation's parks was produced in 1914, when the Corporation was responsible for 800 acres of parks. Traditional methods of maintenance have long since disappeared, along with much of the vast workforce which diligently tended the flower beds and lawns.

In addition, a historic lack of investment has led to a decline in the state of the parks, open spaces and woodlands in the city, a situation mirrored the length and breadth of the country.

However, over the past 12 years in Edinburgh, new initiatives have been implemented to ensure that parks, open spaces and woodlands not only continue to be of value, but are developed and improved.

Parks are part of our lives, socially, physically, psychologically and add to the quality of life for the community. These initiatives reflect the changing demands on open spaces, which were often created long ago, made by today's population. For example, nature conservation is now a fundamental part of many management policies.

Botanical collections have been established jointly with the Royal Botanic Garden and a training centre for people with learning difficulties has been established.

Footpaths and cycleways continue to be developed along strategic routes. New community woodlands are being planted. Peat is no longer used as compost for landscaping works.

Edinburgh recognises the value of the natural environment and is committed to its improvement as a recreational resource for all.

The city is indebted to the Bank of Scotland, Tom Farmer of Kwik-Fit, Lothian and Edinburgh Enterprise Limited, and Scottish Natural Heritage for their generosity in enabling this book so expertly written by Ian Nimmo to be published.

I am confident the tremendous wealth of knowledge, both environmental and historical, that has been amassed will serve as a catalyst for a re-awakening of interest in parks, open spaces and woodlands and encourage citizens and visitors to contribute their views and play a role in the future development in what, in my view, are among the city's most precious natural assets.

Steve Cardownie

Councillor Steve Cardownie,
Convener, Recreation Committee,
City Chambers, Edinburgh.
March, 1996.

Acknowledgements

DURING the research and writing of this book I have received much help and many kindnesses from an army of well-wishers, but I particularly want to thank: the staffs of the National Library of Scotland and Edinburgh Central Library and district libraries; Mr Roger Jones, Executive Director of Recreation, for the support shown for the whole project; the Edinburgh *Evening News* for permission to use some of their pictures and material; the Council's Countryside Rangers Service, with a special thank you to their leader, Carol Huston; the Park Patrol and the ready support of Malcolm Fife, who also took many of the excellent photographs; Mr Bill Stout and his camera; The Royal Botanic Garden for the use of their picture; Mr John Travers of Inch House for access to his historical files; Mr Ian Woolard for his help with research into park acquisitions and dimensions; Aileen Bruce for her material on allotments; Mr John Munro, the Council's Countryside Manager, for his advice and enthusiasm; Mr Bob Watson for his historical knowledge and love of trees; Mr Keith Logie, the Woodlands Management Officer, for his valuable historical contribution on the city's trees; David Patterson of the City Arts Centre; Struan, my son, who helped so readily with research.

I am also indebted to Edinburgh's gardeners, horticulturalists and writers past and present who have touched on the city's green places over centuries as well as today's park users whose paths I have shared in rain, snow and sunshine and enjoyed their company. Most of all I would like to thank Jim McKay, the Council's Parks Manager, who set me on my journey and gave me assistance at every turn. Thank you all.

Ian Nimmo

First published in Great Britain in 1996

by The Recreation Department, City of Edinburgh.

17 Waterloo Place, Edinburgh, EH1 3BG.

Text and photographs copyright: The Recreation Department, City of Edinburgh.

Reproduction of paintings by kind permission of the City Arts Centre, Edinburgh

All rights reserved.

Designed by Ian Nimmo and John Bennett

Repro: Centre Graphics, Livingston   Print: Ivanhoe, Musselburgh

The publishers gratefully acknowledge the support of the Bank of Scotland; Mr Tom Farmer of Kwik-Fit; Lothian and Edinburgh Enterprise Limited; and Scottish Natural Heritage in making this book possible.

Contents

By the Water of Leith . . . Edinburgh through the eyes of artist Patrick Nasmyth (1787-1831).

Before the streets came . . . the Nor' Loch and St Cuthbert's Church were on the North side of the Castle Rock where Princes Street Gardens stand today.

Living Heritage

EDINBURGH'S love affair with parks and gardens, trees and landscape, dates back to King David 1 midway through the 12th century. Edinburgh then was little more than a stronghold on the Castle Rock with a slow-flowing stream meandering through the marshy valley at its foot, where the railway runs today. King David ordered that 15 acres of the marsh be drained and flowers, trees and bushes planted.

It is recorded that the "King's Garden", as it became known, prospered and gave pleasure to David and his courtiers, who enjoyed strolling in this first-recorded landscape garden in Scotland's capital. Of course, the monks in the nearby ancient church of St Cuthbert's were also keen gardeners, but their efforts were designed more for the pot than as an attraction to the senses.

As the centuries passed, Edinburgh grew in ever-increasing density down the defensive high ground of rock that leads to Holyrood. Private gardens off the High Street extended down the slopes on either side, but as the population of the Old Town expanded these gardens slowly gave way to housing. Outside the walled city, large houses and estates were created, some were fortified. Tiny, remote villages came into being like Broughton, Leith, Dean, Restalrig, Pilrig, Duddingston, Liberton, Colinton, Canonmills, Jock's Lodge, which took its name from an eccentric doctor who built a hut for himself there, and further afield was Craigmillar beside its castle, and distant Corstorphine, which some say is named after Torphin, the great Saxon hero. Inevitably, some of the large houses in the vicinity of the old walled city began to develop gardens, partly because they were aesthetically pleasing, some because they were already located in many acres of parkland and a garden was seen as improvement, others because a garden became fashionable and a declaration of family wealth. Some were created because the owners merely wished to follow man's compulsion across the world and through the ages to shape the land to be productive or artistic. The Meadows and Bruntsfield Links were under control of the city and were largely used for markets, fairs, recreation, and for firewood and water supplies. The early villages had their own greens or glebes and the houses tended to be strung out so that the inhabitants were always virtually in open countryside. The need for open space as we know it today was hardly a consideration. The village greens were in reality the first parks.

In the mid-18th century, the view from Edinburgh Castle ramparts northwards to the Forth was one of almost uninterrupted farmlands, fields of wheat, rough grazing, country lanes, woodland copses and only occasional houses. But at least some gardening was taking place because strawberries and cream were on sale for Sabbath strollers from the Old Town at the cottage called "Peace and Plenty", which stood near today's Royal Bank of Scotland's head office in St Andrew Square.

In the Old Town itself, particularly in the Canongate area, there were gardens running north and south on both sides of the Royal Mile and the restored 17th-century garden through Dunbar's Close is a delightful example.

Some of the noble country houses recognised by the Edinburgh citizenry of the times were Gayfield House off what is now Leith Walk; the battlemented Craigcrook, the imposing

---

No better on the face of the earth

"Already there are noble public parks in the Queen's Park, with its admirable carriage drive, the Meadows, the Links, the Calton Hill, Princes Street Gardens; many open spaces everywhere; above all, a situation so generally blessed and so varied in level, that we get a greater number of nobly extended views, and a larger share of fresh air than any other city of equal size on the face of the entire earth"

— from *The Scotsman*, 1854.

Ravelston House; the ancient house of Roseburn, which once gave hospitality to Oliver Cromwell; the fashionable villa of Marionville at Restalrig and the turreted and historic house of Craigentinny, whose fine garden was once the joy of the wealthy seedsman William Millar. These were some of the Edinburgh landmarks in the days when Princes Street and Princes Street Gardens were merely the top of a wind-swept valley of rough grassland and outcropping rock.

It was at this time the over-crowded Old Town broke out from behind the confines of its defensive wall to build its splendid New Town in Georgian magnificence on that exposed ridge. Based on George Street, with its principal parallel flanks of Queen Street to the north and the single-sided Princes Street overlooking the Castle and the fretwork skyline of the Old Town, architect James Craig's masterplan was rightfully acclaimed for its sense of space and the harnessing of Edinburgh's natural hilly contours to create planning drama. And as one of its fundamental virtues Craig understood and adopted sensitively the landscape use of the garden.

Craig's original plans envisaged the development of the hanging valley of Princes Street Gardens as an entity, although no indication was given of how the ground would be treated. The formal green open spaces at either end of the high-and-wide George Street were focal points in Craig's plan of the great facing squares dedicated to St Andrew and Queen Charlotte. And as the New Town spread north, east and westwards, gardens and parks also became priorities for subsequent planners so that it was said of Edinburgh by those who came to view its delights from around the world, if there was one European capital which knew how to handle green open space and have regard for trees and the heritage bequeathed by nature, then it was the capital of Scotland. This was the time of Edinburgh's "Golden Age", when creative thought blossomed as Scotland emerged into peace from centuries of

"A winter canter in the morning around Rotten Row is as good as a cold bath at Inverleith" — Town Councillor in debate on horse riding in Edinburgh parks.

A lazy summer's day on the Meadows about 1810.

civil war and religious strife. Suddenly men of genius — great writers, philosophers, artists, scientists, engineers, architects, men of law and letters — were stepping in profusion on Edinburgh's stage. The hallmark of this remarkable period of the "Enlightenment" was a great starburst of creativity, energy, confidence, curiosity and a quest for excellence. As part of that general search for excellence the focus also turned on Scottish formal, informal and landscape gardens.

Queen Street Gardens, translating a large slice of countryside to the centre of the city, were therefore carefully planned into the aspiring New Town, along with the small green "lungs" at Drummond Place, Moray Place and Ainslie Place; the value of the valley of the Water of Leith was recognised even then and below the Dean Bridge it was turned into a kind of romantic nymph-of-wood-and-stream paradise, complete with the classical St Bernard's Well; Regent Gardens, Royal Terrace Gardens and the tiny Regent Road Park, which hug the lower eastern flanks of the Calton Hill, were designed to continue the impression of cascading greenery.

The Calton Hill, of course, was the planner's dream come true, lifting its green head above the city to declare Edinburgh's affinity with its environment, as it looks across to the Castle on its rock and the crouching jade lion of Arthur's Seat, sitting in its royal park, and towards the green hills at Craiglockhart, Corstorphine, the Braids and Blackford, all of which comprise the seven hills of Edinburgh.

Even in those times Edinburgh demonstrated a commendable sense of caring for the environment. Lord Cockburn, the celebrated judge, one of those who steered the development of the New Town and a vital spark in the continuance of the Edinburgh "Enlightenment", remembered with pain how the woods around Bellevue, between York Place and Canonmills, met their fate at the hands of the builders' axes: ". . . the trees were instantly cut down", he recollected. "They could not have been permanently spared, but many of them might, to the comfort and adornment of future buildings . . . trees never find favour in the sight of any Scotch mason. I remember people shuddering when they heard the axes busy in the woods and furious when they saw the bare ground. But the axes as usual triumphed". That lesson has taken two centuries to be learned — and some have not learned it yet.

Lord Cockburn provided a further valuable comment on Edinburgh's sensitivity towards its green places when he wrote about the extension of the New Town northwards of Charlotte Square, where he had made his home: "It was then an open field as green turf as Scotland could boast of, with a few respectable trees on the flat, and thickly wooded on the bank along

Listen to the music . . . the crowds gather in Princes Street Gardens in 1905 to hear the music wafting upwards from the old Ross Bandstand.

the Water of Leith . . . How glorious the prospect, on a summer evening, from Queen Street! We had got into the habit that the mere charm of the ground would keep it sacred, and were inclined to cling to our conviction even after we saw the foundations' digging. We then thought with despair of our lost verdure, our banished peacefulness, our gorgeous sunsets. But it was unavoidable. We would never have got beyond the North Loch, if these feelings had been conclusive. But how can I forget the glory of that scene! on the still nights in which, with Rutherford, and Richardson and Jeffrey, I have stood in Queen Street, or the opening of the north-west corner of Charlotte Square, and listened to the ceaseless rural corn-crakes, nestling happily in the dewy grass".

It was from sentiments like these that great gardens grew. Although south of the Border, the development of the English landscape garden by the landed gentry was recognised throughout Europe and copied by many, Scotland's own creative flair by its wealthy classes was acknowledged even in the late 16th century. It was William Adam, the early Scottish architect and garden designer who commented: "The risings and fallings of ground are to be humoured and generally make the greatest beautys in Gardens".

Through the 17th century and certainly in the 19th century, Scotland's taste in garden style and character was a steady progression as Scottish lairds indulged themselves by trying to improve on nature or, at least, supplementing it with imposed gardens or man-created landscapes on both Highland and Lowland estates. Well-known architects like Robert Adam and Robert Lorimer tried their hands at landscape gardening, and even the romantic Sir Walter Scott had an influence so that Scottish gardens properly tended to reflect grandeur and climate, mountains and mist, rather than Constable's English countryside or the sublime sunshine of Greece or Italy. *The Scots Gardener,* Scotland's first gardening book, was published in 1673 and many of the techniques described in it remain relevant today.

Much of the land during those early days of Edinburgh's development outside the Old Town was owned by wealthy property owners or trusts. They measured their possessions in acres. In the main, before the streets came, this land was used largely for crops and grazing, but some had large houses and around the houses

Around 1800 the gardens of Redbraes were so beautiful that holes were made in the hedge so that the passers-by could catch a glimpse of their charms.

were fine gardens. For example, an early 19th century map indicates the Earl of Moray owned a large estate where Moray Place stands today, along the Water of Leith and also at Lochend; land beyond Silvermills, where the old distillery was situated, is simply stated on the map as "Mr Stein's"; Mr Jamieson's was to the north and east of Canonmills; it continued until it marched with Mr Fullerton's, which abutted with Miss Clerk's, which ran through to Mr Dickson's, who had Mr McDonald as a neighbour at Powder Hall, which was how it was spelt before it became a single word. The Rocheid property was south of Inverleith, and the delightful, secluded Rocheid Path, behind the Colonies at Glenogle Road on the far bank of the river below Inverleith Terrace, is an echo across three centuries of the dynastic family of Rocheid who lived there.

That same old map shows large areas marked "The Property of Heriot's Hospital" and "The Property of Trinity Hospital". Over the years these two enlightened trusts have provided distinctive service to Edinburgh, allowing the city to develop on their properties, yet holding the reins of control tight enough to act as guardians of the city's natural heritage. Keeping control under pressure is seldom easy. Sensitivity to the environment is not uppermost in the minds of developers and speculators and these two trusts, along with some others, have played an important part in helping to fashion their city.

Public parks were the next stage of Edinburgh's green development. It can be claimed, of course, that the first public parks stemmed from the old common grazing grounds, and the first public park in Edinburgh was the Borough Muir, gifted by David l in the 12th century. But it was the Victorians who are to be thanked for Edinburgh's splendid legacy of parks and open green places and the appreciation of them.

The Victorians believed that as cities grew and developed parks must grow with them for the sake of the health and well-being of the people. At least some of this credo was motivated by the appalling conditions of the inner-cities of the day caused by overcrowding, troops returning from the wars, the drift of country people to

town in search of work and growing industrialisation. It was also coupled with the concern that unless the masses had outlets from their dreary lives and access to fresh air and exercise they might well become restive.

The Edinburgh Police and Improvement Act of 1854 indicated the way ahead: "It shall be lawful for the Commissioners, and they are hereby authorised and empowered, to purchase, feu, lease, or otherwise acquire, such lands in or adjacent to the city of Edinburgh as they shall think suitable for public parks and bleaching-greens, and all proper and necessary access thereto . . ." The increasing build-up of housing and people meant that Edinburgh's open spaces were no longer visible from windows nor were they just round the corner. As the sight of greenery became more distant as the city expanded — into Haymarket, Gorgie, Dalry, Newington, west and central Leith — the need to create places of recreation that were also pleasing to the eye began to be re-understood.

At first, appreciation was slow. The quickening of the pace of acquisition of land for parks was driven by two clear-cut requirements — the increasing dissatisfaction of Edinburgh people with their living conditions and the poor state of hygiene in the developing city. To its great credit, once the need was recognised, Edinburgh threw itself into providing the kind of parks that brought fresh air, green open spaces and bright sunlight into the city.

One of the first truly public parks in the whole of Britain was East Princes Street Gardens. When this little nursery and private garden, with its flowers, bushes, paths and a key charge, were taken over by the old Town Corporation when the railway lines arrived, it was properly hailed as a major achievement. Although it was a small site of long standing the act of throwing it open to the public reflected the mood and will of the citizens. But how much more difficult to identify entirely new sites, estimate their suitability and usage, then acquire them against sometimes fierce opposition — and eventually allocate funds and turn them into parks. It was an enormous task and the subject lent itself to passionate debate.

The Scotsman at the time reflected some of the issues: "Will they be big or little parks? Aristocratic or vulgar? Should there be one grand park or many little ones? Should they be solely grass parks or with flower beds? Can the costs really be justified? What about rights of access for the public or are they merely to be looked at but not entered like the Meadows? Should they be developed quickly or in small portions over many years?"

The newspaper also made its own comment: "The object it is intended to promote is excellent . . . it is a matter of much importance to the town, the interests of which may be materially advanced by a judicious application of the

Plan for a new park

A suitable site for a West Park is still available along both sides of the Water of Leith, between Queensferry Road and Coltbridge and it might be extended either over part of the land of Murrayfield or on other available flattish spaces suitable for playgrounds. A water-side carriage and a riding way throughout the whole length would also be a great service, as it would form a short and easy access between populous districts near each extremity, which can only be reached by inconvenient, steep and very circuitous routes".

— From a new park proposal by William Gorrie, 1870.

Dunbar's Close Garden off the Royal Mile is laid out in the style of the 17th century and kept as an exquisite green oasis in the heart of the Old Town.

funds in question, while on the other hand their mismanagement will be not only an immediate, but a prospective and long-continued source of evil by throwing discredit on all similar schemes in future . . . the views of professionals should be sought and hearkened to . . . parks should be instrumental in bringing together the most widely-diverging classes so as to let them know the good there is in each other".

The building of public parks was a visionary, pioneering initiative and an act of faith, first steps in the field, so to speak, and doubters and detractors as always were quick to make their voices heard when trying to peer into the unknown. Access and distance was an issue which clearly gave cause for concern in an age when most gardens were private under lock-and-key and public transport was horse-and-carriage.

For example, a proposal by the Lord Provost, in conjunction with the Trinity Hospital, for a public park at Blinkbonny, elicited the objection that because it was located a mile-and-a-half from the city centre " to nine-tenths of the inhabitants a park so situated might almost as well, for ordinary purposes of enjoyment, be in London or Paris".

Almost 20 years later, with the debate over the siting of proposed parks still exercising the minds and patience of citizens, the *Edinburgh Courant* published the following heartfelt plea from a frustrated William Gorrie on October 30, 1870: "From remarks made at some of the recent municipal meetings, the renewal of the agitation for providing a public park in the north, and another in the west of Edinburgh, may shortly be looked for; and this cannot be set about a day too soon, for the rapid spread

---

Worst site in Edinburgh

"The proposed site of a park between Comely Bank and Buckingham Terrace, with extensions planned westwards is the worst site in Edinburgh. It faces north; it has steep slopes upon which the sun scarcely shines between September and March; it is exposed to all the winds; and apart from views of Fife from upper parts, it has no prospect of the city".

— A speaker at a public debate in Edinburgh, 1870.

The way it was . . . children's play-time in the east Meadows around the old chain maypole towards the end of last century.

Sunday stroll . . . this was the peaceful Sabbath scene on Blackford Hill around the turn of last century when ground-sweeping dresses were in vogue for ladies and men sported straw boaters for their walks in Edinburgh's countryside.

Take a break . . . and bread and cheese was the main lunchtime fare for these park workers at the turn of the century.

Grass cutting 1900 style . . . it was a slow and laborious process, but in today's terms it would have at least been recognised as 'environmentally friendly'. The picture was taken in the Meadows.

"How difficult it is to get access to the King's Park for the weary street-sore foot. Here is a large population in a poor district close to the healthy, airy grounds, yet purposely debarred by artificial impediments making distant what nature placed at hand. The sole access to the King's Park is at St Leonards. It consists of a contemptible lane, dirty, narrow, steep and ill-paved. And yet it is the principal entrance to the only Royal Park in Scotland". — From The Scotsman, 1854.

of house-building is already threatening to absorb, or at least generally encroach upon, the best sites for public parks in these districts. "Some have affirmed that aspiring at the attainment of both a north and a west park is grasping at more than is ever likely to be required, and therefore I suggest that instead of two, an intermediate situation should be chosen for one park only, which would be equally accessible to the inhabitants of both districts. But surely the inhabitants of these gayest and richest portions of the Scottish metropolis neither want the will nor the means for providing these indispensable recreation and health-promoting pleasure grounds, were the matter properly laid before them".

In this case, the proposed north park became Inverleith and much pleasure it has provided for generations of Edinburgh folk of all ages and interests with Edinburgh Castle and Arthur's Seat heaving up behind like some spectacular stage set on the skyline.

The Victorians idea of an outing to the park was a genteel affair. On Sundays it was expected of the whole family that they would take air and exercise, but in a civilised, sedate manner, decorum and dignity displayed at all times. It was an age of hats, of all shapes and sizes, including head coverage even for the children. It was also an age of bustles, grass-sweeping dresses, outrageous hats and parasols for women, who paraded them all on their park perambulations, husbands on arms.

Victorian parks were social events, arrival by horse and carriage, fashion parades, family days, bandstands, elaborate picnics, flying kites, adventure lands for small offspring and they gave grace, colour and laughter to the gardens.

What those far-sighted Victorians did not envisage was the extraordinary success of their parks. People flocked to them. And as time passed, the citizens of Edinburgh, as is their wont, demanded enhancements — walkways, trees, woodlands, flowerbeds, adornments and with the trees and bushes came birds and wildlife in country habitats at the heart of the city, which added their own attraction. Then the call was for sports facilities, football, hockey

and rugby pitches, tennis courts, bowling greens and children's playgrounds. To the undying credit of the city fathers — then and now — resources were found to meet the demands so that Edinburgh's public parks were as good as, if not better, than anywhere in the country and the envy of most.

But if the 19th century was noteworthy for the development of its parks and lifestyle, which put an even fairer face on the city, then the 20th century has been notable for the explosion of sport centres with the creation of facilities to support them. The encouragement to take fresh air and exercise was in the first instance taken up by the middle class and upwards, but as the parks became more accessible and seen to be genuinely public for everyone, they became enjoyed by all. Soon informal games led to challenges between one street or part of the city with another, organised sport began to be played seriously and Edinburgh hurled itself into the sporting stakes with a will.

Before World War l, for example, Mr John W. McHattie, superintendent of parks and gardens, was able to report that Inverleith Park boasted two gymnasia, one for boys and one for girls; two bowling greens; four tennis courts; two golf courses; horse riding facilities round Rotten Row; football, cricket and shinty pitches and a changing pavilion, partitioned to provide a section for elderly men to use as a reading room. The yachtsmen at Inverleith Pond, complete with admirals' caps, drew crowds to observe naval manoeuvres with their models.

In 1914, Mr McHattie had around 40 parks under his supervision. Today the Council is responsible for more than three times that many parks and play areas, including parks in Currie, Balerno, Ratho, Newbridge, Kirkliston and South Queensferry. In the perspective of those early doubters at the outset of the great Victorian parks enterprise, when anything beyond the ends of Princes Street seemed remote, Balerno could just as well have been in Australia or on the moon.

Yet some potentially handsome parks were also swallowed by houses before the sites could be secured; some parks were planned but never reached fruition, some were absorbed into bigger parks, some have changed their names, others have lost status and some — like Princes Street Gardens, Saughton, Inverleith and the Royal Botanic Garden — are now known far beyond Edinburgh's boundaries.

Those early Victorian pioneers would have been surprised and thrilled at some of the developments today. They could not have foreseen, for example, the popularity and far-reaching effects that the game of golf has had on the look and feel of the Capital. Like some of Edinburgh's famous school playing fields, they splash great swathes of green across the face of the city to force back the encroaching streets

---

Capital debate as war rages . . .

The beautiful little natural, wooded dell of Rocheid Path is in a state of neglect. Trees and banks are being spoiled by children running wild, burrowing under the banks and even mutilating trees with axes and knives. The Arboretum railings are hopelessly too low and the Tanfield end is not railed at all. The modern theory is to trust the people. It is a beautiful one no doubt, but it does not work. As long as small boys and girls have a "happy hunting ground" so long will such beautiful spots continue to be despoiled. Nothing will prevent the trouble except adequate railings.

— From *The Scotsman* letters, March 11, 1940.

and create their own visual and environmental impact. In the old days, when golf was first played on Bruntsfield Links, there were many complaints about Capital citizens having to jouk hurtling golf balls and in a verse at the time tried to get their own back:

Gowfin' a' the day,
Done nae work ava',
Rinnin aboot wi' a bag o sticks
Efter a wee bit ba'.

The growth, development, scale and quality of golf courses in Edinburgh since the turn of the century is a phenomenon. The Capital boasts 28 courses today, six owned by the city itself. Considering the size of Edinburgh it is a staggering total and they, too, help to project the impression of a bright green city.

From the 1900s to the commencement of World War One, the growth of public parks had slowed. Edinburgh's built-up area, which had exploded with a 50 per cent increase between 1870 and the turn of the century, merely reflected the 12 per cent growth between 1900 and the outbreak of the Great War. Attractive community parks were created at this time, of course, mirroring the developing residential areas of the city like Spylaw, Redhall, Bloomiehall, Rosefield, St Marks, Redbraes and Morningside parks.

After 1920, the look of Edinburgh began to change in character, sprawling away from the old high-density tenement blocks, into neat rows of bungalowlands and low-density Corporation estates. While this new Edinburgh began to spread, as part of policy open spaces were in-built to provide green city lungs of grass, trees and bushes. Those tenement canyons devoid of greenery or outlook, became regarded as mistakes of the past and not for repetition. Where possible, even those areas that had previously been neglected were included in the "greening" of the city. Although the demand for new parks had lessened as the Capital's growth subsided, nonetheless such parks as Figgate Burn, Carrick Knowe, Braidburn Valley, Whinhill, Campbell Park, Colinton Mains Park and Orchard Gardens were all acquired by the city around this time. Since World War Two, Edinburgh has seen further improvements in the layout of both public and private housing schemes with a conscious effort being made to return to those green beginning times by building in open space as a fundamental element of the city environment. They take the form of incidental, informal spaces, backgrounds of trees, grassy green lagoons among the houses, easy-on-the-eye arbours, shrubberies and greenswards to sit or play or, as in the old days, "tak' the caller air". Between the end of the World War Two and 1970, for example, the city not only continued this policy, but went further by actively trying

to provide open space and facilities into areas that had been less well provided for in the past. It was during the late 1950s and 1960s that such parks as Jewel, Bingham, Southfield, Dovecot, Gracemount and Fairmilehead were acquired, which in total provided Edinburgh with a further 29 parks and almost 670 acres of additional open space since the end of the war.

And from the perspective of a century-and-a-half ago, who could have foreseen the day when ordinary people would own their own gardens? Yet Edinburgh citizens — inspired by their own city — are nowadays among the keenest gardeners in the world, many of them experimenting with exotic plants, trees and bushes, not only in their own little, unseen, green patches behind the streets or in their allotments, creating personal expression formal and informal works of gardening art, but also in miniature gardens that surprise and delight in New Town basements. And who could have imagined 50 years ago, never mind 200 years ago, the development of the garden centre offering unprecedented choice and advice?

The identification of Edinburgh's Green Belt, so much in tune with the attitudes expressed by Lord Cockburn and others during Edinburgh's "Golden Age", is a further significant step in underlining the Capital's commitment to the environment. This encircling countryside with its unique linkages to the inner city and surrounding countryside is now also part of Edinburgh's green heritage be protected. Edinburgh as "a work of art" is dependent on its setting and maintaining the scale and identity provided by that setting. As the city continues to grow, as it has always done, to bring areas of "pure" countryside within its urban fabric, the question is inevitably posed — does the vision and will still remain to maintain the traditions of yesteryear and keep faith with the enlightened benefactors who have gone before? Or will the short-term perspectives of the speculators, developers and econonomists expunge the advocations of those who would follow in the footsteps of William Adam, Lord Cockburn, Sir Walter Scott or the caring old planners and architects who first fashioned the New Town? At least part of the answer is that there is no other city in Britain more dedicated to the task and the development of the Capital's parks and gardens remain one of Edinburgh's prides. Faith must also be expressed in the tradition and high standards that have gone before. Through two

Dig for Victory!

As part of the Government's campaign to make every yard of ground productive for the war effort it is announced that some parks and golf courses may have to be ploughed up to grow vegetables.

Did you know that if potatoes are peeled raw there is a loss of about a quarter pound in every pound?

When cooked in their skins they are such a valuable food they can be used instead of bread. Make your gardens grow!

Ministry of Information advice in 1940 as published in the *Evening News*.

The road to Leith . . . this is the scene looking from Picardy Place before the New Town was built. Gayfield House near today's Gayfield Square is in the foreground set in farm country. The familiar view of the Fife coast remains the same except oil tankers have replaced the sailing ships.

centuries there has been a consistently enlightened approach to the environment in Scotland's capital and it is laudable that during the industrial growth of the 19th century, when most other towns were expanding with little regard to amenity or recreation, Edinburgh was in the forefront of park acquisition.

Indeed, one of the first environmental campaigns fought was back in the 19th century to stop quarrying on Salisbury Crags because it was disfiguring the face of Arthur's Seat to provide "calsey stanes" for road making. And given the land values and the general materialistic attitudes of today, when the creation of public open space is more difficult than it has ever been, the acquisition of Ravelston Woods and Craigmillar Hill is a clear statement of the commitment of those in public service who still wish to maintain the traditions of more enlightened times.

Edinburgh's commitment is well underlined by the fact the city's unique landscape features, providing its special character and ethos, have been fought for and kept free from development through dedicated recreational use and are now surely safely integrated for all time.

Improvement nowadays is won by consistent, hard striving in a difficult economic climate, yet at a time when environmental considerations have never been better understood. It is a fact, however, that if Edinburgh's parks, gardens and open spaces are to look their best and be properly developed in the years to come it will take more financial resources than have been available in the last half century. It is also an irony that when the public pressures and demands for environmental, amenity and recreation improvements have never been higher, our society has produced an element of wreckers for whom parks and gardens are there for wanton destruction.

Yet Edinburgh remains undaunted. The hard work and innovation brings its own satisfaction because to a large extent green Edinburgh has substantially helped to make Scotland's capital acknowledged as one of the most beautiful cities in Europe with a reputation world-wide and a quality of life that is among the best in Britain.

Edinburgh's green assets are emeralds in the Capital's crown, created by the city for its citizens and still a joy for all who use them.   ✿

Seasons

BEFORE spring's first flush in Edinburgh the last of the wintering goldeneyes, pochards, teal and tufted ducks are heading out of Duddingston Loch. With a mighty flapping from the Cramond Foreshore curlews, turnstones, peeweets, oystercatchers and other waders join that great super highway in the sky towards the breeding grounds. In Princes Street Gardens a more famous bird — the mechanical cuckoo on the flowerless Floral Clock — is assembled and given an oiling ready for May. The appearance of the first snowdrops and crocus in city parks, before the green tinge has touched the hawthorns, has thrushes and blackbirds seeking high branches at the Hermitage of Braid and the woods ring with their morning and evening chorus. Only the wrens reach a louder note, while the squirrels begin their nose-to-tail races through Cammo trees 70 feet overhead. The buds on the elms, sycamores and limes begin to fatten and on that first Sunday in March, as the saying goes, twig-in-beak rooks are rebuilding their old nesting haunts in the Meadows with much cawing.

Yesterday nothing, today the merest movement. Almost imperceptible. The slightest stirrings. But almost certainly, yes, definitely, there is a greenness. Then it all happens fast. Across the city, winter is sent scuttling, those snowdrops and crocus splash parks in white, yellow and purple as they open fully to the spring sun; daffodils suddenly shine gold-bright from Castle Hill, then explosions of whites and pinks as Edinburgh's cherry trees burst forth, a car-stopping show down Colinton Road, a radiant glow at the back of St Marks, white confetti at East Pilton Park.

Spring in Edinburgh is clang of spade on stone as Capital gardeners set to work with a will or a groan; more figures on park benches, more cars in garden centres, more languages in Princes Street Gardens as the visitors join the scene, more chirrupings and rustlings in trees and bushes in parks from Saughton to the Royal Botanic Garden, more pressure on the city's

Inch Nursery as the sowing season begins in earnest.

Spring is rising trout in the Water of Leith, droning lawnmowers, full-throttle tractors in Edinburgh parks with the grass flying as another cutting season begins. It is nesting coots at Figgate Pond, a traffic hold-up as an early family of mallards cross Bonnington Road. And there is an incident at Pilrig Park: "Look, lads, you're no' allowed to practise golf in the park and I've chased ye before. Ye could injure somebody, okay. So what's your names?", asks the park officer.

"Walter Scott", says one boy.

"Robert Burns", says the other.

The change into Edinburgh's summer dress is easy and natural. But there is a special time, towards the end of May into early June, when Edinburgh looks its finest. A time when all foliage reaches a zenith of lushness, when the greenness is still spring-tender and full summer is rich in promise but still a week-or-two away. It is a time when even the air seems fresher, Edinburgh's images appear sharper, more defined, perhaps a trick of Edinburgh light and the season, a phenomenon seen but not understood, and for those who appreciate it is wonderous.

Now is the time to walk the Braids and Blackford Hill, to behold Edinburgh below as Marmion once surveyed the same scene, only now the oil tankers are in the Firth, but the yachts are sailing like swans; it is a time to stroll the soft, leafy paths of the Dells of Colinton and Craiglockhart or Ravelston Woods or the River Almond and gaze and gaze at the trees, sense the spirit of the woods and listen to the sounds — scrapings, rustlings, murmurings that are unintelligible but could be a mouse in the dry grass, a weasel on the prowl, a rabbit thumping the earth in warning, a wasps' bike in the bramble; then the alarm signal from a blackbird or magpie as privacy is invaded, raucous squeakings at feeding time from young sparrowhawks high above, the two-

tone plaintive call of a bullfinch, the sharp bark of fox at sundown, the grunt of a badger foraging at dusk, the screech of a hunting tawny owl locating his partner, and the distant reply.
Summer days are white clad figures on the cricket fields at Union Park, Inverleith, the Meadows, Colinton Mains, Roseburn and the Inch; a seat in the sun listening to the music wafting upwards from the Ross Theatre in Princes Street Gardens and the unmistakable sweet sound from childhood memories as the giant carousel, with its brightly-painted wooden chargers, gently carries today's small, wide-eyed passengers around and around in the shadow of ancient St Cuthbert's Church.

Down on ocean Inverleith the children sail the park in wooden HMS Edinburgh in the play area, while at the East Fettes Avenue end the petanque players strike boules with a metallic click on the French-style piste as a Grand Prix reaches a climax. Summer days are the scent of roses at Saughton, sailing model yachts at Inverleith Pond, riding the Braids, stretching luxuriously full length in Princes Street Gardens soaking up sun, a putting challenge at St Margaret's Park — a step back through time in the little, shady garden laid out in 17th-century style at Dunbar's Close in the Canongate, where the ghosts of Edinburgh's past still stroll.

Snatch of conversation from an Inverleith park bench as two elderly visiting New Yorkers rest their bunions and engage a friendly park officer in conversation: ". . . and that garden seat you are sitting on", says the park officer, "came from Holyrood Palace. Do you know what that means? It means it's the Royal Family's Edinburgh residence. And that means the Queen hersel' has probably sat on that same seat". The Americans exchange glances of astonishment and reverence and wriggle themselves more firmly on the bench.

Some say autumn brings Edinburgh's trees their finest hour — perhaps their finest hour is still half a century away as the city plans for a tree-colourful future. As the evenings shorten, colours ebb from flowers and the trees change character and dress, mellow tints of ochre and bronze and reds and golds declare the turn of the season across city parks and woodlands, unless Jack Frost nips in early when the maples flame scarlet.

In that in-between time, before summer's greenness and bright colours reluctantly bow out and autumn asserts, Princes Street Gardens knows one last night of blazing, dazzling, fantastic colour as the Bank of Scotland brings the Edinburgh International Festival to a crescendo with a fireworks extravaganza that takes all the colours of spring, summer and autumn and hurls them skywards above Edinburgh Castle in one breathtaking, explosion of light and sound and excitement. Then winter declares firmly it will not be denied. Slowly at first — and October is still fair — but the bright leaves of summer at last begin to sear, falling flags ankle-deep where the wind has caught them, crisping under foot, curling in smoke upwards through the trees as the sun lowers. Those summer-attraction squirrels in Princes Street Gardens are now without audience, but they puff out their new winter coats ready for the dark days to come.

The wavering Vs in the sky along Edinburgh's fringes are returning greylags bound for Westwater and Portmore and other Border reservoirs, but some splash down for a night's lodging at Duddingston Loch. At the Gyle, five football pitches are in use, four at Inch and a score of Hearts-Hibs encounters are being settled with jackets for goalposts in parks across the city. Dark evenings are black, leafless branches above Craiglockhart Dell etched on a lighter-black sky like the spires and towers of the Old Town; a slashed bowling green and a joyrider's dumped car at Victoria Park.

Winter arrives in the mirk. Yet somehow the haars, the smirring rain, the horizontal sleet make Edinburgh's historic past more believable than in bright summer sunshine. Cauld, dark and dreich is the stuff of ghosts and they look down from the closes of the Old Town, ancient teeth chittering above the sound of the wind as darkness falls.

It takes a million lights to make a city, and they are all spread out below, in strings and clusters, the flowers of the night. Except for those black voids seen from on high that spread out across much of the city's face — black pools, black ribbons, black seas, black holes of nothingness, separate but sometimes flowing and linking to make larger giant voids that are Arthur's Seat, Corstorphine Hill, Ravelston Woods, Craiglockhart, Blackford Hill, the Braids and the raven's wing to the north that is the Forth. In daylight summer they are green, in winter sometimes blue-white, with the tracks of Edinburgh's wildlife upon them.

These are the parks and gardens and hills and woodlands and open spaces that are Edinburgh's heritage.

Even in winter, they have their own stark beauty and changing moods, harsher perhaps, less welcoming, but there is only a cold month to pass before the rooks carry those first nesting twigs to the Meadows again and the green snowdrop shoots reach upwards in the surety of another Edinburgh spring.

SPRING on Castlehill.

SUMMER in the piazza at West Princes Street Gardens.

AUTUMN in Ravelston Woods.

WINTER on the Meadows.

City of trees . . . the northern panorama from Blackford Hill but the whole of Edinburgh is the Park Patrol's patch.

On patrol

PAPA Two calling. Hello, Andrew, it's me!", the radio handset announces. "Just letting you know a boy is stuck up the Castle Rock. Contact the police, please. But I might manage to have him down before they arrive. Over."

"Papa Nine here, Andrew. There's been a break-in at one of the sheds. They've rummaged around a bit, but it's too early to say if anything's missing. Forced the lock with an iron bar. Checking and I'll come back to you quick as I can. Out."

"Papa Five, Andrew. Some geezer is chucking a boomerang all over the Meadows. There's been complaints. Some near misses. I'm on my way. Out."

Andrew is Duty Supervisor of the Park Patrol. His office is in a hut behind what was once the old red-roofed farmhouse at Inverleith Park. It would be too pretentious to describe it as the nerve centre of the operation, because his is an informal regime, radio procedure less than correct, sometimes non existent, everyone knows everyone, the banter and good spirits reflect long associations and trust. But there is no mistaking the firm control behind the disembodied radio voices or the dedication to duty.

The Park Patrol is in the frontline of dealing with the public. They handle the public's concerns and the problems throughout more than 150 of Edinburgh's parks and play areas 365 days a year.

Theirs is a job that demands a special range of talents: they must be diplomats and ambassadors for the city, know when to be firm in upholding park rules and the law, but also when to defuse situations timely before the punches fly; they must be practical, as familiar with the parks as their own back gardens, ready to answer questions about their park's history or even individual monuments as assuredly as they deal with an an injured swan at Inverleith Pond, a dumped car at St Mark's, a runaway horse on the Braids, or a broken leg at a football match at Bingham.

Experience, practicality and sound commonsense are perhaps the key attributes of the men and women of Edinburgh's Park Patrol — and they earn their experience the hard way.

On the ground, so to speak, are around 27 officers who have designated parks of their own to look after.

During the summer it is permanent back-shift, most finishing around 10 pm. It is their responsibility to ensure their parks are run efficiently, which also means collecting cash for the hire of football, rugby and cricket pitches, checking teams are on the right pitches and that pavilions and dressing rooms are in a satisfactory state.

They are also the eyes and ears of their parks. They keep a sharp look out for all kinds of problems because timely reporting of a vandalised fence, a troublesome piece of equipment, a crumbling wall or a damaged tree can prevent a worse problem. It is true, almost every untoward happening in their green domains, small or significant, is laid before them for consideration — be it an injured bird, a gang of rowdy youths, a broken window, a damaged swing or a lost child.

In their distinctive white vans, the Mobile Park Patrol operate in close liaison with their colleagues on the ground. Thirty years ago, many of the smaller parks and play areas had park keepers of their own, but pressures on manpower and resources made this an impossible service to maintain. Now those white vans make regular checks on the unmanned areas, operating on Edinburgh's four points of the compass — Edinburgh North, South, East and West. And they know their patches as well as they know Princes Street.

It is non-stop work: check, report, move. They can cover a hundred miles a day and encounter exactly the same problems as their static counterparts. Out-of-the-way corners of the city, allotments, the caravan site at Silverknowes, parks and play areas, the Cramond foreshore are all part of their beat and when problems arise, with the help of their radios, they can be

They are the eyes and ears of the parks, they know their patches as well as they know their own back gardens and every happening in their green domain is laid before them.

All's well. . . a mobile patrol officer reports to Control at the Inverleith Park base from one of the familiar white vans.

there in an instant. They co-operate well with the police, see things that might escape others' attention, the unusual, the quirky, sometimes it is to report merely that a park light has failed — but they know it's important because parks change character after dusk and it could mean danger to someone.

At one time, based in York Place, the Park Patrol, which was set up in 1975, had also helped with the staffing for putting, bowling greens and the Ross Bandstand and assisted at the city's golf courses. But following a re-organisation in 1992, they now concentrate on their present duties with the help of a manager, an administrative assistant and four duty supervisors.

The job remains full of surprises. They never quite know day-to-day what they will encounter next or where. It ranges from the amusing to the gruesome. Sometimes they attract criticism as spoilsports, stopping boys fishing in the Figgate Park, or practising golf swings on cricket pitches or playing football on bowling greens. But they know it would take only one drowning, one person to be struck on the eye with a golf ball where no golf was authorised, one bowling green ruined because of inattention and the calls for the Parkie's blood would have telephones jumping. Such is the perversity of the park-going public that around 4,000 people are warned by the Park Patrol every year for breaking regulations.

Nonetheless, the Park Patrol still manages to keep the best of relations with the public at large. Sometimes events occur where they need the public's help. It has never been refused. Those who visit Edinburgh's parks on a regular basis recognise the difficulty of the job, the effort that goes into making a success of it and the worth of the officers. They have seen parkies stop yobs from heaving rocks on to the

railway lines, chase frisky, escaped cattle with a yippie-ay-oh, round up straying sheep, escort the anti-social from Princes Street Gardens, help a terrified youngster out of Blackford Pond when the ice gave way, comfort a screaming toddler who had mislaid his parents. They have even read headlines of how they handled an unexploded bomb.

Yet the role of the Park Patrol is changing. As the millennium approaches and the need for even greater involvement with the public increases with a range of new duties — from the care of the natural environment to the explanation of local history — their role will be less custodial, more one of interpretation and education for all park users. In the future the Park Patrol will be a point of contact for information on all of the city's parks, open spaces and woodlands for both citizens and visitors as well as an important link with local communities about their concerns and aspirations for development of their patches.

Of course, the Patrol will still deal with those unusual and awkward situations — like wayward hurlers of boomerangs on the Meadows. "Papa Five again, Andrew", says the voice from the radio handset. "I've had a word wi' the boomerang man. He's awa hame. Out". Papa Five is laconic. He does not bother to give details. For him it is merely routine stuff. But he could have said — and it would have been right— that he approached the boomerang man with a confident stride and a firm manner.

"Hey, Jimmy", says Papa Five "you're going to brain somebody with that thing. And it's no' coming back tae ye. Ye cannae chuck a boomerang about the Meadows. Too many people here. Somebody'll get hurt".

"Aye, okay, okay", says the boomerang hurler. "So where can I go to practise it, then?"

"Australia", suggests Papa Five gently. ✿

Trees

AT the last count there were a million trees in Edinburgh. It is not a figure plucked from the clouds. For example, in the Meadows there are 536 elms, 447 sycamores, 160 maples, 195 cherries, 117 ash trees, 95 limes, 67 whitebeam, 19 gean, 11 willows, 10 beeches, 5 poplars and 4 horse chestnuts. That is the kind of scientific precision with which Edinburgh's tree stocks are measured, and they are further categorised by their diameters — 28 elms between 50 and 60 centimetres wide on Bruntsfield Links, 27 ash trees and 32 sycamores over 60 centimetres wide. And so on across the city.

The problem with trees is that they can grow on you. Edinburgh citizens can walk past 7 metres of leafy glory every morning for years without really noticing. But if someone says remove it — even for the best of reasons — then suddenly that tree becomes a precious wonder, more

beautiful than a poem, as the poet says, to be nurtured and protected. And they are hooked. Edinburgh folk are like that: for years they seem to appreciate the city's trees undemonstratively in silence, until a speculator tries to take out a grove on the quiet — and then Edinburgh rises up in defence, ready to do battle on their behalf to the last leaf.

It is hardly surprising after a quick look around that Scotland's capital is one of the most tree-rich cities in Europe, much of it bequeathed as heritage from once great country estates and tree plantings by far-sighted city fathers of old that has helped to set the tone and character of Edinburgh. It is impossible to put a value on this heritage because it is irreplaceable. Perhaps the best way to estimate the value of Edinburgh's trees — the magnificence of the natural woodlands on Corstorphine Hill, at Ravelston Woods or Cammo, the huge variety

A mixture of trees in their full summer glory at Spylaw Park in Colinton beside the Water of Leith.

The forest that we might have walked through 5000 years ago in what is now Edinburgh would have been dominated by oak, ash and wych elm. The woodland would have contained lesser numbers of birch, holly, rowan, crab apple, aspen, gean, hazel and hawthorn.

and splendid specimens in city parks, even the trees in Edinburgh's built-up areas, among some of the finest street displays in Britain — is to imagine the city without them.

It is unthinkable. And that is why in Edinburgh the removal of a single tree is viewed with such suspicion, why the ravages of Dutch Elm Disease have caused such concern. And it is also the reason why the Council's tree strategy for the future is now in the forefront in this country with a commitment to develop city woodland down to community level.

The past mistake of placing so much emphasis on a single tree species like the elm will never be repeated. Like the fetish for planting Japanese cherry trees after the Second World War, Edinburgh will never again plant so many of a single type that is likely to shed its glory within a week of tasting Edinburgh's prevailing wind.

What will happen in the future is that Edinburgh will develop a diverse range of species and, as part of that same policy, the Capital is destined to become a city famous for its autumn colours to rival the fresh greenness of an Edinburgh spring.

The great landscape painters saw trees as something so beautiful that they had to be committed to canvas. The enlightened landscape architect sees trees as part of the essential ingredient of the city plan, to be used as mass to fill voids, in vignette street exclamations, as a stage set sensitive to tree forms, heights, textures and colour. At least that is how it should be. But these are the aesthetic pleasures of the trees and their contribution to Edinburgh's environment is essentially practical: they purify the air we breathe, they form the city's wildlife habitat, bind the soil, provide shelter from wind and dust and even stifle noise pollution.

The growth of cities, the removal of open space, the needs of modern living have put both trees and cities under pressure. Edinburgh has handled the pressures better than most, but they come at a time when the tree plantings of last century are passing their prime — and trees do not grow quickly. Simultaneously, in so many cities, countryside and nature are becoming remote. Edinburgh is one of the frontrunners in trying to correct these problems so that more and more in this city people are becoming aware of their environment, the need for closer contacts with nature and more people and communities are becoming involved.

The story of Edinburgh's woodlands began when the ice retreated 10,000 years or so ago. Soils had been moved around by the ice-sheets and there was much exposed rock and clay. Firstly, this would have been colonised by pioneer plants with air-borne spores such as lichens and the moss Rhacomitrium, found in Scotland today on exposed mountain tops. The first woody plants to follow were probably

willows and birches, hardy trees with small, mobile seed that could easily be dispersed. Alder and aspen would have colonised the banks of rivers, streams and lochs. It would take many hundreds of years of soil formation by the pioneer species, and slow progress northwards through a Britain still connected by land to France, for the heavier seeded long-lived climax trees like wych elm, ash and eventually oak to reach dominance in the Lothians. Scots Pine was never a major woodland component in this area unlike Western and Highland Scotland. Scots Pine expanded 8,000 years ago from northern pockets which had survived the Ice Age, and subsequently invaded Scotland from Ireland via Galloway 7,000 years ago.

Oak, ash and wych elm became the dominant trees because they were best suited to the fertile mineral soils formed in the Lothians, and because once they become established, they are not subject to invasion by other trees species. Sycamore is the modern threat to woodlands comprised of these native trees, but it was not introduced until much later. Beech grew to be dominant in the warm, chalky soil of southern England, but never reached Scotland until taken there by man.

Four thousand years ago, the Scottish climate changed dramatically, as it became much wetter, leading to the formation of peat — and leading to the loss of woodland in many areas. The pine stumps found emerging from eroded blanket peat all over the Highlands date from this time and were probably not lost as a result of human activity. Many old birch stumps of this period have been found preserved in peat bogs in central Scotland so it seems likely that at least some changes were brought about in the drier south region.

The stable forest that we might have walked through 5000 years ago in what is now Edinburgh would have been dominated by oak (both sessile and pedunculate), ash and wych elm. The woodland would have contained lesser numbers of birch (both silver and downy), holly, rowan, crab apple, aspen, gean, hazel and hawthorn. Shrub species like blackthorn, elder and guelder rose would also have been present. Water bodies would have been surrounded by common alder, grey, goat and crack willow. The woodland would have been home to wolves, brown bear, European beaver and wild ox.

Humans have had an effect on every square centimetre of Edinburgh. There is no area that has not at some stage in the past been cleared of trees, although some areas have suffered less from interference than others.

Tools found on the sites of prehistoric settlements in Edinburgh date back to Neolithic times 5000 years ago. The clearance of woodlands may have begun around this time in order to create grazing for domestic stock. A contemporary experiment performed in Norway

The green and the gold . . . autumn colours touch the Meadows with the tall spire of the Barclay Church in the background.

Spring blossom . . . looking over the treescape in Princes Street Gardens to the Old Town on its rocky ridge.

Touch of
the Orient
. . . a
Japanese
maple
becomes
a pink
umbrella
in
Lauriston
Castle
grounds
beside the
pond.

Woodland path . . . all the pleasures of the countryside are found on a stroll over Corstorphine Hill.

showed that the stone axes were surprisingly effective tools for the felling of trees. Artifacts found dating back 2500 to 3000 years ago included quern stones, used for the milling of grain, so it seems likely that woodland would have been cleared for the purpose of growing crops.

By the time the Romans invaded 2000 years ago, much of the woodland in the Lothians would probably have been cleared. Pollen records for the Bearsden Roman Fort show that much woodland had already gone in the west of Scotland and there is little to suggest in the agriculturally rich soil of the Lothians things would have been very different. Immediately following Roman occupation some areas may have reverted to woodland as fields were abandoned and the displaced population migrated north, but in the first millennium AD it would never have returned to the extent of 7000 years ago. Indeed, as populations settled in the areas colonised by the Romans, clearance may have continued to reduce the amount of woodland.

In the middle ages there were undoubtedly large forests maintained in the Lothians. The forest of Drumsheugh was possibly the principal one, and was a hunting area for royalty. There must have been continual pressure on the other remaining woodland from domestic stock and firewood cutting, but there are also signs of woodland management and by the 17th century it was observed that in the grounds of Dalkeith Palace there were ancient oaks with giant stools, which had developed from centuries of coppicing. By the end of the 17th century, how

ever, natural forests had become seriously depleted due to the clearance of land for agricultural purposes.

The Government commissioned John Evelyn to report on the problem which he did in the form of a book called "Sylva, or a Discourse of Forest Trees and the Propagation of Forest Trees and Propagation of Timber in His Majesty's Dominions", published in 1664. Evelyn appealed to the landowners extolling the virtue of trees for timber production and also their aesthetic qualities in the development of park lands in their extensive private grounds.

Two events occurred at the same time as the publication of Evelyn's work. Firstly, the renaissance in art, music and literature in Europe brought about a new awareness of the natural landscape as expressed in the arts of the day and this resulted in a move away from the formal garden settings of the past.

Secondly, the old system of strip farming was abandoned and landowners enclosed their open fields with hedges and walls. Less productive and poor draining land was planted with trees, which not only created woodland for timber production, but shelter for crops and livestock. Yet by the time General Roy was compiling detailed maps of Scotland in 1750, there were few significant areas of woodland remaining. The Water of Leith valley persisted as a woodland because its steep sides prevented much use being made of it for agriculture. Other familiar Edinburgh woods such as Corstorphine Hill had been cleared for grazing and the plantings here and at the Hermitage of Braid date from the late 18th and early 19th centuries.

A panorama of Edinburgh observed from Calton Hill and drawn in great detail in 1792 records the relative paucity of woodland in Edinburgh at this time. Trees persisted in field boundaries and river valleys and it was not until shortly after, when a fashion for landowners to plant trees, particularly beech, began in earnest. There are still many old beech trees in the city which date from this period. The fashion for the planting of elms came a century or so later when Edinburgh had become polluted and the Victorian improvers found a tree which could thrive in the city reek. It was at this time Edinburgh became a centre for the breeding of improved strains of elm under the then curator of the Royal Botanic Garden, James Macnab. Many of these trees exist in their maturity today in Inverleith Park, the Meadows and Bruntsfield Links. Some may be the finest specimens still growing in Britain and, in a few cases, they are unique.

The industrial revolution brought with it different priorities as far as towns and cities were concerned — preoccupation with economic growth and a move by large numbers of people from the countryside to the cities and towns. They became cut off from the countryside, epi

From the *Evening News*, 1994. Dutch Elm Disease was first identified in Edinburgh in 1976.

Council controlling deadly tree beetle

JIM WILSON considers the success of official axe-men in their fight against a beetle that's threatening city trees

OFFICIAL tree fellers are winning the battle to control a lethal flying beetle threatening city trees.

KILLER OF THE ELMS

■ Dutch Elm Disease is carried by a flying black and brown beetle called Scolytus Scolytus, which breeds beneath the bark of trees.

■ The 1/4-inch-long beetles spread the disease by carrying spores. The fungus spreads quickly, particularly in hot weather when the beetle flies further — and elms are "choked" to death.

■ First signs of the disease are top shoots withering. Eventually leaves turn dark yellow, then brown.

demics were common and poor living conditions coupled with ill health caused major concerns. It was out of this background, a developing social conscience the motivation, that public parks were created for recreation and to provide relief for those in the captive conditions of factories and mills.

In common with other cities in the United Kingdom, Edinburgh has planted few trees compared with numbers planted in the late 19th century. After two world wars and the depressions of the 1920s and 1930s trees took a low priority. But at last, particularly over the last five years, there has been an awakening to the problems confronting Edinburgh's even-aged tree stock and there is now a determination to take vigorous and positive action.

Edinburgh's objective is clear-cut — to establish a multi-aged treescape for the city involving a wide range of species that will achieve a balance between the physical, economic, social and spiritual needs of the city.

To achieve this objective, yet simultaneously to continue to enjoy Edinburgh's elms for as long as possible, the rigorous sanitation felling policy of trees infected by Dutch Elm Disease is the only way forward and it can prolong the life of the elm population for many years.

In arboricultural terms this means also that other species, which have completed their life cycle and are in decline, must be removed as part of a phased programme to allow for the establishment of new and young trees to provide that dynamic and diverse treescape the city seeks for the future.

It means tree planting schemes are a priority. It means creating new community woodlands across the city. It means every park will have a natural area, which will involve further planting. The timber needs of the parks and walkways will be met by even more plantings, which could eventually see a new city forest created within Edinburgh's Green Belt.

The consultation and involvement of Edinburgh citizens is vital — the sites and the biology of the different tree species must meet the wishes of local people.

It will mean a substantially higher profile for the whole environment in Edinburgh — trees, open space and wildlife — which will result in a better understanding and appreciation of the countryside within the city. It will be pursued through schools and commemorative tree schemes as part of the learning process. The dividends will also be realised in the future.

The commemorative tree scheme can be of great help to the city. In the past it has been a commendable tradition to accept donated garden seats from members of the public. Many Edinburgh parks are full of them. In Princes Street Gardens, for example, there are row upon row.

But nowadays it is more than acceptable to

Trees . . . sunshine, shade and children on Leith Links.

Trees . . . a little of everything in the depths of Colinton Dell.

Trees . . . silhouettes beside the seaside at Cramond foreshore.

Notable Edinburgh trees

Edinburgh has many splendid specimens of trees hardly known to Capital citizens far less its visitors.

Some are the oaks and metasequoia at Cammo, sweet chestnut at Davidson Mains Park, hornbeam at Silverknowes and walnut in Inch Park. Of special note are Edinburgh's elms, which remain some of the finest in Britain and continue to grace Inverleith Park, Princes Street Gardens, the Meadows and Bruntsfield Links. Attractive avenues of Wheatley elms survive at Ravelston Dykes, Comiston Road and Queensferry Road.

The dawn redwood, previously thought to exist only in fossil form until found growing in China in the 1940s, can be seen in Princes Street Gardens along with Asiatic birches, notable for their white bark, the maiden hair fern tree, the southern hemisphere beech and Dawyck beech from the Borders. A few of Edinburgh's trees have historical associations:

The Corstorphine Sycamore is one of Scotland's best known trees and a source of local folklore. It is the original sycamore of a variety now seen widely throughout Edinburgh and has been covered by a preservation order since 1955. It is reputed to have been brought to the city by a monk in 1429.

A legend claims that it was under this tree that Lord Forrester, owner of the ancient Corstorphine Castle, was murdered with his own sword by his spurned mistress, his dead wife's niece, to whom he had promised marriage. She was arrested, escaped from the Tolbooth dressed as a man, but was later recaptured and hanged in 1679. Her ghost, known as the White Lady of Corstorphine, is said to appear wailing under the sycamore with a blood-encrusted sword.

A further legend claims that Lord Forrester had buried treasure under the tree, but when a villager tried to dig it up a voice from the tree called on him to stop. No one has dared to steal it since.

In 1988, at the instigation of the Corstorphine Association, an elaborate system of cable bracing was designed and attached to the tree to save it being toppled in a gale. It remains to this day.

The Sixpenny Tree in Colinton was a lime situated at the north end of Redford Road at the junction with Colinton Road. It is uncertain how it came by its name, but it may have been because it was where the papermakers from surrounding mills met to pay their 6d dues. It is also suggested the name could have reflected the cost of pies and beer from the local inn.

Another story claims it was one of several standing trees involved in an auction sale, but the auctioneer's lunch in a nearby cottage was ready before all the trees were sold. When the cook heard only one tree was left she bid sixpence and bought it herself so that the meal would not be spoiled. An inspection of the tree in 1994 revealed that it was quite hollow with little sound wood remaining and it had to be felled. However, a similar new young lime was planted to replace it.

The Colinton Cedars were brought to Edinburgh as seed from Aleppo in Syria around the middle of the 18th century by the brother of the famous Lord Provost of Edinburgh, George Drummond. The brother, who was consul at Aleppo, had the cedars planted in a sheltered part of Colinton Castle grounds, which later became Colinton House and is now Merchiston Castle School.

The Blacksmith's Tree is a copper beech on the Corstorphine Road by the old smiddy.

Queen Mary's Tree was named after Mary, Queen of Scots, who reputedly planted the tree around 1561 on one of her visits to Craigmillar Castle. The last remnant of the tree fell in 1974, but in 1938 another Queen Mary planted a tree of the same species nearby at the Little France caravan site and thus Queen Mary's Tree lives on.

The Mound Christmas Tree is gifted annually from Hordaland Regional Council in Norway. It is a Norway spruce and measures 20 metres in height. A former Lord Provost, Dr John McKay, visited Hordaland to select the first tree.

receive a dedicated tree or trees instead, which assists in upgrading parks, heightens awareness of the environment and provides a lasting pleasure. In some cases companies step in to help and a notable example of this kind of assistance is the way that Tom Farmer, of Kwik-Fit, stepped in to replace the diseased elms in East Princes Street Gardens with semi-mature trees. This act of generosity was much appreciated and it went a considerable way to lessen the visual impact of the loss of the elms.

Although no tree is felled only for its timber because it is of more value standing, the vast increase in tree felling made necessary by removing infected elms acted as a catalyst for the Council to establish a sawmill in 1985. It allows felled timber to be naturally utilised for path edging, fencing posts and other items and there may be a possibility in the future for manufacturing items from wood

Of course, trees will not be hurried. Even planting trees now for their autumn colours will not present the city in its finest red-and-gold array until the middle of the 21st century. But by then Edinburgh's tree heritage will have been re-established with our own native trees, with exotic species in special places, trees everywhere and for everyone that will make another Edinburgh talking point and a joy for both citizens and visitors.   ✤

On watch with the Countryside Rangers

THE mystery declared itself half-way up the 100-step spiral staircase inside Clermiston Tower, which stands on the high point of Corstorphine Hill. A tiny fledgling blue tit, light as thistledown, lay dead on the 53rd iron step without a mark to indicate how it died.

The second mystery was revealed six steps later. This time it was a young coal tit, fully feathered and ready to fly, but also unmarked and unaccountably dead. By the time that little, encircling platform at the top of the tower had been reached the count was three dead blue tits and two dead coal tits.

So what happened? Had they been attacked on their first trial flight by a sparrowhawk or kestrel? Or perhaps by an owl or crow? But they were all inside the tower. Could their parents have been killed and the chicks starved to death? Had their parents somehow brought unsuspected poisoned food with the inevitable consequences?

Here was one of nature's unexplained minor

tragedies and the discussion among the three members of the Council's Countryside Ranger Service was serious. "I don't like unsolved mysteries like this", said Fergus. And suddenly — it seemed as if by engaging body-spin like a Steve Hendry snooker shot — he had left the safety of that little perch and launched himself outwards and upwards, dizzily spreadeagled like a fly on a wall, to climb to the very pinnacle of the tower to discover if the answer to the dead birds was there.

Perhaps it was merely a small incident in a busy day in the life of this highly-motivated, committed and self-sufficient little band, but they were giving the matter due concern.

Already that day they had escorted a group on a lecture tour around Cammo, fished a submerged and corroding gas cylinder from the Braid Burn, painted silhouette bird shapes and written captions for a new information display. They had also prepared a script for an historical tableau in Colinton Dell, considered characters and costumes and located the precise where

abouts of some of the Hermitage of Braid squirrels for a TV documentary. On the same patrol, a newly-fallen ash tree blocking a path was noted and overhanging branches were snipped all along the route to make it easier for public access.

A Ranger's week begins with a 9 am Monday conference like a thousand other business meetings taking place in the city. It is an update on matters arising, a briefing, reporting and discussion get-together, informal but business-like, minute taking, and setting the Rangers' agenda for the week ahead.

Around the table, in a bright upstairs room in the Rangers base at the Hermitage of Braid, Chief Ranger Carol and the four members of her team set the week rolling:

The badgers are very active in a certain site within the city; poison hemlock has been sighted, identified and action taken on Corstorphine Hill; broken glass found scattered and removed from a path in Braidburn Valley Park; display boards are wanted for a project on Leith Links; a "flasher" has been seen at Cammo and the police informed.

Who is free to take a group with an interest in birds along the River Almond Walk next Thursday? Fine, then that simplifies the staffing for the Burdiehouse Burn walk with seven kids and six adults. A wasps' byke has been found in the old stables at Cammo and giant hogweed is on the march at Warriston; two foxes, a weasel and a heron have been observed at various Edinburgh locations and, oh, another fox has been refusing to acknowledge traffic lights on Leith Walk; ah, and bad news, mountainbikers are on the loose again — apart from breaking down our woodland paths they're going to break someone's neck, if not their own; we need to talk through the Cammo Safari on Sunday and make sure the slides are ready for Plants for People on Friday.

From the window of their sunny meeting room at least 24 species of birds can be observed, but the Rangers hardly need to look up from their discussions to establish recognition. The surrounding woods are alive with the sound of birdsong and most are instantly detectable by

their "call signs" to the trained ear of the Rangers. Even as they hold their meeting, a wren — the wee bird with the loud voice, says Carol — is heard musically above the soft cooing of the wood pigeons as a grey wagtail gymnastically catches flies on the lawn.

The business of the day is carried along briskly, efficiently and thoroughly with Carol holding the reins and giving direction. Every member of the team is involved and active, working to a clearly-defined management plan.

Motivation is the key. Weekends appear to be given up without demur for a project that interests, enthuses or is simply needed. Being a Ranger is not so much a job as a way of life. Their knowledge — above and below ground, about plants, fungi, birds, mammals, trees and local history — is now overlaid with other skills designed to give them expertise in environmental management, which means conservation, interpretation, education, safety for the public, community involvement, site-surveying and recreation management.

The Rangers are also people-friendly because they have an important message to impart and much of their influential work is involved with others, lecturing, demonstrating, persuading, solving problems, giving leadership to help local groups better appreciate and improve the environment around their own patches.

Not least important, is the sterling work they undertake with children, catching them young with all kinds of stimulating ploys — from building bird boxes to woodland walks with everything from bats to badgers as teaching aids.

Part of their work is designed for the 5-14 Environmental curriculum, which they hope will develop in youngsters a respect and understanding of the countryside that will pay dividends in years to come.

The Scottish Countryside Rangers Service had its formal beginnings in 1967 with the Countryside (Scotland) Act. The Scottish Countryside Rangers Association was founded in 1974 and training was also established.

The need for the kind of service provided by them was immediately recognised, its aims caught imaginations, local authorities began to lend support and the value of the Rangers has grown in scale, respect and importance ever since.

With the creation of Scottish Natural Heritage in 1992, the Rangers now work in a new partnership but with many of the same objectives and common aspirations. For years in Edinburgh, part of the large south east region, there was only one Ranger, but it is an indication of the firm commitment of the Council to the environment that they now employ five. The range and scope of their duties also increases.

The term "conservation" nowadays has so

The Hermitage . . . the visitor and all-year Countryside Ranger Service base in the Hermitage of Braid.

many interpretations, but to add to the general understanding that it is the preservation and protection of those features of our environment thought to be of value to society — like fine buildings, landscape and wildlife — such further dimensions now impinge on the Rangers as the impact of the law, the use of resources, the disposal of by-products and, inevitably, the controlling of costs by sensible budgeting.

The modern, fully-trained Countryside Ranger is now a complete and true professional.

In a green, tree-rich city like Edinburgh, with its vivid historical past all around, an architectural showpiece and a wide variety of wildlife at its core, the importance of the environment and need for conservation is obvious. Yet the very fact of the Capital's green wealth, compared with so many other cities, makes the responsibility for supporting and sustaining that heritage even more keenly felt.

To maintain its high standards and the city's environmental wellbeing, it is important there is vigilance and a free-flow of updated information. For the Rangers this means a rolling report on wildlife, trees, bushes, plants and activities and it is in this respect their patrol system is of paramount importance.

Formal, no-fuss reports are completed every time a Ranger monitors an area, even the smallest details are noted, for they help to build up an overall picture and fill in gaps like jigsaw pieces. The information gleaned from the patrols helps to keep track of the wildlife in an area and eventually produces more effective and enlightened management.

A stroll with a Ranger is to view Edinburgh from an entirely different perspective. It is not that the poetry in the early June greenery at the Hermitage of Braid or its fine-lace treescapes against a January snowfall is lost to them. The very fact they are Rangers perhaps makes nature's wonders more acutely appreciated.

But apart from the spiritual, the Rangers also see dimensions beyond the obvious and know where and how to look: the terror of a rabbit mesmerised by the gyrating dance of a weasel on Corstorphine Hill; the dipper successfully rearing her brood in a soggy nest after a spring spate on the Almond; the dreaded tell-tale signs of another doomed elm on the Meadows; the satisfaction of a flycatcher taking residency in a Cammo bird box; the despair at the upturned white bellies of trout on a stretch of the Water of Leith, with the milky-white stains of the pollution still in the quiet pools; the exhilaration of watching an injured kestrel take to the wing again; the pleasure in discovering regeneration of trees in Colinton Dell; the concern over what caused those untimely deaths of blue tits and coal tits on Clermiston Tower; the joy of passing on Ranger knowledge and inspiring enthusiasm in the eager young faces of a new generation of future Edinburgh citizens.   ❀

Look what I've got! Rangers river dipping in the Braid Burn.

It's a squirrel! Family nature ramble in the Hermitage of Braid woods.

Action! As Capital citizens of all ages . . .

Green action at St Margaret's Park as the bowlers demonstrate their skills.

Football action at Hunters Hall Park as an on-target header skims the bar.

. . . take to the city's parks and golf courses

Cricket action at the Meadows as the bails prepare to fly.

Baseball action as a touch of America catches imaginations at Hunters Hall Park.

Golf on the roof of Edinburgh, acting the clown,

Club action on the Braids as Edinburgh's golfers get in the swing.

Nature in action as a Countryside Ranger explains the wonders of the woodlands to a group on a ramble.

a stroll in the woods . . . it's all part of the scene

Children in action as an intrepid cycle safari heads out across Inverleith Park.

Clown action . . . be ready for anything at the Scottish International Children's Festival in Inverleith Park. This group came all the way from Argentina.

Memorial to a favourite doctor . . . the fountain in Abercorn Park erected by the patients and friends of Portobello doctor Hugh Dewar at the turn of the century.

On the roof of Edinburgh . . . a jogger pauses for breath and a look at the view from the indicator on top of the Braid Hills.

String of Emeralds

A BIRD'S eye view of Scotland's capital from the ramparts of Edinburgh Castle confirms it as a green city of parks, trees and open spaces. The parks are one of the city's delights — and prides. They come in every shape and size and use. From showpiece parks like Princes Street Gardens, Saughton, Inverleith or the internationally-famous Royal Botanic Garden, to small but important community parks like Jewel or St. Mark's, countryside parks like tiny Newcraighall, imposing parks like Lauriston Castle, woodland parks like Cammo, even seaside-walk parkland like the magnificent Cramond foreshore. Every Edinburgh park is different in look, shape and character. The following is an alphabetical record of the main parks and where to find them:

Abercorn Park

Situation: Bordered by the north side of Abercorn Terrace, Pittville Street, John Street and Elcho Terrace, Portobello. Area: 2 acres (0.81 hectares).

This unpretentious little park, known locally as Daisy Park, has been one of Portobello's pleasures for many years. Nowadays it is a quiet place for a stroll, or a chat on its seats of wisdom where the old folk meet, where toddlers take first steps and strollers along the Prom

seek shelter when the sea wind bites. During the last war local residents also took cover in the park because this was where the air raid shelters were located.

Abercorn Park was acquired from the General Assembly of the Church of Scotland in 1897 and it was here, in the old days, as part of Portobello Links, that son-of-the-manse Thomas Ord performed his celebrated equestrian acts in Circus Virtuoso to the delight of the enthralled throng. The highlights of this gentleman showman's display from his snow-white charger were rapid changes of costume without dismounting, hurling discarded costumes in all directions as he appeared first as a vivid green Irishman, then a sailor, a soldier, a tipsy fishwife and, at last, as the climax — a Highland chief. His act was not a solitary affair because it was in the days when Portobello was one of the jewels of the Forth and city folk made their way there in thousands.

Nowadays Abercorn Park is enjoyed by locals and visitors. Lined by elm, whitebeam, holly, almond, hawthorn and sycamore trees, new plantings of birch, acer and sorbus, with some presented park seats, rosebeds and a display of spring bulbs, it contains an interesting fountain reflective of the time when local people demonstrated their appreciation more readily than today. The fountain is in memory of local doctor Hugh Dewar, who cared for the sick in the area from 1866 to 1914. It was erected by "his grateful patients and numerous friends who deplore the loss in the prime of his manhood of a kind friend and a skilled and beloved physician".

Facilities: Park benches. On bus route. Access for disabled.

Allison Park, Kirkliston

Situation: Off Carmel Road at the junction with Pentland View, behind Kirkliston Primary school. Area: 13 acres (5.265 hectares).

Surrounded on one side by woodlands, Allison Park, named in honour of William Allison, farmer at Newmains and Almondhill, is divided into two sections: at the Carmel Road entrance, the park is dedicated for play and contains a pavilion. The second section is a football pitch with raised banks at the sides for spectators. This area is planned for development but will eventually be replaced by two other football pitches. The whole park is fenced, including the two separate sections, but an opening allows players access to the football field from the pavilion's changing rooms. There are two play areas: a well-equipped adventure area for older children and a separate safe play area for small children with seating. In addition, a popular skateboard rink attracts young people to practise and display their skills.

Allison Park came into the Council's hands in two stages: firstly, land was acquired from the Secretary of State for Scotland in 1984 and also in 1988 from the Marquess of Linlithgow and is well-used by all ages. Leading from the park a hard and lit path crosses what is known as the Back Braes to link with Cotlaws off Gateside Road. Here is another world entirely, delightful woodlands of oak, sycamore, silver birch, rowan, beech, larch, elder, hawthorn, woodland glades and leafy paths. One of the paths leads to Pike's Hole, known more often nowadays as Pike's Pool, home for a pair of swans, nesting mallard, coot and waterhen, with a special wet area at the top end where dragonflies skim the reed beds in summer. A path traces the pond on its west side by a ferny bank with a mixture of oak, sycamore, rowan and bramble. A distillery tapped Pike's Hole water as far back as the early 19th century and the lade and sluices are still in use today by an associated company, although its distilling days are over.

Above Pike's Hole and its woodlands the Back Braes continue as a large, attractive grassed area which was once Gateside Farm land, now offering easy access from Cotlaws, an old name for what is now the Gateside estate. It is a pleasant place for children to play, local residents to stroll or walk their dogs and it, too, has been bordered with new plantings of silver birch, ash, oak, rowan and sycamore, with the sound of birds ringing from their branches. The M9 between Edinburgh and Stirling roars nearby, but the noise is quickly filtered into nothingness by the trees.

Facilities: Allison park: Pavilion, 1 football pitch, two play areas and skateboarding. Back Braes: Woodland walks. Off bus route. Access for disabled.

Atholl Crescent and Coates Crescent

Situation: Straddling the road between Shandwick Place and West Maitland Street off the western extremity of Princes Street. Area in total: 1.11 acres (0.44 hectares).

These twin Georgian crescents of elegance were part of Edinburgh's New Town western development and substantially completed by 1825. Some of the first houses of this section of the New Town were built on meadowland, but there was a reluctance by Edinburgh people at the time to take up the feus because the houses seemed so distant from the city centre.

Both crescents today face each other across the main approach road into west Princes Street and their fronting gardens provide a welcome splash of green in what is one of the busiest parts of town. Atholl Crescent Gardens passed into the care of the Corporation in 1948, but the minute of agreement between the Corporation, the Atholl Crescent proprietors and the George Heriot Trust were never executed and therefore they were reaffirmed in 1957. Coates Crescent came into the then Edinburgh Corporation's administration and care in 1949.

Bordered by low walls with hawthorn hedging at the rear both contain attractive trees, including lime, elm, oak, hawthorn, hornbeam, Himalayan cherry, Asiatic birch and sycamore. Coates Crescent is also home to an important statue of William Ewart Gladstone (1809-98), the former British Prime Minister with strong Edinburgh connections.

Designed by J. P. MacGillivray in bronze it depicts Gladstone in Chancellor's robes surrounded by allegorical and biblical female figures, while two boys hold a laurel wreath with a Greek inscription. The gardens were upgraded and a major replanting of trees carried out in

1992 by the Council in conjunction with Lothian and Edinburgh Enterprise Ltd.

Facilities: Garden seats. On bus route. Access for disabled.

Bingham Park

Situation: Between Bingham Avenue and Duddingston View, next to Lismore School off Duddingston Row. Area: 3.36 acres (1.3608 acres).

Bingham Park was designed purely as a recreation area for local use and fulfils this purpose. Basically it is a playing field next to Lismore Primary School where young people can release energy and enjoy the open space in the shadow of Arthur's Seat. It is a popular football venue with a pavilion and although youngsters probably use it most for their various games, it is also appreciated by some older residents as a place to stroll. The Bingham Community Centre is situated within its grounds. Over the years it has had a number of owners, including the Abercorn Estates, the Wauchope family, and the National Coal Board before passing to Edinburgh District Council.

Facilities: Two football pitches and a pavilion. On bus route. Access for disabled.

Blackford Hill and Hermitage of Braid

Situation: Rising to a height of 539 feet, Blackford Hill and the Hermitage of Braid is bounded by Blackford, Cluny Gardens, Midmar Drive, the Hermitage of Braid itself with Craigmillar Park Golf Course to the east. Access to Blackford Hill is by Observatory Road, Cluny Gardens, the Hermitage of Braid and Blackford Glen Road. Area: 157.3 acres (63.7065). hectares.

It was from Blackford Hill that Sir Walter Scott's Marmion surveyed the spires of the Old Town below and Burns strolled with some of his new-found friends of rank after his first

book of poems was published. Edinburgh has developed and changed unrecognisably since those days, but much of Blackford Hill is left unaltered. It remains wild and wind-blown, a large slice of countryside within the city, a place to be alone or to enjoy with the family, hear a woodpecker or watch a hunting kestrel. It is an important part of Edinburgh's natural heritage. What is also of importance is that good management and sensitivity to the area, its needs and environmental considerations have now assured it will be secured for the pleasure of future generations.

The views out across the city in all directions can still hold visitors and locals spellbound as the Blackford panoramas extend over the Forth to the distant Lomond Hills above Loch Leven in Kinross, southwards to Allermuir and Caerketton in the Pentlands, to the Lammermuir and Moorfoots, and eastwards to the Bass Rock and the North Sea. Blackford Hill is one of the largest — and one of the finest — open spaces controlled by the Council. It was created from the oldest rocks in the city, when the lava flowed across a red sandstone desert 400 million years ago. The hill is classically "crag-and-tail" shaped, formed from a vast ice-sheet moving eastwards, scratching, scarifying, exposing the rocks into escarpments, gouging hollows and valleys. It carried all before it, including huge boulders still visible, until it began to subside to a gentle slope on the eastern side.

Blackford Hill came into the hands of the old Edinburgh Corporation in 1884, purchased for the sum of £8000 from Lt. Colonel Henry Trotter of Mortonhall. A few years later, the Observatory on the Calton Hill required to be moved from the city-centre glare and three-and-a-half acres were sold for the building of a new National Observatory on Blackford Hill, where it has been sited ever since.

Several other small parcels of ground were bought later, including in 1906 the area known as Egyptfield, which contained Blackford Pond. In the old days all this was part of the Borough Muir and the likelihood is that Egyptfield, which at one time was laid out in ornamental gardens, received its name from the wandering tribes of "gypsies", a shortening of the word Egyptian, from which country they first appeared in Scotland in the 16th century. It is one of the theories that this is how nearby Morningside received such biblical names as Jordan Lane, Canaan Lane and Nile Grove.

POINTS OF SPECIAL INTEREST

The ornamental **Harrison Arch**, at the entrance to Observatory Road, makes an impressive approach to Blackford Hill. It was erected to the memory of Lord Provost Sir George

BLACKFORD HILL . . . it has all the look and feeling of a Highland scene but within a city.

Agassiz Rock on the south side of Blackford Hill is where Swiss geologist Louis Agassiz identified the Ice Age as being responsible for the grooving and polishing marks across the face of Scotland

Harrison, who was in office at the time the hill passed to the city. The arch is constructed of Permian red sandstone quarried in Dumfries.

The **Royal Observatory** moved from Calton Hill in 1896, helped with funding by the Earl of Crawford, who gave it one of the finest astronomical library collections in the world at that time. The Royal Observatory continues with its important and wide-ranging research and has links with other observatories around the world. Its work is displayed in a visitor centre open throughout the week. The professor of Astronomy is the Astronomer-Royal for Scotland.

Agassiz Rock, on the south side of the hill by the old quarries, is where, in 1840, the Swiss geologist Louis Agassiz identified the Ice Age as responsible for the grooving, polishing and erosion across the face of Scotland. A plaque unveiled in 1993 marks the location. Part of the rock which carried the tell-tale scratch marks has, unfortunately, since fallen off as a result of frost action.

The origins of the name **Corbie's Craig**, the outcropping escarpment above the quarries, are lost in the past, but it seems obvious it was the haunt of corbie or hooded crows. It is reassuring that a corbie still frequents Corbie's Craig after many centuries.

The woodlands at the base of the hill and throughout the Hermitage of Braid are of special note. They are typical of trees and bushes that were planted here in the 18th century, and include regenerated species indigenous here before that time, protected by the high banks and, in places, the difficulty of access. The woodlands have continued to regenerate suc

cessfully and a stroll along the many paths and bowers, shows examples of mature trees, trees with their life span over and young saplings beginning to take their places. They include elms, beech, ash, sycamore, oak and, more recently, larch and pines.

The woods provide excellent natural cover for over 90 species of birds and hundreds of different plants and flowers, including celandines, wild hyacinths and delicate wood anemones. Squirrels, rabbits and foxes also make their homes in the woods.

Hermitage House, now a visitor centre and base for the Countryside Ranger Service, was built for Charles Cluny in 1785. With its corner turrets and designer battlements, it is believed to be a reflection of the long-vanished Braid Castle, said to have been sited in the area with references stretching back to the 12th century. It now contains lecture rooms and displays about Blackford Hill, the Hermitage and other Lothian parklands.

Blackford Pond was fashioned by the Ice Age and has been a highly-popular family attraction for years in its woodland setting. It is a home for swans, mallard, tufted duck, moorhen, coots and a statuesque heron, which lives off young perch and frogs. Migrating birds also use it as a stopover and black-headed gulls and lesser-blackbacks have learned there is a ready supply of food from visitors. A good example of community involvement was the role played by Cala Homes Ltd, whose generous sponsorship helped to refurbish the island. It is recorded that it was once a popular skating venue in winter and even a rendezvous for Sir Walter Scott and Lord Cockburn and their friends.

Trees and green space all around . . . the Hermitage of Braid and Blackford in focus.

The **Ice House** at the rear of Hermitage House is a good example of cold storage in days gone by. Over 200 years ago many well-off families preserved meat and game in small, shaded out-houses, packed in ice wrapped in straw to increase insulation. At the Hermitage, the ice was collected by the head gardener from Blackford Pond or other ponds in the vicinity, although sometimes ice was bought in. With luck the food remained fresh into the summer months.

The **Dovecot** is high on the bank on the Hermitage Drive side of the Braid Burn. It has a total of 1965 pigeon boxes. Dovecots were once a common sight in Scotland, where well-prepared pigeon was a table delicacy for the wealthy and many landowners had their own safely-guarded supply. In the 16th century breaking into a dovecote was a hanging offence. The Hermitage Dovecot is the second largest in Edinburgh.

The remains of the ancient water pump, situated in the **Braid Burn** behind the old stable block, was used to tap a regular supply from the burn and pump it up to Hermitage House. It was cheap, ingenious, inexpensive and required little maintenance.

The area was designated Edinburgh's first Local Nature Reserve in 1993.

Facilities: Woodland walks (guided by arrangement), bird watching, children's activities, talks, videos and countryside displays, picnic areas, seats. Tea room, toilets in visitor centre. On bus route. Street parking. Access for disabled.

Bloomiehall Park

Location: Off Baberton Avenue and entered by Juniper Park Road, Juniper Green. Area: 6.2 acres (2.511 hectares).

This pleasant little park, to the rear of Juniper Green village and overlooking Baberton Golf Course, enjoys exceptional panoramas across the Forth estuary from its high position. Indeed, many people visit the park simply to behold such a sight — the River Forth spread out below, the Fife coast and surrounding countryside beyond, stretching northwards to the Lomond and Cleish Hills and westwards for 50 miles to the Trossachs. It is a dramatic scene, yet the sweep of the Pentland Hills behind, in sharp close-up contrast, is hardly less appealing. Bloomiehall Park is tucked out of the way so that many Edinburgh folk don't even know of its existence, yet it is a vantage point that affords one of the finest views in the Lothians.

Popular among local people, it came into the hands of the city in 1911, and has other attractions — a popular football pitch, an excellent creative play area complete with a commando-style rope pyramid and an attractive shrubbery, which includes yew, holly, sorbus, privet,

BLACKFORD POND

. . . a product of the Ice Age, it is now a haven for swans, ducks and a host of other birds and a magic place for children. Sir Walter Scott and Lord Cockburn met here. It was once a popular place in winter for ice skating.

rowan, sycamore, lime and willow. A border of sycamores is on the north side and there are park benches and a gravel path.

Facilities: Football pitch, play area, and benches. Access for disabled.

The Braid Hills

Location: Bounded by Braid Hills Drive in the north, Braid Road and Buckstone in the west, Frogston Road in the south and Alnwickhill in the east. Area: 231.5 acres (93.7575 hectares).

The Braid Hills rise to a height of 675 feet and afford spectacular views on all sides. They are partially covered in whin, wild roses with patches of bramble, a sheer delight for the beholder, but at times a curse for the golfers when the Braids attract the kind of windpower that bends tee-shots. It is a phenomenon known to every Braids regular who wields a club up there in the clouds — along with scorching sun, raging downpours, North Pole blizzards and at times impenetrable fog. It has been said the four seasons of the year can be encountered on the Braids in a single round. The Braids have been called "the father of municipal golf courses" and they remain one of the most popular and challenging.

Edward l camped here in 1298 on one of his forays northwards and Cromwell surveyed the city from its heights, an eagle's perspective before laying his campaign plans to take Edinburgh Castle in 1650. But the battles for golfing glory, pride of club and silver trophies, tactical manoeuvrings and all-out assaults over terrain that would daunt a goat, have long since eclipsed events in mere history books.

From this lofty perch Edinburgh's great good fortune and heritage is at once declared and remarked upon by today's observers — the great swathe of almost unbroken green open space that stretches from the Braids, across Blackford Glen to Blackford Hill, leads into Craigmillar Park Golf Course, through to the Inch Park and Edinburgh University Sports Ground, then broadening and diffusing into the green area around Craigmillar Castle, Prestonfield Golf Course and on to Arthur's Seat and Duddingston. Most cities would lend their souls for such an inheritance.

The Braids were purchased by the Edinburgh Corporation in 1890 with authorisation from the Edinburgh and Police Extension Act "to be used in all time coming for the purpose of a public park and pleasure and recreation ground for the use of the inhabitants of Edinburgh". At that time the transaction did not include the whole of the Braids as we know them today and some 22 acres along the Liberton Road were

leased. As the years passed, further leasings and acquisitions took place and when the country was gripped by golfing fever there was no better site to construct a golf course. The first of the Braids courses was opened by Lord Provost John Boyd on May 29, 1889. The golfers from those distant times would hardy recognise the place today — now with two testing 18-hole courses, excellent facilities, including a fine clubhouse, changing rooms, professional help and an entertainment suite.

Although more than 70,000 golfers play the Braids every year and they are home base for a number of well-known Edinburgh golf clubs, one of their characteristics is that in spite of the large numbers of golfers who use them and the fickleness of Scotland's weather, the fairways and greens are kept to a very high standard.

It is also reassuring, after all these years, that the Braids continue to fulfil the purpose for which they were first purchased. From the beginning they have always attracted walkers and that tradition continues. In the past the interests of golfers and walkers have not always been easily accommodated, but nowadays both respect each other's rights of access and their separate pleasures of tramping this high and special place within the city where the larks still sing. Nowadays the Braids is the only park in the city where horse riding is permitted. On the highest point an indicator pinpoints local landmarks, hill ranges and distant mountains as far away as Ben Lomond, Ben More above Crianlarich, Beinn A Ghlo by Blair Atholl and the Sidlaws near Dundee. Erected in 1995 as a plinth set on three legs of Dumfries red sandstone, the indicator provides a 360-degree sweep, and includes height, distances and information about how the landscape was fashioned and major historical events. The indicator was financed and designed by local residents George Russell and John Bartholomew.

Facilities: Walking, golf, riding. Near a bus route. Access for disabled.

Braidburn Valley Park

Situation: Bounded by Comiston Road and Greenbank Crescent. Area: 27.5 acres (11.1375 hectares).

This delightful, elongated park forms a natural hanging valley below the busy Comiston Road. A stroll through Braidburn Valley Park is like a walk in the countryside with its steep sides, the Braid Burn overhung in parts by brambles, willows and hawthorn and with the Pentland Hills spreading across the southern horizon.

Acquired in 1933 for the city, a handsome pair of iron gates, once the entrance to Comiston

THE BRAID HILLS . . . the wilderness viewed from Blackford Hill with the Pentland tops in the background.

BRAIDBURN VALLEY PARK . . . looking across the Braid Burn to Hillend and the Pentland Hills.

BRUNTSFIELD LINKS . . . a green place to relax and enjoy but there are still those with golf clubs as a reminder of the glory years.

House, with the initials of King George and the Queen Mother set into them, form the northern Greenbank Crescent main entrance. Some say the contours of the valley at this point create an optical illusion to give the impression that the Braid Burn is flowing uphill, before it disappears from sight under Comiston Road to continue its way through to the Hermitage of Braid.

Trees are one of the features of the park and landscaped sensitively so that the sense of countryside is enhanced. Groves of cherry trees, a stately fringe of Wheatley elm along Comiston Road, a miniature woodland of elm, beech, sycamore, holly and a shrubbery at the main gate lend the park interest and depth. The wilderness area of hawthorn, elder, bramble, ivy and dog rose on the bank behind Greenbank Crescent Gardens is a natural habitat for wildlife and the park is full of birdsong. A notable feature are the hornbeams which form a frame to what was the old open air-stage. Country-style paths run on both sides of the burn, across three bridges and the grassy ridges on the western bank marks what was once the seats when Braidburn Valley Park had its own open-air theatre. A close look at the quiet pools in the burn reassuringly confirm that minnows and small trout continue to thrive there. With the rolling Pentlands as a backdrop, the sound of the burn, the country paths and the attractive treescape it could be a Peeblesshire glen.

It is a much-used and attractive park, a favourite strolling area for local people, those with dogs to exercise and family outings. Benches are placed at intervals along the main path. Braidburn Valley Park is a natural extension of the Hermitage of Braid and a possible site for a municipal arboretum, where indigenous tree species could be established. It is another of those important Edinburgh parks which continues the green linkages between the hills in the south to the sea.

Facilities: Walking paths, park benches. On bus route. Access for disabled.

Brighton Park

Situation: Off Brighton Place, bounded by Brighton Crescent and Sandford Gardens. Area: 2.1 acres (0.8505 hectares).

Brighton Park retains some of the atmosphere of old Portobello, when it was a fashionable seaside resort and many of the well-to-do of Edinburgh society had a summer home in the town or even preferred to take its bracing air as permanent residents. The Brighton development dates to 1823 and the park, though small and essentially a sitting-out area, still reflects some of the elegance of the buildings around it. The 18th-century stone sundial, which sits in a corner beside Brighton Place, merely adds to the impression of a past age.

It is nowadays a place for a quiet stroll to take the air, a seat in the sun to peruse the morning papers, chat to friends or contemplate the mass of Arthur's Seat. Surrounded by a privet hedge, Brighton Park has a fine shrubbery of varieties of holly, cotoneaster, berberis, hawthorn, forsythia, flowering currant and other shrubs and bushes bordering its central green sward. There are also peripheral displays of roses and a spring bulb show. Those who live in neighbouring streets are fortunate to have such a pleasing garden on their doorsteps.

Facilities: A pathway and park benches. On bus route. Access for disabled.

Bruntsfield Links

Situation: Bounded by the south side of Melville Drive and extending beyond Whitehouse Loan to Bruntsfield Place, Terrace and Crescent. Area: 36.2 acres (14.661 hectares).

Bruntsfield Links is the easterly part of what was the famous old Borough Muir, where in 1513 King James lV reviewed his troops before they set off to the fatal field of Flodden. The Borough Muir or Myre was gifted to the "Magistrates, Council and Community of the City" by David l of Scotland and once extended westwards from what is now the Dalkeith Road area to Merchiston, and southwards to the Pow Burn.

In those ancient times, not only did the moor abound with oak trees, but outlaws and Edinburgh outcasts made it their home. It was not a place to be caught after dark, but the Scottish nobility once used it for their hunting ground, when deer and wild boar were plentiful.

"Great stone quarries" are recorded on the site and old Edinburgh Town Council minutes indicate that one Patrick Carfrae, deacon of the masons, was given permission to dig for stones there in 1599. Quarrying continued on the Links for at least 200 years and rightful concern was expressed from time to time about their depth and danger.

Up to 1878 it was upheld by the magistrates and Council as a portion of the Common Good property and in 1741 an important priority was declared in the contract with John Hog, who had been given permission to "dig for stanes" for the refurbishment of tenements at the Luckenbooths. On no account, he was instructed, must he interfere in any way or on any part of the Links used for "the citizens' diversion and recreation in the golf".

"The Gowf" took precedence over everything, from stopping a road being built through the park to the prevention of exercising horses. Even Sir Walter Scott, in his capacity as secretary of the Royal Edinburgh Light Dragoons, was informed that drilling his troops on the Links' most hallowed golfing turf would not be permitted. The Links became the home of several golf clubs, the most ancient being today's Royal Burgess club, which traces its roots back to 1735.

 As the city expanded and increasing feus were allocated, first houses and then the streets began to eat into this important green space, until the Edinburgh Improvement Act of 1827 called a halt to the encroachment. Those dearly-defended 30 acres today are one of the prides of the Bruntsfield area with their splendid presentations of elm, sycamore, maple, ash, lime, white

beam and other varieties like cherry, hawthorn, chestnut, crab apple and oak. They make summer a visual treat. Apart from a stone seat at the highest point, bearing initials and several dates, the oldest being 1848, there are no reminders of the past other than the popular putting green at Bruntsfield Place. But like those ancient golfers who swung their way with vigour across the Links that same pleasure of a stroll over one of Edinburgh's green delights continues today for local residents and visitors alike.

Facilities: Short golf course, putting, walks, benches and toilets. On bus route. Access for disabled.

Burdiehouse Burn Park

Situation: Off Captain's Road, following Burdiehouse Burn, divided by Lasswade Road and Gilmerton Dykes Street. Area: 14.5 acres (5.8725 hectares).

Created when the Burdiehouse and Southhouse housing schemes were built in 1955, Burdiehouse Burn Park follows the natural valley of the burn, which forms a green trail for several miles across the city.

The park is designed to provide space, a leisure outlet and freedom to roam for the residents of these two schemes and its position high above the city on its southern edge, with fields and the Pentland Hills beyond, creates a sense of open countryside.

It has been identified as a site for the development of a community woodland project. Burdiehouse Burn is a natural feature, a dirt track follows its route and on its far bank an uncut, wild grassland area is a small child's adventure ground. Burdiehouse Primary School is situated within the park at its top end.

At the southern section of the park there is a natural amphitheatre and it is here football and other games are played. A safe play area for young children is attached to the community centre.

Wood sculptures are placed around the park — a giraffe's head, a giant dragonfly, a canoe, a totem pole, an otter, a small monster with a happy grin on its face — which add interest to the pleasant stroll along the burn.

On the other side of Lasswade Road, where the park continues, and over Gilmerton Dykes Road, trees and bushes become an increasing feature along the line of the burn. Although the park ends near the foot of Gilmerton Dykes Crescent in a pleasant setting of sycamores, hawthorn, hornbeam and elder trees, with scattered pink and white dog roses, a narrow right-of way track continues past towering banks of sycamore, ash, cherry, elder, holly and hawthorn, overgrown ground cover of bramble and some wild raspberry, with the scent of mint close to the burn bank. The path leads to Ellen's Glen in its woodland setting. It is remarkable that such a rural scene, alive with birdlife, the open park and its winding burn, can be sustained in what in reality is a densely-populated part of town. Plans for a new community woodland will help to transform the more exposed elements of the site.

Facilities: Football, a community centre and safe play area. On bus route. Difficult for disabled.

Cairntows Park

Situation: On the busy junction of Niddrie Mains Road, Duddingston Road West and Craigmillar Castle Road. Area: 4.4 acres (1.782 hectares).

Also known as Craigmillar Park, this tiny green handkerchief of grassland, little more than a village green, was owned by the Liberton Trust and purchased by the Council in 1992. It may be basic in amenities, but it nonetheless remains highly popular and bursting with activity. In a densely-populated part of town, it attracts young and old to stroll or play games safely on the grass and is fenced off from the surrounding busy roads. Football is one of its main interests and there is a pavilion and small pieces of equipment for young children. Young maples have been planted and a fine avenue of elms still makes an attractive summer sight.

Facilities: A football pitch, pavilion and play area. On bus route. Access for disabled but some entrances with steps.

The Calton Hill

Situation: Calton Hill is bounded by Regent Road, Royal Terrace and Greenside. Area: 22.2 acres (8.991 hectares).

The Calton Hill, that rocky little knoll rising to

355 feet above sea level, almost at the east end of Princes Street, provides Edinburgh citizens with the finest grandstand view of their city. This was Robert Louis Stevenson's favourite prospect, a "field of monuments", as he called it, with stunning panoramas at every turn of the head. The story of Scotland has virtually unfolded around its tree-clad slopes, where the gorse and broom shine bright yellow in springtime, and it remains a special place in Scotland's capital with a fascinating history of its own.

Its commanding situation above the city has singled out the Calton Hill for special treatment through the centuries and it hosts a number of important monuments.

Perhaps the most significant and certainly the most dramatic are the 12 classical columns in Craigleith sandstone of the National Monument, erected to those who fell in the Napoleonic Wars. The Monument, partially constructed during Edinburgh's "Greek" period, turns the Calton Hill into a mini Acropolis. The width of the paths to the top of the hill bear witness to the effort and difficulty of hauling up the huge blocks, which was reportedly accomplished by 12 horses and 70 men. The spread of the New Town along its eastern flanks and the creation of Regent Road has tended to size down the Calton Hill's perspective, but its slopes stretch down to Abbeyhill, Calton Road, with its cliffs and crags, and the aptly-named Hillside Crescent off London Road is merely a further extension.

It is suggested the derivation of Calton or Caldoun is a hill covered in bushes, but it could also have been from the Gaelic Choille-dun. From earliest times the summit seemed devoid of trees, as it almost remains today, and superstitions abounded about the reason, although it seems Calton Hill elves, who foregathered there at the sound of the Fairy Boy's drumbeat, had a clearly established connection. Even hazel trees planted in recent times failed to survive, although on other parts of the hill ash and sycamores flourish robustly. It has been called the Black Craig, probably from the Gaelic dhu in respect of its dark volcanic rock, also the Dow Craig, and the high knoll on the south side was the Miller's Craig. A public hanging took place on the hill in 1554 and the City Accounts at the time read ". . . for taking of ane gret gibet furth of the Nether Tolbooth, to haif hangit hommill (beardless) Jok on. . . Item for chords to bynd and hang him with . . . ". A Carmelite Monastery once stood in Greenside, but it is now long gone without trace.

One of the first recorded involvements with the Town Council was in 1456, when King James ll granted "Edinburghers" a tract of ground called the Greenside "for the purpose of holding tilts and tournaments thereon". It later became the

CALTON HILL . . . and sunset throws the Capital landmarks of the Nelson Monument and the National Memorial into silhouette.

Calton Hill cannon . . . it has a colourful history dating back to Portugal in 1622 but also saw service in Burma.

site of a lepers' hospital and such was the fear in those days of that dreaded disease that the punishment for those who tried to leave was a hanging. As a chilling reminder a gibbet was erected in the hospital grounds. In 1725, after the Town Council purchased the Caltoun Craigs from Lord Balmerino, a charter was obtained from King George 1 turning it into a Burgh of Barony.

Apart from the building of the Bridewell by Robert Adam in 1795, to partially replace the squalid old city jail in the Canongate, it was the expanding eastern development of the New Town that began to change the face of the Calton Hill.

With the difficult spanning of the gorge by the Regent Bridge in 1819, Georgian splendour began to attire Calton Hill's wind-swept flanks. The new buildings broke the gridiron pattern of the first New Town based on George Street with its recurring theme of parallelograms, and were fitted instead to the changing contours of the hillside. The classically-magnificent Royal Terrace, with its Ionic and Corinthian colonnades, stretches for a quarter-of-a-mile as a single block of one facade, while Regent Terrace displays Greek Doric porches, iron balconies and railings. But what is also important is that the buildings have been softened and their attraction enhanced by the fresh green shades of gardens and trees all around.

Indeed, the terrace gardens reach high on the hillside and were even used as an inducement to tempt would-be householders out of central Edinburgh and across the gorge. They were envisaged as the Calton Hill Pleasure Ground and in 1830 Regius Professor of Botany and Keeper of the Royal Botanic Garden, Robert Graham and Dr Patrick Neill, a well-known botanist and horticulturist, gave professional advice about design, trees and plants. They remain today a private pleasure ground, rich in birdsong, and although Whisky Row, as it was once called because many of its wealthy merchants could watch their cargoes sail up the Forth from drawing room windows, may not nowadays so easily view the Forth for trees in summer foliage, it is a small price to pay for their delight and beauty of the country landscape.

Over the years, a number of important monuments, memorials and landmarks have been erected on Calton Hill, which those early city planners chose almost as a symbolic site to display all that was finest in the extraordinary classical flowering in the second half of the 18th century. The most interesting of these adornments are:

The **Nelson Monument** was the first memorial to be placed upon the bare hilltop to commemorate the exploits of Lord Nelson at a time when the Napoleonic Wars were vivid in the minds of the people. Designed by William Burn in 1807 it is over 30 metres high and built in six sections like an inverted telescope. Above the entrance sits a carving of Admiral Cordova's flagship, with its 112 guns, which Nelson defeated at St. Vincent. At one time, Nelson dinners were held here, but the old traditions are still maintained on Trafalgar Day in October when the flags are flown to spell out Nelson's famous message: "England expects that every man this day will do his duty". Visitors remain intrigued to note that every time the One O' Clock Gun is fired from Edinburgh Castle, a time-ball falls from the top of the monument as if some crackshot on the ramparts was incapable of missing. The tower is also used as a guide for Forth shipping. The contours of the hill at this point, when viewed from Holyrood, are claimed to form a profile which resembles Nelson.

The **National Memorial** to commemorate those who died in the Napoleonic Wars was planned as a replica of the Parthenon. It is identified as the "ruined Greek temple" observed from Princes Street that catches the eye and imagination of visitors. Designed by William Playfair and C. R. Cockerell, the foundation stone was laid by George IV in 1822 amid booming cannon and cheering crowds.

The grand scheme did not catch the imagination of the public who were expected to help to meet the cost with a subscription. In spite of the initial enthusiasm and effort — it took 12 horses and 70 men to haul the giant stones to the top of the hill — only the base and 12 columns were completed. When it became clear no further funds were forthcoming, the scaffolding was removed and it has remained in its unfinished state ever since. Nonetheless, this classical folly lends tone and drama to the Edinburgh panorama and nowadays it is seen as a valuable and historic backdrop.

The **Old Observatory** was built to a less-than-distinguished design by James Craig in 1792. It was never used for the purpose for which it was created and was eventually turned into a fortified tower occupying a corner of the **New Observatory's** boundary wall.

The New Observatory was the work of William Playfair in 1818 and again reflects Edinburgh's flirtation with classical Greece. It consists of a 62-feet central cross, with four projecting pediments supported by six columns fronting the four points of the compass. At the southern corner there is a small monument to John Playfair, president of the Astronomical Association at the time, who was the architect's uncle and professor of mathematics at Edinburgh University.

The Dugald Stewart Monument to the Professor of Moral Philosophy at Edinburgh University, lecturer in mathematics, astronomy and renowned mind of his day, was based on the monument to Lysicrates in the Acropolis. It overlooks Princes Street at the top of the Waterloo Place stairs and is shaped as a cupola with nine fluted Corinthian pillars with a central urn.

The **Burns Monument** on the south side of Regent Road, opposite the old Royal High School building, and at the top of the track known as Jacob's Ladder, is again a circular Corinthian temple by Thomas Hamilton, built in 1830, with a roof in a somewhat bigger version of the choragic monument of Lysicrates. At one time it contained a small collection of Burns artefacts but these have now been removed to other Edinburgh museums. It was originally planned to serve as a shrine for the Flaxman statue of Burns.

The **Old Royal High School** building on Regent Road was carved out of the hillside in the likeness of the Temple of Theseus in Athens and designed by former Royal High pupil Thomas Hamilton in 1825. The Royal High School has always played an important part in Edinburgh and includes among its former pupils Sir Walter Scott, three Lord Chancellors an Archbishop of Canterbury as well as many famous names in almost every profession. It was felt something classically special should be created for the removal of the school from the Old Town to the New Town and, as a result, it is one of the most magnificent representative buildings of Edinburgh's Greek period. Presently it belongs to the Council and has been linked with the possibility that one day it will house a Scottish Assembly or even a Scottish Parliament.

Calton Jail was at the top of the cliff above Calton Road where St. Andrew's House stands today. All that is left is the castle-like block that was the Governor's house and Bridewell. It declares something of the times that even a prison building had to be of architectural excellence and therefore the celebrated Robert Adam was chosen as architect and the Bridewell was completed in 1795, although the wisdom of placing a jail on such a prominent site and so close to the city centre was debatable. Lord Cockburn thought "it was a piece of undoubted bad taste to give so glorious eminence to a prison". There was a platform on its roof for the execution of prisoners and the Calton Hill above provided another grandstand view of the proceedings. The jail closed in 1925 and the last woman to be hanged there was Jessie Kean, the Stockbridge child murderess.

The **Calton Hill Cannon**: the old brass cannon aimed at Princes Street, which features in many of the photographs taken from the hill, has a colourful background. It was made in Portugal in 1622 and found its way to the Portuguese East Indies. The Burmese captured it from the King of Arakan in 1785 and the inscription in Burmese on the cannon records the action. In 1885 it came into British hands after the capture of Mandalay and was eventually given to Edinburgh. At one time there were six cannons on Calton Hill, but the need in 1940 for scrap metal for armaments saw the others consigned to a further if less glorious war-like use.

St Andrew's House is the home of the Scottish Office where the Secretary of State for Scotland and his ministers hold sway with their senior civil servants. It remains an important building in the genre of the 1930s.

The **Singing Stars Plaque** at the entrance to the Calton Hill at Waterloo Place is little known but commemorates three Scots who found fame on the world stage in the 19th century: John Wilson made his name as a tenor in Covent Garden and Drury Lane and was popular as a singer of Scots songs; John Templeton was another tenor acclaimed in Drury Lane and opera houses around the world and David Kennedy also began as a baritone chorister who concentrated on the songs of Scotland.

Facilities: Viewpoint, bus and car park, park benches. Off bus route. Access for disabled.

Cammo Estate Park

Situation: Bordered by Cammo Road, off Queensferry Road and Cammo Walk on the western edge of the city. Area: 100 acres (40.5 hectares).

The story of Cammo House and its gardens is deeply woven into Edinburgh's history. At the height of its fame it was the epitome of elegance, yet the glory faded, first into disrepair as its last private owner allowed the estate to wither, then even the great house fell from its previous riches into ruin. Some believe Cammo was the infamous House of Shaws in Robert Louis Stevenson's "Kidnapped", others say it is haunted, but in its ruined state today, with its once splendid trappings of greatness still echoing loudly from the past, it has been reborn under the direction of Edinburgh District Council, who have turned the estate into a fascinating and unusual city park, a haven for wildlife in its setting of woodland, meadow and marsh.

Cammo Park was Scotland's first attempt to create a landscape garden inspired by the 18th-century land owner and visionary Sir John Clerk of Penicuik. Cammo's antecedents are in the 14th century, when it was church owned. At one time it was part of the Abbot of Inchcolm's estates, but it came into the hands of the Bishop of Dunkeld in exchange for Cramond Tower. It is recorded as a fine house built at Cammo in 1693 by Sir John Menzies, before the lands passed to Sir John Clerk in 1710. Sir John

CAMMO ESTATE PARK . . . the fall of the House of Cammo is part of Edinburgh's history but its grounds still flourish.

CAMMO HOUSE . . . the ruins of what was once one of the most celebrated homes in Scotland.

immediately began to refashion the whole estate. He introduced new ideas and concepts, even utilising the poorest ground for "wilderness" areas as habitats for wildlife. He collected specimen trees from around the world, created copses, arbours, stately woodlands and tree-lined avenues, designed to present sudden, surprise vistas of the Pentland Hills and pastoral vignettes of the surrounding countryside. Among the flower beds there was a "Portugal Garden", the location of which is now lost, as well as a vegetable garden, tree shelter belts and an attractive canal feature for winter curling, which was a home for ornamental ducks. Sir John turned Cammo into a Scottish showpiece.

The estate, which was much larger than it is today, was sold to James Watson of Saughton in 1741, who renamed it New Saughton, but much of Sir John's pioneering work was consolidated during the 131 years it was in the care of the Watson family. It was during this period that the pinetum, a Victorian fashion, was created to the west of the house and the stables, east lodge and walled gardens were built. It was the epitome of a successfully-run Scottish country house and estate in the grand manner of the 19th century. At the height of its splendour, the Watsons

employed nine gardeners, seven labourers and 22 domestic servants, fine carriages came and returned, pulled by immaculately-groomed high-steppers, and glittering dinner and garden parties were common Cammo occasions.

In 1837 the Watsons sold their New Saughton paradise to Edinburgh brewer Alexander Campbell, who split the estate but promptly restored the original name to his portion — Cammo. The property passed to the Maitland-Tennant family in 1891, but the financial resources were just not available to maintain Cammo in its accustomed grand style. Slowly Sir John Clerk's "wilderness" areas, planned 150 years previously, invaded the whole estate, the house fell into disrepair, the buildings and grounds became increasingly dilapidated. Mrs Maitland-Tennant and her son, Percival Louis, began to withdraw from public gaze and assume the mantle of Edinburgh "characters", that well-known breed of Capital worthy that overlaps into eccentricity and surmounts social divisions. Mrs Maitland Tennant, who lived to the grand old age of 92, became styled the "Black Widow" of Cammo because of her predilection for sombre dress and there are still those who remember her dark, shadowy figure in a recess of her carriage as it passed between

Cammo and the city. Latterly, Percival took to a caravan on the estate and a large family of household dogs continued to live in the crumbling house. On Percival's death in 1975, Cammo was bequeathed to the National Trust for Scotland, but by that time the once-great Cammo House was past preservation.

But the story did not end there. Although the house had to be demolished after damage by two malicious fires, the foundations were made safe and the estate feued to Edinburgh District Council to enhance plant and wildlife environments and as a teaching resource for the public at large. The Countryside Rangers provide a popular guided tour from their Cammo base at the entry gate, financed by builders MacTaggart and Mickel, with displays and an information service.

The former glories of Cammo are there for all to see, with many of the 123 tree species, avenues, paths, lawns, glades and even the canal pond still in place. It remains another of Edinburgh's special places of natural beauty, with a colourful history and now again an important habitat for wildlife, which includes 64 species of birds and mammals. Among the multiplicity of trees — sycamore, elm, ash, cherry, black poplar, oak, lime, yew, copper beech, sweet and horse chestnut, larch and Scots pine — and among the smaller elder, holly, rhododendrons, hawthorn, engulfing bramble, beds of stinging nettle and marshland, there are nesting kestrels, sparrowhawks, owls, carrion crows, magpies, treecreepers, wrens, spotted flycatchers, blackcaps, a variety of tit and finch families and, down by the canal pond, water hens and sometimes a heron. Some of the ancient oaks may date from Sir John Clerk's time.

Cammo is a natural den for foxes, rabbits, weasels, grey squirrels, badgers and small mammals and there are those who come with a checklist for the 148 species of plants which include cuckoo flower, marsh marigolds, dog's mercury, enchanted nightshade and monkshood. Carpets of snowdrops and bluebells are eye stoppers in spring. Cammo's sheltered environment also makes it a habitat for insects, while the meadows are a play and breeding area for many butterflies. The sounds of Cammo at any time are worth a moment of personal silence.

At the turn of this century the fields around Cammo were home to Cammo Golf Club, which moved to Dalmahoy in the 1920s. The unusual-looking farmhouse on the estate was, in fact, the old Cammo clubhouse.

Facilities: Visitor Centre, guided tours, lectures and car park. Still to be seen from the estate's days of 18th and 19th-century elegance are the ruins of the house, the stables, piggery, walled garden, canal pond and the water tower. On bus route. Car parking. Toilets. Access for disabled but some of the paths rough.

All enquiries should be made to: The Countryside Ranger Service, 69a Braid Road, Edinburgh, EH10 6JF. Telephone: 0131 447 7145, Cammo telephone number: 0131 317 8797.

Campbell Park

Location: Off Woodhall Road on the western extremity of Colinton and below the Edinburgh by-pass. Area: 8.1 acres 3.2805 hectares.

Campbell Park, named after the local farmer at Woodhall farm, who gifted the ground to the community, was dedicated as a recreation area for community use in 1936. During the winter months it is a venue for football and children have the use of a safe play area. A pavilion has been provided for changing. The boundaries of the park are marked by a hawthorn hedge and railing, with sycamore and elder trees.

Traffic hurtles along the city by-pass above, but the park remains a peaceful island with impressive views of the Pentland Hills to the south. In the valley below, the young Water of Leith makes its way down to the Forth. Campbell Park is part of the strategic green route that stretches from the sea to the hills.

Facilities: Three football pitches, pavilion and play area. Off bus route. Access for disabled.

Clermiston Park

Location: Off Drum Brae Drive, bordered by Clermiston Drive and Clermiston Gardens. Area: 14.0 acres 5.67 hectares.

Like nearby Drum Brae Park, Clermiston is one of the highest parks in the city with the summit of Corstorphine Hill only a short distance away. Clermiston makes no claim to be other than a community park providing an open space for games, a place to stroll and relax for young and old. However, like its near neighbour, it provides from its vantage point a magnificent panorama of the Forth estuary and Fife coast. To the west the peak of Ben Lomond can be seen some 50 miles away and the Pentland Hills make an impressive southern backdrop. The park has surrounds of mixed cherry trees, whitebeam, sycamores and rowan. A small avenue of young trees flanks a shortcut path at its northern end. Kicking a ball remains a passion for Clermiston's young men, who have a football pitch in the park available to them with a pavilion. The old tennis courts make a useful cycle area. With those sweeping vistas all around it is little wonder the park is well used. The land was acquired for the city in 1956.

Facilities: One football pitch and a pavilion. On bus route. Access for disabled.

Colinton Dell

Situation: The main entrance is off Lanark Road beside Colinton Church in the old part of the village below Bridge Road spanning the Water of Leith. Other entrances include Boggsmill Road, Katesmill Road and the old Colinton railway station at Spylaw. Area: 45 acres (18.225 hectares).

Colinton Dell is now a section of the recognised Water of Leith Walkway, where it enters a dramatic gorge, but it has been known as a tree-clad, beautiful and lonely place through the centuries. The entrance is beside the old Colinton Parish Church, where once Robert Louis Stevenson's grandfather was the incumbent. A plaque on the wall marks it as being part of today's Stevenson Trail. RLS had only happy memories of Colinton, particularly the manse garden and the surrounding countryside. Colinton Church celebrated its 900th anniversary in 1995.

Colinton, or Collingtoun as it was known in ancient times, means "village in the wood" and on descending the path into Colinton Dell the impact of trees is immediate. They enclose in green gloom then suddenly there are streams of bright light and dapplings on the path and steep slopes where the sun spills through the trees high overhead. The trailing branches almost touch the river as it tumbles, rushes and splashes then eases into peaceful dark pools before suddenly becoming urgent white water again, the foam flying.

This is indeed poet's country — or an artist's challenge — dripping rainforest one moment, the pungent scent of wild garlic pervading, then the calm of a church, birds singing lustily in the sunlight, then a twist of the path into shadow, a chance encounter of the unexpected at any moment — the flutter of a wren, the brown flash of a weasel, the glimpse of a receding fox or even the bobbing white tail of a startled roe deer.

The woodlands are classified as ancient or long-established and the regeneration process had continued long before Stevenson strolled there, before the Spylaw snuff man James Gillespie, founder of Gillespie's hospitals and schools, walked that narrow path in the 18th century and perhaps even before some of General Monk's troops — now the Coldstream Guards — made their way through it on their way to attack Redhall Castle in 1650. The most

common trees in Colinton Dell woods are ash, lime, elm, birch, willow and hawthorn, but higher on the banks are oak, yew, holly, hornbeam, cedar, sweet chestnut and beech.

The protection afforded by the high banks and thick undergrowth make it a natural habitat for a range of wildlife. More than 80 species of birds have been recorded, including a variety of finches, tits, dippers, ousels, wrens and owls. Likewise, along the water side and up the escape paths, voles, frogs, rabbits, hares, weasels, stoats, foxes and occasionally roe deer have been seen.

Colinton Dell is a special place, arguably the most atmospherically beautiful along the length of the Water of Leith. It attracts many walkers and families and, by the various swing ropes dangling from trees, like RLS there remain many small boy explorers unable to resist its offerings of adventure. Redhall Weir and the old mill site continue to catch the interest.

Facilities: Safe walkways, cycleway. On bus route. Access for disabled but steps at some entrance points.

Colinton Mains Park

Situation: Bordered by Firrhill Drive, Oxgangs Drive and Oxgangs Road North. Area: 20.8 acres (8.424 hectares).

Colinton Mains Park makes no pretensions at being anything other than a large, community park, a flat green open space for soccer, cricket in season, youngsters playing and where local people can walk or take their dogs for exercise. However, it has a special attraction — the full bulk of the Pentland Hills dominates its southern skyline. The three 15-storey blocks of flats at the park's east end are well-named Capelaw, Allermuir and Caerketton.

It is a dramatic backdrop and another of Edinburgh's hill ranges is also visible — the Braid Hills. It is interesting to note that the name Firrhill, associated with the area, still has a reflection in the tall, dark Scots pines that act as a southern boundary to the City Hospital above the park.

The Braid Burn, complete with minnows, forms the northern boundary of Colinton Mains Park, along with some attractive cherry and sycamore trees and a hawthorn hedge. The northern entry into the park is across a wooden bridge. Cherry trees, which present an eye-stopping display of blossom in May and early June, are a feature, but elder, sloe and prunus are also represented.

It is a much-used park by all ages in the community. The pavilion is located at the west end on Oxgangs Road North with spaces for around 15 cars. The flat surface makes it a popular

CORSTORPHINE HILL . . . a slice of countryside in town. This view from the north side stretches out to the hills of Fife.

venue for football and cricket and it is one of the six parks in the city to have a cricket square. Young children have their own safe play area and there is also a popular bowling green. There is a strong sense of community in the area, the local gala day is held in the park and a fairground in summer. All these activities are given an additional dimension set as they are against the Pentland tops in the sky like a stage backdrop. The park came into the hands of the city in 1939.

Facilities: Three football pitches, a cricket pitch, bowling green and a safe play area for young children. Parking and on bus route. Access for disabled.

Corstorphine Hill

Situation: Rising to a height of 529 feet, Corstorphine Hill lies between Corstorphine Road and St. John's Road in the south and Queensferry Road at its northern extremity. Clermiston Road is on the west side. Area: 112 acres (45.36 hectares).

Corstorphine Hill is one of the seven hills of Edinburgh and its wooded summit is visible from all over the city. Like Arthur's Seat and some other city high areas, Corstorphine Hill was formed by volcanic eruption millions of years ago. It heaved up through a soft layer of rock above the flat plain now known as Corstorphine to create a dramatic sight. The west side of the hill bears the juggernaut scourings of the Ice Age as the great glaciers of 12,000 years ago ground and gouged their way across the hillside to create a glacial "platform". The hard rock on the south side is dolerite and called a "sill" and the softer picrite rock is found to the north.

It is on the western slope that the signs of early inhabitants are found, the unmistakable "cup and ring" circles that mark the settlements of around 1500 - 2000 BC and possibly long before this time. In those days high ground was safer ground, a defence against menacing animals and marauding tribes and Corstorphine Hill had inhabitants from earliest times. It was a strategic perch from which to spy advancing enemies from a distance and the view from

Time for contemplation . . . on the peaceful wooded flanks of Corstorphine Hill looking towards the summit from the east side.

Corstorphine Hill today — framed by tree-tunnel windows in the woods or dramatic opening spectacles at a turn of a path — remains unsurpassed in Edinburgh.

But the importance of Corstorphine Hill nowadays is as a large slice of countryside within the city — wood, scrub, rock and grassland — with the bird, mammal, plant and insect life natural to such an environment. Even in the open countryside beyond Edinburgh, such places are under increasing pressure. To have this kind of wild heritage within a city setting gives Corstorphine Hill a special significance and the Capital a particular responsibility for its safekeeping. That is why Corstorphine Hill, acquired by the city in 1924, has been designated Edinburgh's second Local Nature Reserve, a part of the city to be conserved for future generations to continue to enable Edinburgh citizens to walk its woodland tracks, wonder at the sweeping panoramas of the city below, the Lothians and Fife spread out into the distance, glimpse a woodpecker or a stooping kestrel or listen to the thousand sounds that are part of the forest.

Much of the hill is covered by woodland — fine specimens of beech, sycamore, lime, ash and pine with birch and rowan providing more delicate contrasts. Apart from the ground cover of gorse, raspberry, bramble and hawthorn, at least 144 different flowering plants flourish in its dells and bowers, including such local rarities as climbing cordelias, small balsam and lords and ladies. The hill is a foraging ground for foxes, badgers, rabbits, grey squirrels and small mammals and, in the trees and bushes above, there are nesting sparrowhawks, owls, woodpeckers, a variety of finches, tits and garden birds. It is a remarkable display of native species, including butterflies, moths and insect life at the heart of town, as fascinating in their wild setting as some of the more exotic varieties in Edinburgh Zoo on the southern flank.

Crowning Corstorphine Hill, set among splendid woodland, is the Clermiston Tower, built as a memorial to Sir Walter Scott by William Macfie in 1871 to mark the centenary of his birth. It was presented to the city in 1932 by W. G. Walker on the centenary of Scott's death. A spiral staircase winds inside the tower for 100

Hill with a prospect . . . looking into central Edinburgh and Arthur's Seat from the Clermiston Tower on Corstorphine Hill.

steps to provide an eagle's view of the surrounding countryside and over the woodland canopy below. It is a majestic panorama, well worth the climb, and arrangements for entry can be made with the Council's Countryside Rangers Service, Hermitage of Braid, 69a Braid Road, Edinburgh EH10 6JF. Telephone: 0131 447 7145.

Facilities: Visits to Clermiston Tower and car parking off Clermiston Road and Cairnmuir Road. Off bus route. Access for disabled difficult, unsuitable for wheelchairs.

Craiglockhart Dell Park

Location: Part of the Water of Leith Walkway between Graysmill and where the river flows under Lanark Road. Accessible from both sides of the glen, including off Lanark Road and Craiglockhart Drive South. Area: 6.7 acres.

One of the gems of the Water of Leith Walkway, Craiglockhart Dell was part of the estate of Craiglockhart House. Much of it was planted in the 18th century by Dr Alexander Munro and the present paths and grottoes date from around this time. Those early plantings have grown into a magnificent self-generating woodland wonderland, with the Water of Leith gathering speed at this point to create a constant murmur, while in the longer pools the brown trout break surface with a swirl to feed off the infinite insect life. Above is a veritable tree sanctuary, a lonely Highland or Border glen uplifted and set down in the city, the wildlife with it.

Some splendid specimens of sycamore, beech, fir and larch are found throughout the dell, with a great mixture of hawthorn, cherry, lime, sorbus, willow, chestnut, alder, elder, holly, an undergrowth of bramble, stinging and flowering nettle and, in some of the delightful open glades, foxgloves, fern, dogs' mercury, woodruff and the purple rosebay willow herb has made a claim. It is a perfect example of a forest in continuity, older trees that have reached their life spans, young, sturdy replacements flourishing, tender shoots and saplings reaching upwards and dead trees, some freshly fallen or rotting among the wild plants, form small habitats on their own accounts for insects and slug life, within the larger habitat that is the woods of the dell as a whole. It is nature's cycle for all to see and appreciate.

In such a setting wildlife abounds. Although foxes are rarely seen their musk is suddenly and frequently heavy on the air where they have recently passed. Small mammals like mice and voles, prey for the foxes, as well as rabbits and weasels, are in the high banks. Occasionally, a roe deer will stray into the dell from higher up the river. Up to 80 species of birds have been identified, including dippers, grey wagtails, wrens, a variety of finches, pigeons, and mallard. Many different plant species are in the wood — perhaps approaching 200 — and one of the pleasures for those with an interest in flora is the discovery of something new, deposited by a spring flood or a passing bird. Beside the bridge there are benches and a picnic table.

Redhall Castle and Redhall House, at the upstream entrance to Craiglockhart Dell, have long histories. The castle, built in the 13th century, was torched and razed by Cromwell in 1650. Redhall House, also reduced by Cromwell, was rebuilt in 1756 by George Ingles, who laid out the grounds, planted trees and bushes and created grottoes. The walled garden, owned by the Council, became a tree nursery, but is now leased to the charity Sprout.

Not surprisingly, Craiglockhart Dell is a favourite for visiting Edinburgh people. Water of Leith walkers march it in both directions, it has its share of joggers, small boys are in adventure land, it is a place for family outings and picnics, able to absorb people and noise and provide whatever mood the searcher seeks. Yet among the tall tree canyons it continues to remain a quiet and lonely place.

Facilities: Woodland walks, cycleway, benches and picnic table. Bus route. Access for disabled but very steep slopes.

Craiglockhart Hill

Situation: Bounded by Colinton Road, Craighouse Road and Morningside Grove. Glenlockhart Road divides the hill into two sections. Area: West and East Craiglockhart Hill 87.77 acres (35.54 hectares); Craiglockhart Wood 8.96 acres (3.62 hectares).

Craiglockhart Hill is another of Edinburgh's seven green crowns that rise above the city as natural landmarks, enhancing the Capital's fair looks and helps to form its character. Some of Edinburgh's most delightful woodlands are found around the flanks of its 575-feet top. The hill is alive with wildlife, it is home to one of the city's largest grey squirrel colonies, while Craiglockhart Pond, on its Colinton Road side, is an attraction for a variety of ducks, coots, moorhens, seagulls and even passing coastal visitors. Like Edinburgh's other six hills, the clear and distant views from the summit in all directions are spectacular, but as the path winds upwards it provides many unexpected vignettes of the city below viewed through woodland windows framed by branches of beech, sycamore or fir. Yet partly because access to the hill is limited by the build-up of private property, Craiglockhart Hill's peaceful beauty and far-cast vistas are enjoyed mostly by in-the-know local people.

The name of Craiglockhart is said to derive from Craig-loch-ard, which has a possible reference to what was once known as Corstorphine Loch. It has always been a wild place of steep rock escarpments, rich woodland and acres of gorse above its tree line. Two hundred years ago it was known as a haunt of kestrels and they continue to nest on the hill along with sparrowhawks, owls, magpies and many small birds. Local residents along the edges of the hill are accustomed to seeing foxes in their gardens and, not unexpectedly on such open hillside, also rabbits, weasels and even roe deer make an occasional fleeting appearance.

The quaint old Craig House, part of what was the Thomas Clouston Clinic, one of the most progressive mental institutions of its day, and now to be turned into a new campus for Napier University, dates from 1565 and is claimed to be haunted by a mystical Green Lady. It is recorded how John Kincaid, of Craig House, with followers clad in armour and bearing weapons, burst open the door of a house in Leith in 1600 to carry off Isabel Hutcheon, a widow living at the time in "sober, quiet and peaceable manner . . . dreading nae evil, harm, or injury, but living under God's peace and our sovereign lord's". Over two centuries Craig House has been home to a number of illustrious residents, including John Hill Burton, author of a number of Scottish books, including a history of Scotland and owner of a fine library, which "spilled into every room in the house". The new Napier University campus will eventually have 2,500 students and Craig House fittingly will become a study and archive area, with reception and exhibition facilities.

In 1870 Craiglockhart Poorhouse was opened on the Wester Hill and in 1904 the City Fever Hospital was built, which is now the City Hospital. The Merchants of Edinburgh Golf Club play on both Wester and Easter Craiglockhart Hill and at one time, when the club was founded in 1907, golf balls hurtled from hill to hill. With the development of Glenlockhart Road and the increase in traffic the golfers chose safety first and now walk across the road to a new hole rather than play over it. In the main walkers and golfers go their separate ways and, on Easter Hill, they are parted by a wall and an iron railing.

The Craiglockhart sports centre off Colinton Road opened in 1976 and after being comprehensively upgraded in 1994-95 became the prime Scottish venue for indoor and outdoor tennis.

Although rights of way create debate in the area, the main entrances to Craiglockhart Hill are from the end of Craiglockhart Terrace, beside Craiglockhart Pond, off Glenlockhart Road near its western end and from Craiglea Place off Morningside Grove. A path leads from these extremities through the woods or on to the summit. From the Craiglockhart Pond side the path is rough in places and strong shoes or wellingtons are advised, particularly in wet weather. However, it is well worth the effort as the path trails through woods of elm, lime, varieties of holly, sycamore, hazel, beeches, chestnut, maple, oak, ash, elder, Scots pine, larch, birch and even rhododendrons near the Craiglea Place end. It is another remarkable example of a high, wild and lonely place within the Capital and it gives pleasure throughout the seasons.

There are two main natural viewing stances, the first from the path where it reaches a high point above the Craiglockhart Pond on the rocky hillside — and the whole of Edinburgh's northern panorama is displayed across the playing fields of Myreside and Meggetland, over many of Edinburgh's famous landmarks to Corstorphine Hill, the River Forth and Fife. The second prospect is at the summit where a full 360-degree viewpoint takes in Atholl in north Perthshire, Ben Lomond and the Grampians, Border country to the south, a dominating full frontal of the Pentland range with open sea, Forth islands and the Bass Rock in the east. It is worth the climb and the visit for that one view.

Facilities: Rough hill and woodland tracks, some seating at the Craiglea Place end. Off bus route. Limited access for disabled.

Cramond Foreshore Walk

Situation: It follows the Forth's southerly shoreline from the causeway at Cramond Village along the Esplanade to Granton Point. Area: 150 acres (60.75 hectares).

Here is another of those dramatic Edinburgh contrasts that are such a feature of the Capital's panorama. With the tang of sea salt immediately declaring the Forth has at last arrived at its estuary, the walk along the shoreline on hard paths can be described only as magnificent. On one hand are stunning views across the Firth to the Fife coast until eastwards it disappears into the North Sea more than 30 miles away. Opposite, on the distant southern shore, North Berwick Law rises on the horizon like a desert pyramid. The Lomond and Cleish Hills are to the north and the river points westwards to Kincardine. In one great sweep the eye beholds the patchwork fields of Fife, Cramond Island and the islands of Inchcolm and Inchkeith, The Snab to the left, Dalgety Bay, Aberdour and Burntisland across the water, the rocks and

CRAMOND FORESHORE . . . woodlands by the seaside looking over to the Fife coast and Forth islands.

seapools where the children adventure, the sun worshippers strewn on the sands and among the tussocky grass, the big oil tankers heading for Hound Point with the distant throb of their engines just audible, yachts tacking with the wind, a pair of eider bobbing with the waves, the lulling of waters lapping — and sometimes their roar because the Forth can fast change its mood. It is from here, at the delightful mouth of the River Almond, with its swans, ducks, anchored yachts, picturesque buildings and walk out to Cramond Island at low tide, a worthwhile 50p will ferry seekers of deeper seclusion across the river.

But landwards, over the fence, is a tranquil world of unspoilt meadowland and woodlands, grazing sheep and cattle in a rural setting that stretches up to Lauriston Castle. The path along the shore is fringed with sycamores, hawthorn, elder and ash trees. There are plenty of places to sit and watch the passing scene, with some covered seating in case of squalls. The road leads past a cafeteria, hugging the shore, and winds on to the Granton end, where again the scene alters.

Here it is softer, farther removed from the Firth where the path meets West Shore Road, and there is a flourish of cherry trees mixed with young sycamores and a variety of shrubs like weigelia, cotoneaster and flowering currant. This point is also known as Gypsy Brae and it

is a little park in its own right, the hill behind a backdrop of woodland — hawthorn, sycamore, elder and ash — which acts as a frame and foil to the green swards on either side of the path. It is a place for family picnics, peaceful strollings, but there are also football facilities for the energetic young. The Forth bridges are not visible from the Cramond end, but from Gypsy Brae two spans of the Forth Railway Bridge and a single span of the Road Bridge between lend them an additional artistic dimension of landscaped engineering. There is much potential in the future for further extending this coastal walkway.

As one of Edinburgh's old villages Cramond has the distinction of having the longest known period of human settlement. The Romans had an important station here, the Alauna of Ptolemy, and it was the headquarters of the ll and XX Legions under Lollius Urbicus; Constantine lV, who reigned in 994, was killed on the Cramond beach in 1002 by Malcolm ll, whose army took up a position so that the high wind, it is said, carried the sand into the eyes of his enemies; and the remaining18th century houses continue to provide character and reflect Cramond's past.

Facilities: Cafeteria, seats and space to kick a football at Gypsy Brae. Toilets. On bus route. Parking. Access for disabled.

Cramond sunset at the mouth of the River Almond.

Dalmeny Park/Iona Street

Situation: Off Leith Walk and bordered by Iona Street, Dalmeny Street, Dickson Street and Sloan Street. Area: 2 acres (0.81 hectares).

This little park was formerly known as Iona Street and was first set out as a recreation area in 1902 with gymnastic apparatus provided. It was maintained in the early days by the governors of the Trinity Hospital who passed it into the city's safe keeping in 1922.

Dalmeny Park today is divided neatly into two sections. The recreation area for children continues on the same lines as it did almost a century ago, with various frames, swings and a chute, but now also with a cycle area and a place to practise skateboards. It is well used and safe and a valuable asset in a busy and built-up part of town.

The other section has been turned into two attractive bowling greens called Iona Tree Bowling Green with a well-maintained clubhouse. It has proved a popular and busy rendezvous for the bowling fraternity. The park is surrounded with an iron railing and a mixture of elm, hawthorn, poplar and cherry. This tiny green oasis merits development and improvement in conjunction with the local community.

Facilities: Safe play area, bowling greens. On bus route. Disabled access from Dalmeny Street entrance.

Davidson's Mains Park

Situation: Off Quality Street and Barnton Avenue and behind Queensferry Road. Area: 31.5 acres (12.7575 hectares).

This handsome park comes as a surprise to the uninitiated because it is not immediately noticeable or easily found. It is really a northern extension of Corstorphine Hill across the busy Queensferry Road opposite Barnton Quarry and has all the natural feeling of a wild and beautiful place. Those who make the effort are well rewarded with sweeping grasslands in a mixed woodland setting. Trees are one of the park's

most attractive features. They lend grandeur and a sense of peace to the whole park, but they also create tricks of light and shade and dappling to catch an artist's eye. It is a mixed woodland with natural regeneration and includes chestnut, elm, oak, maple, Wheatley elm, ash, yew, sweet chestnut and whitebeams as big as you will get in Edinburgh.

The ground was acquired for the city from Dame Mary Ramsay-Steel-Maitland in 1922 and today it brings much simple pleasure for its users. It has pleasant walks in the open or through the trees, where in spite of the traffic on Queensferry Road over the wall, the noise is subdued. It is ideally suited for community events.

There is a natural bowl in the centre where children can play ball or team games, but the entire park is their adventure ground. Grey squirrels have colonised the woodlands, magpies, tits and garden birds are in profusion. The park also has a small play area and benches, but the natural beauty of D-Mains, as some people refer to it, is always the main attraction.

Facilities: One football pitch; woodland walks, benches, play area. On a bus route. Disabled access but pathways rutted.

Dovecot Park

Situation: On the south side of Lanark Road adjacent to Dovecot Grove near Kingsknowe Golf Course. Area: 14 acres (5.67 hectares).

Drivers on the Lanark Road have hardly time to lift their eyes to admire this pleasant little park. Yet it would be worth stopping for a few minutes to stroll through it. Created in 1960, Dovecot enjoys an open aspect looking over to Corstorphine Hill and, at the rear, where the bank falls steeply to the Water of Leith Walkway, glimpses of the Pentland Hills are visible through the trees. Basically, Dovecot Park is for football, play and a quiet stroll, but it has been laid out to please the eye with a predominance of cherry trees at the rear and, along its south side, some attractive sycamores on the Dovecot Grove end with an island of mixed hawthorn and sweet-smelling elder. Tucked at a corner is a fine grove of mature birch trees, their white bark an attractive contrast against the wilderness of the bank beyond. A central arm of cherry trees extends into the park above the pavilion.

Where the bank drops sharply to the Water of Leith, a place for mountain goats or small boys blazing trails through the jungle, a delightful wild woodland is established of ash, oak, cherry, hawthorn, conifer, elder, bramble and dog rose. Those motorists on Lanark Road do not appreciate what they are missing in their rush into the city or on their way home.

Facilities: Three football pitches and a pavilion. On a bus route. Access for disabled.

Drum Brae Park

Location: Off Drum Brae North Road, flanked by Drum Brae Terrace and Parkgrove Road, Drumbrae. Area: 10.8 acres (4.374 hectares).

Drum Brae Park, like close-neighbour Clermiston Park, is one of the highest in the city. From its vantage point it displays magnificent Edinburgh panoramas in every direction. Perhaps a community park in a city housing estate may seem an unusual location for such spectacle, but Drum Brae Park arguably presents some of the finest views in Lothian. To the north the Kingdom of Fife lies in sharp detail across the Forth estuary, the twin Forth bridges its gateways; hills and mountain ranges heave into view — the Lomond Hills, the Cleish Hills, the Ochil Hills and, to the west, the unmistakable shape of Ben Lomond 50 miles away, while the oil shale bings of West Lothian, like a miniature range of red mountains, catch the eye closer to hand; to the south the Pentland Hills fill the horizon and, with a turn of the head, Corstorphine Hill with Clermiston Tower lifting above the trees is only a few strides away. This eagle's eye view from Drum Brae Park also confirms Edinburgh as one of the great green cities of parks, treescapes and open spaces.

It was created in 1961 on two levels. During the winter months the top level is extensively used by local youngsters as a venue for football and the park has its own pavilion. The safe play area is also popular throughout the year. The northern slope has been planted with a mixture of stand-alone trees and in copses — beech, birch, sycamore, hawthorn, cherry, rowan and the park's boundaries have been set out with hawthorn, rowan, whitebeam and sycamore trees. A sports centre and swimming pool is planned for part of the park in the future.

Facilities: Football pitches, but not in use. Play area, benches and a popular venue for sledging in winter. On bus route. Access for disabled.

Dunbar's Close Garden

Situation: Off the north side of the Canongate next to Canongate Kirk. Area: 0.75 acres (0.30375 hectares).

Onc of thc Capital's little gems, Dunbar's Close

Garden has been laid out in the style and character of a 17th-century garden and in the historic surroundings of Edinburgh's Old Town, with the Canongate Kirk over the wall, it retains much of the atmosphere of the Edinburgh of three centuries ago. Unlike the crowded High Street area further up the hill, many of the Canongate houses had fine, long gardens running north and south and Dunbar's Close Garden is a good example of the gracious style of those days.

It is a small garden, entered by iron gates, into a forecourt cobbled in setts with four tiny but elegant flowerbeds and sorbus trees. The garden continues on a gentle downwards slope along a gravel path: on the right is a yew hedge grown in an interesting series of recesses, with small flower beds in each; on the left are two sectioned gardens backed by a wall, each with four small beds edged by box parterre, a favourite style of the time. In the first are shaped bushes, the second is a lavender garden. Apple trees have been grown along a wooden fence screening the sections.

A tiny green lawn is at the foot of the garden with cherry, holly, beech and hawthorn marking its lower boundary. Behind the yew hedge are flower and rose beds and creeping ivy.

All the flowers are in the idiom of the 17th century. It is a delightful place of peace with a strong sense of the past and restored from wilderness in 1978 by the charity organisation, the Mushroom Trust. There are plenty of garden seats, some fittingly in stone.

In Robert Burns's day, Dunbar's Close was famous for its oyster cellar. Burns was surprised to find fashionable ladies there washing down their oyster suppers with liberal quantities of ale or punch and ready for a dance to the fiddle, harp or bag-pipc.

Facilities: Garden seats. On bus route. Steps difficult for disabled.

Dundas Park, South Queensferry

Situation: Off Dundas Avenue and Ashburnham Road at the rear of Queensferry High School. Area: 4.84 acres (1.9602 hectares).

Dundas Park, which was acquired for the Council from Lord Primrose in 1962, makes no pretensions at being anything other than playing fields for children and an ideal football venue on the flat.

With the giant spans of the Forth Railway Bridge in close-up beyond its north side, the park is also a pleasant place for local people to stroll and there is a well-used safe play area for young children.

FIGGATE PARK . . . a delight of trees, water and birdlife in the shadow of the crouched lion of Arthur's Seat.

DUNBAR'S CLOSE GARDEN . . . it is one of Edinburgh's little-known gems tucked away off the Royal Mile in the style of the 17th century.

A path at the Queensferry High School side, bordered by cherry trees, hawthorn, ash, sycamore, alder and elder, with brambles and stinging nettles, leads through to Lovers Lane off Scotstoun Avenue.

It is little surprise foxes have been seen for the dense undergrowth forms a natural wildlife habitat. Behind the park is a further deep wilderness area of rough grasses, dog rose, wild sweet pea, thistle and the ubiquitous rosebay willow herb. It is an adventure ground for children and a further natural habitat and playground for a variety of butterflies, moths and insects. A sports centre and two football pitches are in future development plans.

Facilities: 1 football pitch, play area. Off bus route. Access for disabled.

East Pilton Park

Situation: Mid-way along Pilton Avenue, off Crew Road West and bounded by Pilton Gardens on its north side. Area: 7 acres (2.835 hectares).

Pilton Park has an immediately-obvious virtue — it is single mindedly a place for play and where youngsters can expend energy. To allow these activities full rein, this little park, in the centre of an area of high-density housing, has been sensibly divided to allow toddlers and their watching mothers to play or sit at ease in a well-equipped play area while older children separately have the run of the park, which includes a commando-style slide on rubber tyres and football pitches in season.

The ground was acquired from Dame Ramsay-Steel-Maitland by Act of Council in 1931 and has been put to good use by local residents. It is busy, popular and effective as a neighbourhood park and makes a pretty picture in the spring when the bordering cherry trees are in full pink and white blossom.

Facilities: Play area, park benches and two football pitches. On bus route. Access for disabled.

Fairmilehead Park

Situation: Off Comiston Road and bordered by Camus Avenue and Pentland View on the north side. It is also known as Camus Park. Area: 7.8 acres (3.159 hectares).

Fairmilehead is a leafy residential part of the city and Fairmilehead Park is well named. Trees are one of its most attractive features. Sycamore, beech, conifer, elder and holly are all represented, some in small pieces of woodland that are a-twitter with birdlife in summer. Trees and bushes from the private surrounding gardens add to the pleasure, in particular a fine copper beech. A rough, overgrown area with rowan, birch, conifer and dog rose provides natural ground cover so that it is hardly surprising foxes are reported to be among the neighbours. It is a part of the city known for its many natural springs, resulting in a small pond on the north side, which supports the kind of nature conservation regimes that Edinburgh is trying to introduce where possible. A further wet corner runs under the trees entering Pentland Drive.

Fairmilehead Park, which came into city ownership in 1964, is essentially for walking, playing, sitting out and quiet contemplation from one of the benches. Distant glimpses of the Fife coast between the trees and bordering houses catch the eye. There are hard paths for walking, it is much frequented by local residents and the whole park has a pleasant atmosphere. A safe play area is an obvious attraction for younger children and the park is popular with local nursery groups.

Facilities: Safe play area, paths and benches. Off bus route. Access for disabled.

Figgate Burn Park

Situation: Off Duddingston Road and behind Northfield Drive, with the railway line as its north eastern border. Area: 27.83 acres (11.27115 hectares).

Tucked out of sight behind Portobello High School and Duddingston Primary School, this is

HARRISON PARK . . . a pleasant surprise in the centre of the city that has had to fight for its survival against development.

one of the most attractive small parks in the city. Tadpole-shaped, with the delightful tree-fringed Figgate Pond in the "head", the elongated "body" follows the line of the Figgate Burn in a pleasant and secluded woodland setting, with feeding mallard dabbling in the burn and the trees and bushes alive with birdlife. Apart from the waders in the Figgate Pond, which was once a clay pit, pigeons, magpies, chaffinches, a number of tit species and starlings with favourite tree holes, at least one family of owls, blackbirds and thrushes from the neighbouring gardens all make the park their haunt among the beeches, oaks, chestnut, ash, lime, some conifers and sycamores. ➤

Around the pond, where for generations parents and grandparents have taken small children to feed the ducks, nature is seen in action in close-up as coots nest on branches where they touch the water and, farther out on the island, water-hen and ducks claim a home. The hanging willows so close to the pond and beside the burn in the rough ground below Mount Castle Bank could be taken as a scene from a Cezanne painting along some placid, rural French riverside. In the background, the bulk of Arthur's Seat dominates the skyline to lend drama and aspect to the park's natural beauty and peace.

The charms of the Figgate Burn Park, which became Council acquired in 1933 from the Abercorn estate, are well appreciated by people living in the locality. It is a popular walking area for all ages and where dogs can also run, although timely notices at the entrances remind dog-owners of their responsibilities for this is a park to be enjoyed by everyone. In the spring, daffodils are a splash of early colour along the edges of the park before the fresh greens of the trees and bushes make their appearance.

The Figgate Burn is crossed by several bridges and over one of these a path leads up to a safe play area and a small playing field shielded by trees. This welcome spur off the main park allows children to have a playing field of their own, without interfering with the rest of the park or unwanted adults straying into their own patch. It overlooks railway sidings, which is another source of interest for them. The 1143 (8th Edinburgh) Squadron of the Air Training Corps has a hut at the Hamilton Terrace entrance.

Facilities: Walks, bird watching, children's play area. On bus route. Access for disabled but steps on Mountcastle Drive North entrance.

Gardner's Crescent

Situation: Off Lothian Road between Morrison Street and Fountainbridge. Area: 0.35 acres (0.14 hectares).

Although the building of Edinburgh's New Town was completed centrally by 1840 the style continued to appear in various streets and buildings throughout the city for many years. Gardner's Crescent was one of these, but it was speculative in anticipation that the western development would reach further than was finally achieved. Gardner's Crescent therefore stood alone and, apart from the "colonies" style housing of the facing Rosebank and Rosemount Cottages, the rest of Edinburgh developed around it in this corner without distinction. In front of the crescent a tiny garden was created to complete the half-circle and it has been kept as a neighbourhood green patch ever since, coming into the city's hands in 1886 as amenity ground "for the public benefit and advantage".

A line of the original railings remains at the rear, a low wall borders the busy Gardner's Crescent road side with a mesh fence beside the tarmacadamed path. Cherry, sycamore and elm trees make an attractive display and a line of park benches are set against the railings. Gardner's Crescent garden provides a pleasant touch of greenery, a place to sit in a busy part of town and is appreciated by both residents and the many city folk who use it as a short cut as they walk between Morrison Street and Fountainbridge.

Facilities: Garden Seats. Near bus route. Access for disabled.

Gayfield Square

Situation: On the westerly side of Leith Walk opposite Elm Row, between Union Street and Annandale Street. Area: 0.93 acres (. 38 hectares).

This tiny green rectangle surrounded by the bustle of one of the busiest parts of the city had illustrious beginnings. The aristocratic Gayfield House stood at the top of Leith Walk and Gayfield Square, earlier known as Gayfield

Place, and had its own share of celebrities, including lords and ladies, knights and earls. In 1819 a well-known Lord Provost, Kincaid Mackenzie, entertained Prince Leopold, afterwards the King of the Belgians, in his house on the west side of the square and Archibald Bennet, at No. 1 became physician to Emperor Alexander of Russia and the Imperial Guard and was knighted for his services. But perhaps the most notable neighbours of Gayfield Square today are the officers of Gayfield Police Station on the west side.

Nowadays Gayfield Square serves as a valuable community park and a place to sit in summer with the atmosphere of the old days still reflected in the classic New Town buildings all around and some still retain their elegant fanlights and attractive iron balconies. The grey frontages of the houses act as a foil to Gayfield Square trees — elm, sycamore, hawthorn, almond, ash, whitebeam, birch and some fine rowan. Bordered by a stone wall and the old iron railings, there is a small shrubbery at the Leith Walk end and the entrance is at the opposite side. Edinburgh Corporation assumed custody and management of the ground in 1886 under the powers of the Edinburgh and Municipal Police Act of 1879.

Facilities: Garden seats. On bus route. Access for disabled but small raised kerb gives some difficulty.

Gilmerton Park

Situation: Off Ferniehill Road, Gilmerton. Area: 5 acres (2.025 hectares).

The official title may be Gilmerton Park, but for local people it is still known as The Dell, a name going back for as long as anyone can remember. The unevenness of the surface is because old quarries were once worked here, later filled by dumping, although some soft ground subsidence has remained. If the park is little more than a few green grassy acres that provides open space for children to play, local residents to stroll, walk their dogs or as a short cut to school or the shops on Moredun Park Road at the foot of the hill, it is unquestionably a park with a view. From its high vantage point the Edinburgh panorama from Gilmerton Park is dramatic. In the middle distance is historic Craigmillar Castle, Arthur's Seat and the Salisbury Crags, the rocky spine of Edinburgh's Old Town leading up to the Castle with the Tolbooth St. John's and the great crown of St. Giles' clearly visible; westwards is Blackford Hill with its observatory and, away to the south-west, are the rolling Pentland tops. Across the Forth the Fife hills are the northern backdrop and the ever-widening Firth melts into the open North Sea to the east. Two strategically-placed seats take full advantage of the scene for it is something to be savoured.

The park, which has an irregular shape, stretches down to meet the school playing fields at the bottom of the hill, with the life of the community gathered around it — houses, homes for the elderly, the community centre, library and a football pitch with pavilion. Gilmerton Park was acquired by Edinburgh in 1964. It is much used and, for such a small park, space and distance are its predominating features. A few lime, elm, ash and sycamore trees are near the Ferniehill Road end and a hard path divides the park leading from Fernieside Gardens to Moredun Park.

Facilities: Park benches, hard path, one football pitch. Off bus route. Access for disabled.

Gyle Park

Location: Mid-way along Glasgow Road on the south side behind St. Thomas's Episcopal Church. Area: 52.8 acres (21.384 hectares).

Hidden behind the Glasgow Road on the outskirts of the city, The Gyle is one of the Council's largest parks. It is unequivocally dedicated to sport. But such is the Gyle's southern aspect, with the whole range of the Pentland Hills panorama dominating the horizon in one giant sweep, with Arthur's Seat, the Braids, Blackford Hill and Corstorphine Hill all part of the same spectacle, that it also attracts those who simply want to pace the park's boundaries to admire the view.

The Gyle's wide-open sense of space and distance is arguably unrivalled by any other of the city's parks. Not that it will be much considered by the many football and rugby teams who come to do battle there. At weekends the rugby pitches are regularly used by Corstorphine Rugby Club, while various football league and friendly games are also played. Other rugby and football clubs use the park during the week and there are changing facilities in a large pavilion.

Part of its boundaries are marked by sycamore, rowan, sorbus and ash trees, with paths and benches to the west and south side. It is popular with joggers and dog-walkers and a safe play area also makes it an attraction for young children.

The Gyle Park, under city ownership since 1953, has become a considerable city asset with its popularity as a sporting venue and those magnificent views. To meet the demands for pitch sports and the needs of the local community Gyle Park may see recreational developments in the future.

Facilities: Eight football and four rugby pitches, a pavilion, play area, paths and benches. On bus route. Access for disabled.

Hailes Quarry Park

Location: Off Murrayburn Road, Dumbryden Drive, next to the Union Canal, Longstone. Area: 30 acres (12.15 hectares).

Situated behind the Union Canal, Hailes Park is one of the Council's largest parks. Its beginnings were as the old Hailes Quarry, opened in 1750, and its light-coloured calciferous sandstone was used in the making of Edinburgh's Georgian New Town. At its peak Hailes Quarry employed 150 men, with over 100,000 tonnes of rock extracted each year and spanned 300 acres to a depth of 100 feet. The quarry was flooded in 1949, but deemed a danger to children and, as part of the infilling process of this huge site, it became a city dumping ground and tip. It was from this unlikely start that today's green and pleasant acres were fashioned. A number of large rocks have been placed at different locations within the park as a reminder of the area's past.

With its quarry background, Hailes Park forms a natural bowl looking towards Corstorphine Hill with easy access for the fringing Longstone estate flats. Bordered by cherry, rowan, poplar, hawthorn and birch trees, scattered with woody islands and landscaped in the centre as a mini-woodland of oak, birch, rowan and alder, the park has all the feel and look of the countryside.

The whole park is an ideal playground for children, with two play areas for small children and, in keeping with the central theme of wild woodland, various pieces of commando-style equipment have been placed strategically around it. The size of the park, with its large areas of rough-cut grass, make it an attraction for walking and jogging on gravel paths with glimpses of the triple spires of St. Mary's Cathedral and Donaldson's School through gaps in the buildings. Separated from the park by a thick hedgerow, the Union Canal is another attraction with its ducks and water fowl and weedy-green waters with their wilderness backdrop of ash, bramble, hawthorn, rowan, chuckling magpies and a variety of small birds.

Hailes Quarry Park came into Edinburgh District Council's jurisdiction by a series of acquisitions beginning in 1967 and finally by leasing over two acres from Lothian Regional Council.

Facilities: Benches, two play areas and commando style equipment. Near bus route. Access for disabled.

Harrison Park

Harrison Park is split by Harrison Road, Polwarth, and is bounded by the Union Canal, West Bryson Road, Harrison Gardens and Ogilvie Terrace. Area: 17.5 acres (7.0875 hectares).

Harrison Park first came under control of the Corporation in 1886 with a 15-year feu of 13.92 acres from George Watson's Hospital. An additional 1.375 acres were feued in 1902 for a bowling green and playground. It is interesting to note from old records that in the year of the First World War "expenditure on the formation of the bowling green, road and drain charges, and fees of feu charter have been £219 15s 3d". The wages of the staff to look after the bowling green, tennis courts games area and football pitches were an annual total of £159 9s 8d. The income from the rent of rubber shoes for the bowling green was £7 1s 8d.

It is a pleasant, well-used little park in the heart of the city with the tree-lined walkway along the bank of the Union Canal a particular pleasure like a tiny wildlife reserve with willow trees that seem to defy the law of gravity. Nesting ducks, coots and other waterfowl create interest for all ages. The Harrison is an all-purpose park, a place to walk, or jog, or sit in quiet peace, or for children to play football or cricket, or to run the dog, yet designed and segregated so that each activity does not encroach unduly upon the other. The tennis courts, like the bowling greens, have been popular now for a century. There are rose beds along the front of Ogilvie Terrace and flowers and park benches on the south side of the dividing Harrison Road. The park's trees are mostly cherry and limes. On the other side, the park continues with a safe play area and bowling greens tucked neatly in to a corner.

Harrison Park is one of those unexpected Edinburgh surprises. Set in an area of the city which nowadays is partly residential and partly industrialised, it could so easily have been swamped as the city developed along with the accompanying pressures on open space. It remains a testimony to the city planners of old for creating it in the first place and to the residents and city councillors who have had to fight over the years to keep their precious green acres out of the clutches of speculators and industrial developers.

Facilities: Tennis courts, bowling greens, one football pitch, play area, games area, toilets. On bus route. Access for disabled.

Haugh Park

Situation: Down Braepark Road, off Whitehouse Road, Barnton, or by foot from Cramond Bridge Hotel across the Almond by the old Cramond Brig. Area: one acre (0.405 hectares).

Although Haugh Park was acquired by the city in 1890, the majority of people in Edinburgh hardly know of its existence, far less where it is located. In old Scots "haugh" means low, level ground beside a stream, which is an excellent description of this tiny park close to the River Almond on its east bank and between the old and new Cramond Brigs.

Nowadays, perhaps it barely meets the definition of a park, but it is a delightful place nonetheless, planted with a shrubbery of viburnum, hawthorn, roses and young trees and, for such a small park, it has a large and popular play area for young children. There is also limited car parking, benches and picnic tables. A visit to Haugh Park is like a trip to the country.

A few strides from the River Almond Walkway, the park has a quiet, rural atmosphere overlooking a field at the foot of Braepark Road. The park leads on to a picturesque close-up of the river from a stone viewpoint. Here the Almond forms a pool at a bend in the river and the sight in both directions is idyllic.

Downstream is the old Cramond Brig, with its antecedents stretching back some four centuries. Sir Walter Scott gave this area immortality with his tale of how "Jock Howieson" was gifted the lands of Braehead for saving King James V from a fight. There was only one condition — whenever the king passed that way a basin and ewer were to be offered to him by Jock's descendants. Nearby is Braehead House where Scott's little friend "Pet Marjory" spent happy holidays.

Haugh Park is located in another of Edinburgh's tree-rich areas — trees down the Braepark Road approach, splendid beeches, oaks, chestnuts, rowans, sycamores by the water, a wilderness bank behind the park of silver birch, rowan, lime, ash and bramble. The quiet hum of traffic is heard as it crosses the new Cramond Brig, but at Haugh Park and its delightful woodland surrounds the atmosphere remains of peaceful tranquillity.

Facilities: Car parking, benches, picnic seats and children's safe play area. Off bus route. Access for disabled.

Hillside Crescent Gardens

Situation: Facing London Road opposite Royal Terrace Gardens with Brunswick Street, Hillside Street and Wellington Street radiating from it. Area: 1.45 acres (0.58 hectares).

By the time the Calton Hill area of Edinburgh's New Town was being planned around 1818 the popular development of this elegant new green-field Edinburgh was to the west rather than east of Princes Street. The Calton Hill concept by William Stark, who had an affinity with trees and saw them enriching the area, was aimed at winning back the eastern appeal of the fast-growing city.

Unfortunately, Stark died before his plan could be put into effect, but his pupil, William Playfair, one of Scotland's most celebrated architects, took up Stark's ideas and became the architect for the proposed extended New Town between Edinburgh and Leith. Regrettably, its grand concept never achieved the quality of the building on the hill itself, but Hillside Crescent remains as one of the few examples of what was in the original plan for this part of town. True to Stark's feeling for trees and open space a small garden was planned to fit into the cres-cent, still with its New Town-style classical columns and remaining attractive iron balconies on its Leith Walk end.

Hillside Crescent Gardens today are in three sections, separated by hard paths and surround-ed by a low wall where the bases of the original iron railings remain visible. At each end of the gardens small sections of the railings are still displayed to indicate how it once looked. The gardens are now surrounded by a mesh fence. The central section is mostly open grass with a few maples, limes and elms. But the end sec-tions have fine displays of horse chestnuts as well as lime and elms trees to create a little woodland area in miniature, threaded by paths and there are garden seats handy. Facing the busy London Road, one of Edinburgh's main eastern arteries and the old stage coach route, the gardens are an important continuation of the greenery of the Calton Hill, through Royal Terrace Garden and over the busy London Road. They give pleasure to residents, strollers and even the passing motorists.

Facilities: Garden seats. On Bus route. Access for disabled.

Holyrood Park

Situation: Holyrood Park is unmistakable because it is visible from all over the city. Arthur's Seat stands at its centre, encircled by the Queen's Drive and the Palace of Holyroodhouse stands below its northern flank at the foot of the Old Town. Area: 650 acres (263.25 hectares).

For a city of its size it is remarkable that Edinburgh should have a mountain wilderness at its core as if somehow a Highland scene had drifted down from the north. The volcano origin of Arthur's Seat is still obvious as it lifts its green head 800 feet above the city, although most people interpret its western view as a crouching lion ready for the spring. But its sheer bulk and distinctive aspect — a park-in-the-sky — immediately declares itself a "green city" symbol of Edinburgh.

Apart from its imposing shape above the city, Holyrood Park remains an important prehistoric landscape with a wealth of geological, archeo-logical, historic and natural interest, with the mark of man etched on its face from earliest times. The centre of the volcano, which formed Arthur's Seat some 350 million years ago, is at the Lion's Head and the Lion's Haunch. But it was the earth-shattering, crunching and grind-ing process as continents collided several mil-lion years later that created mountains and the shape of Arthur's Seat and laid bare its secrets for all to observe.

The fluted rock columns known as Samson's Ribs, for example, above the old Wells o' Weary, were formed inside the volcano. The escarpment below St. Anthony's Chapel show the layers of lavas and volcanic ash as do the rocks on the Queen's Drive.

The final fashioning by nature of Arthur's Seat was left to the fierce forces of the Ice Age as vast tracts of ice and debris gouged and scoured their way west to east to form chasms and hol-lows that eventually became Hunter's Bog, Duddingston Loch, Dunsappie Loch, Dry Dam and St. Margaret's Loch. The long, deep cleft on the western slope, known as the Gutted Haddie, was caused by a remarkable waterspout in 1744 that also flooded Duddingston Loch and destroyed part of a house as it gushed downhill. Traces of the earliest inhabitants are seen in the cultivated terraces above Dunsappie Loch, which could date back to the Bronze Age. There are even sites where homes once stood near the terraces, and east of Dunsappie Crag and above Hunter's Bog, there are the tell-tale marks of settlements. The sites of several hillforts are also visible westwards of Hunter's Bog, at Samson's Ribs and around Dunsappie Crag. They cover several periods, but the oldest probably goes back to the Iron Age.

SALISBURY CRAGS . . . a dusting of fine snow enhances detail of the Arthur's Seat wilderness at the heart of the city.

ST ANTHONY'S CHAPEL
. . . all that is left of the little
chapel above St Margaret's
Loch. It is said its beginnings
go back to the 15th century
and it once held a light to
guide Forth sailors.

Winter sunrise . . . and the bird community on Duddingston Loch at the foot of Arthur's Seat prepares for another day of survival.

Arthur's Seat took its name from the 6th century King Arthur, as legend has it, but it could also be from the Gaelic Ard-na-Saigheid, which means the height of the flight of arrows. The park, where there had been periods of recurring forest spanning millions of years, was winning royal approval in the 12 century as a hunting tryst, but it was the founding of the Abbey of Holyrood by David l in 1128 that began the association with royalty that continues to this day.

Holyrood increasingly became attractive as a royal residence rather than the Castle, with its easy access to the hunting grounds, and the Abbey's guesthouse was eventually built into a fine palace. James V added Arthur's Seat and its park to Holyroodhouse in 1541, an enclosure of about five miles in circumference, where debtors could find sanctuary from their creditors for 24 hours.

The names of many of Scotland's famous historical figures are linked with Holyrood Royal Park. Mary, Queen of Scots held a banquet at the foot of Arthur's Seat in 1564; Prince Charles Edward Stewart — Bonnie Prince Charlie — and his Highland army camped below the Rock of Dunsappie before the Battle of Prestonpans; Walter Scott and philosopher David Hume frequented the park "for reverie" and Sir Walter, one of Scotland's great writers, held that the view from the Radical Road below Salisbury Crags afforded the finest view of Edinburgh; and one of the most spectacular events held in the park took place in 1860 before Queen Victoria and 100,000 spectators as the great Scottish Volunteer Review was held.

Changing weather . . . and the mist begins to envelop Arthur's Seat.

When the Black Plague struck the city in 1645, many of those infected were taken out to what was then known as the King's Park, where a hutted village sprang up below Arthur's Seat and those who died were buried there in an attempt to contain the pestilence. The park has been the site of foul murders like the infamous surgeon Nicol Muschat, who cut his wife's throat on a stroll to Duddingston in 1720; duels like the celebrated case of city tailor William Mackay, who ran-through a soldier with his sword, but paid the price with his own life when the prosecutor proved Mackay had been the aggressor on the basis that he was not a gentleman; and even an historic mutiny took place on Arthur's Seat by the Seaforth Highlanders in 1778, where they built a defensive bunker between the Lions Haunch and the cone.

One of the last of the pagan festivals is still innocently carried out on the hill on Mayday. With its roots stretching back to the worship of Baal, or Fire, it is still the custom to climb to the top of Arthur's Seat in darkness to watch sunrise break over the city. Many of the old names associated with the park through centuries are still used: Haggis Knowe, Whinny Hill, the Cat's Nick, Galloping Glen, The Dasses, Windy Goule, Hangman's Knowe, Girnel Craig, the Sclyvers, Samson's Ribs and the Gutted Haddie continue to be recognised locations. Other points of interest include:

Duddingston Loch: The largest of the three lochs in the park, and the only natural one, extends to some 7.9 hectares and was declared an important bird sanctuary in 1923. Many of the birds found in the park tend to home in Duddingston Loch and the connecting reedbeds of Bawsinch.

Dunsappie Loch: It was created on natural marshy ground in 1844 by draining a nearby burn into it. Situated off the High Road in a prehistoric setting the little shallow loch continues to attract visiting ducks and geese and is a popular picnic spot. At one time it was used by the monks of St. Anthony's Chapel as a fish pond in the 15th century.

Hunter's Bog: It was the wet area between Salisbury Crags and the Dasses, although it has been long since drained. At one time a wild and desolate place, where locals did not tarry, it was turned in to a firing range with an army garrison in 1858 and continued as ranges through both world wars.

Queen's Drive: Laid out for Queen Victoria in 1843, it took four years to encircle the whole park, sweeping away many dividing walls and some unsightly buildings to provide magnificent views of the city. During the excavations one of the largest boulders recorded in Scotland was found, said to have been wrenched from the ground and carried by the movements of the Ice Age from Corstorphine.

Radical Road: Constructed along the foot of the Salisbury Crags in 1820 and named after jobless and disaffected west-country weavers brought in to build it. At that time there was a proposal to "sow the cliffs with odoriferous and flowering plants" as well as the "rarest heaths from the Cape of Good Hope and other foreign parts".

Salisbury Crags: Most likely named after the Earl of Salisbury, who commanded Edward lll's invading English army in 1336. There are also theories the name comes from the Scots "saugh" or French "saule" — a willow, in conjunction with the Scots "brae", meaning a hill or incline. When the Radical Road was being constructed, the Earl of Haddington saw the spectacular rock formations as an opportunity to quarry the rock and sell it to pave the streets of London. As keeper of the Royal Park, it was viewed as an act of greed, an abuse of his power and a despoilation of Arthur's Seat. The quarrying was stopped after what was one of the first and successful environmental campaigns in the country.

St. Anthony's Chapel: The origin of the ruined little chapel or hermitage on outcropping rock above St Margaret's Loch is unclear, but generally it is understood to have been dedicated to St Anthony the Eremite in the 15th century. It is also claimed to have been built to guard the nearby holy well and is connected with Knights Hospitallers of St Anthony in Leith. A night-time light was once kindled there to help sailors find their bearings in the Firth of Forth.

St. Margaret's Loch: This picturesque little lochan or pond, a favourite of ducks, geese and young children, is artificial and was built in 1857.

St. Margaret's Well: Dedicated to the saintly Queen of Malcolm lll, the well stood at the south end of what was the great Forest of Drumsheugh. However, during the laying of the North British railway line it all but disappeared under Waverley Station and it was "flitted" in 1862 to the Salisbury Crags. The other St. Margaret's Well is situated at the foot of the Castle Rock.

Wells o' Wearie: In the old days when the water wells in the Old Town ran dry Edinburgh folk had to walk to the Powburn or queue at the Well-house tower at the foot of the Castle Rock for their supply. When water was really scarce they walked to the wells below Samson's Ribs on the south side of Arthur's Seat. They well deserved their name, remembered in that haunting old Edinburgh song, "The Bonnie Wells o' Wearie".

Facilities: Parking, picnic areas. Road through park closed on Sundays. Limited access for disabled.

Hunters Hall Park

Situation: Bordered by Niddrie Mains Road on the north side, The Wisp to the east and the Niddrie estate on the west, surrounding the Jack Kane Centre. Area: 70 acres (28.35 hectares).

Like some other Edinburgh parks, names change or fall into disuse and although Hunters Hall Park remains its official title this large stretch of green on the edge of the city is also called Niddrie Park, the street maps name it Niddrie Policies and others call it the Jack Kane Centre, although the park was there long before this sports complex was built in 1975.

It is a wide and handsome park, dedicated to sport, but also with much more to offer. Its open aspect looks across to the full eastern flank of Arthur's Seat, the Pentland Hills in the distance and, beyond The Wisp road, the open countryside. A woodland path follows the eastern and southern border of the park through a wilderness area of hawthorn, elder, bramble, holly, dog rose, but also with some fine beech, sycamore, oak, lime and elm trees, with sorbus, rowan and yews at intervals. Not only does this strip of woodland form an excellent and attractive border, but it is a natural habitat for birds and small mammals and well-colonised by rabbits. Nesting pigeons, magpies, and garden birds successfully rear their broods in spite of the presence of children below, who use dens and impenetrable jungles as a playground.

At the rear of the Jack Kane Centre, a copse of mixed sycamore, ash, Scots pine, oak and chestnut provides a landscape feature. Chestnut, sycamore, beech and elm are found as attractive stand-alone trees or in small groups in the northern part of the park, which lend it softness and depth.

Although a pitch is provided for followers of rugby it is king football that holds sway. There are 11 grass football pitches, back-to-back in rows that indicate the volume of involvement, but also the scale of the park because Hunters Hall seems able to swallow them all and there is plenty of room for everyone. Changing facilities are available in the Jack Kane Centre, opened in the name of the former and respected Lord Provost Jack Kane, OBE. The Centre forms a valuable community focus as well as providing a range of sporting and leisure facilities, including a cycle speedway track and BMX track for youngsters.

Part of what was the Wauchope Estate, the park was acquired for the city in 1955 and is particularly attractive for children. In the main, it is a large, flat, safe park with a section of the Niddrie burn flowing at one side and the children have the run of its 70 acres. The BMX track is clearly a success and a large and spreading concrete tree root full of tunnels and

HUNTERS HALL PARK . . . is one of the city's main sporting venues but it includes many specimen trees including this fine beech.

By the side of a lonesome pine . . . a play area full of tunnels and children's hidy-holes near the Jack Kane Centre in Hunters Hall Park.

INCH PARK . . . a panoramic view looking over a fine treescape to the flank of Arthur's Seat in the background.

INCH HOUSE . . . as it is today and the scene some 200 years ago when it was host to the most famous in the land.

hideaways is a popular meeting point. There is a small safe play area for young children located near the main entrance.

Here is a community park on a large scale, with easy access from Niddrie and Greendykes estates for those who want to walk, play sport, jog, be alone or take part in the Jack Kane Centre's many activities. It is a welcoming park.

Facilities: 1 rugby pitch, 11 football pitches, all-weather area for hockey or 5-a-side football, cycle speedway track, BMX track, the Jack Kane Centre's facilities, children's play areas. On bus route. Access for disabled.

Hyvots Bank Valley Park

Situation: Dissected by Gilmerton Dykes Street, the park's extremities are off Lasswade Road to the south and Hyvot Loan to the north. Area: 12 acres (4.86 hectares).

This long, thin park with a view follows a natural declivity and is almost a kilometre in length. It is divided by the busy Gilmerton

Dykes Street. The southern and highest portion affords a dramatic cityscape, Arthur's Seat and the Salisbury Crags dominating the foreground with the Fife coastline and hills to the north. Edinburgh's many landmarks declare themselves from the Old Town and beyond — St. Giles', the Castle, the spire of St. John's Tolbooth and St. Mary's Cathedral. The Pentlands Hills are the backdrop at the rear of the upper park, which is dedicated as a place to stroll, for youngsters to play games and as an open space in the centre of a housing estate.

Lower Hyvots Valley Park, which does not enjoy the same spectacular views at ground level, is nonetheless interesting because the flats are built within the park itself, without fence or barrier. It makes a large and much-used backgarden, playground and neighbourhood park combined, with ash and cherry trees, roses and varieties of hedging peeking over the backgardens of the houses on Gilmerton Dykes Drive. The park, which was created in 1955, runs parallel with Burdiehouse Burn Park a few hundred yards to the west.

Facilities: Hard path walk by burn. On bus route. Very steep access for disabled.

Frame of roses . . . a corner of Inch Park near the rugby pitch showing the park's wide-open spaces and some of its attractive tree collection.

Inch Park

Situation: Bordered by Old Dalkeith Road, Gilmerton Road and Glenallan Drive. Area: 61.1 acres (24.7455 hectares).

Inch is the old name for an island or a piece of low-lying land near a river or burn, and the spacious Inch Park fulfils that definition with a section of the Braid Burn still running through its northern edge. But in the old days it is also recorded how Inch House was once surrounded by a moat, entered by a drawbridge and during periods of heavy rain it became an island cut off by flooding.

Part of that band of bright green within the city that embodies the Braids, Blackford Hill, Craigmillar Park and Prestonfield golf courses, as Edinburgh's boundaries begin to merge with the countryside in the south and east, it is a large, handsome park on two levels with trees an obvious special feature — tree-lined paths, tree-studded green parkland, copses and bordering woodland in wide variety. The pupils of Kingsinch School and Liberton Primary School, set in the park's southern edge, may be too young to appreciate the setting and historic connections, but there must surely be a later benefit to have their early education in such surroundings — the Pentland Hills on the horizon, the wind in the grove of stately beech, elm and ash trees beside the schools and the run of such a delightful park behind them. Equally, the residents along Glenallan Drive are fortunate to have such an outlook with such ease of access — no fences, just a step across the road — to such a large and attractive front garden.

The top level of Inch Park is given over to rolling grassland, kept short and set off by some fine sycamores, elms, beeches and, along the Cameron Toll side, a border of mixed beech, rowan, yew, sweet chestnut and varieties of holly, which acts as an attractive screen.

The lower section is dedicated to sport, the home ground for Lismore Rugby Club and Mitre Cricket Cub. A grass square and an artificial square for cricket is available along with two football and two rugby pitches. The pavilion is close to the Inch House, where limited parking is available. It is an active section, where much training for all the sports takes place as well as matches played.

The lower park is also graced by some magnificent beeches, chestnut and sycamore and, at various corners and borders, cherry, ash, horse chestnut, elm, copper beech, hawthorn, birch, sorbus, sweet chestnut — even a monkey puzzle tree — add to the park's general good looks. The Braid Burn, clean enough after its passage round the city to support small fish and other water life, creates a further interest just behind Old Dalkeith Road. And as an out-of-sight crowning glory to the park, it is the location of Inch Nursery, the plant production centre that services all the city's parks and gardens and, through Enable Services, is also now a training centre for those with learning difficulties (see chapter on Flowers of Edinburgh). Behind its concealing beech hedge, thousands upon thousands of flowers, trees and bushes are being prepared to take their places to enhance the attractive face of Edinburgh.

The lands of the Inch, once known as the King's Inch, were granted to the monks of Holyrood in the 16th century and Inch House dates back to 1617. The initials of its first owner, James Winram, are carved on one of the window pediments along with those of his wife Jean and dated 1634. George Winram, who became Lord Liberton, was mortally wounded at the Battle of Dunbar fighting on the Covenanting side. The house then passed into the hands of the distinguished Gilmour family in 1671, starting with Sir John Gilmour, who became one of Scotland's great judges and a Member of Parliament for Mid-Lothian. Three generations of Gilmours represented Edinburgh in Parliament, the first to the Scottish Parliament and the others to Westminister after the Union. The family linked with the Littles of neighbouring Liberton to become Little-Gilmours and the Gordon-Gilmours extended the house in 1891, adding such 19th-century fashionable details as turrets and oriels. Over the centuries, Inch House has been host to royalty and nobility, the distinguished and the famous; over centuries glittering social occasions have contrasted sharply with the clash of swords and, in the uncertain days of the Forty Five, Hanoverian troops were garrisoned there.

But times change — in 1946 the house was sold and for a time became a school as Edinburgh's "model housing scheme" was built. Now Inch House is a community focal point, a popular adult education and community centre, providing a range of activities run by a locally-elected management committee — football training, yoga, keep-fit classes, weight-lifting, photography, mums-and-toddlers groups, old folks' club, carpet bowling, even a venue for would-be pop stars. It is a far cry from the pomp-and-ceremony days and perhaps it was impossible for those great statesmen and celebrities of old to have foreseen the time when the local people of Inch would take over their stately home or arrive by motor car or taxi along lighted paths. Yet Inch House has survived, in the same grounds that adorned it centuries ago, while other noble houses have become museums or rubble. Inch House today is being put to good use, providing valuable services and much pleasure to many and a major new play area is underway.

In fact, the whole entity of Inch park is a major Edinburgh asset. With a blink of sun it is a contrast of light and shade, the shining green of meadowland, the pastel green of the beeches with their slate-grey barks, the limes and oaks, the broad hand-like leaves of the chestnut, the spikes of the hollies, the needles of the conifers and the dark, rich purple leaves of the maples. But it is at dusk when the shadows have lengthened, or on those dark winter days when the mist swirls or the haar sweeps up from the Forth, that the ghosts of Inch's past are closest to hand.

Facilities: Two football and two rugby pitches, a cricket square, pavilion, park benches, lit paths and play areas. On bus route. Access for disabled.

Inverleith Park

Situation: Bordered by Inverleith Place, Fettes Avenue and Arboretum Road. Area: 54 acres (21.87 hectares).

Inverleith Park is at the heart of one of the most attractive large open spaces in the city which includes the Royal Botanic Garden, the splendid private grounds and sports fields of The Edinburgh Academy, Stewart's & Melville College, Fettes College, George Heriot's at Goldenacre, the Grange Cricket Ground, and the fields of Broughton High School and the police headquarters on Fettes Avenue.

With the slender spire of Fettes College reaching for the sky above the trees like some Transylvanian castle and the towers and spires of the Royal Mile, the silhouette of Edinburgh Castle and the crouching lion of Arthur's Seat and the Pentland Hills filling the southern horizon, this is obviously a very special part of the city. But this huge green oasis is not merely a pretty picture: the playing fields and wide-open parklands are alive with activity and the most active of all is Inverleith Park with its sense of space, town and treescape drama.

Inverleith Park means so much to so many people of all ages with different needs and interests that it almost has separate communities of its own. It is a popular place for walking and exer

cising dogs; a venue for bowlers and there is also a short-hole golf course; a cricket square; it is training ground for a variety of sports from soccer, hockey and rugby and it is a joggers' delight; a place for sailing boats and Sunday picnics; a centre for that old French game of Petanque; there is a much-used children's play area, one of the first of the creative new breed to be introduced in Edinburgh; a place for flying kites and also for quiet contemplation — for its scale tends to swallow people and there is always a corner for seclusion, yet more than 400 events take place annually in the park.

Its striking central avenue, grand entrances, handsome trees — elm, lime, sycamore, ash, poplar and a line of some fine mature birches in the south-east corner — its secluded bowers, abounding wildlife, the sheer scale of such an open space in a city, bestow Inverleith with a sense of grandeur.

In the north-west corner a small encampment of sheds and glasshouses signal that the allotment gardeners are also in action on what was once a 19-hole pitch-and-putt course in the early days. Inverleith Park is also the centre of the Park Patrol service, whose white vans are a familiar sight as they keep a watchful eye on the city's parks and play areas. There is a particularly attractive children's play area in the park and popular bowling greens.

Inverleith Park came into the hands of the old Corporation in 1889 when it was purchased from Mr Charles Rocheid for £33,500 and a farm came with it. From the beginning, the Corporation understood the potential of the gem they had bought, and developed it vigorously. Paths, roadways and drainage were quickly underway, greenhouses, the construction of a pavilion, separate gymnasia for boys and girls, two bowling greens, four tennis courts, two golf courses and a ride for horses were constructed. Even shinty in those days was encouraged.

It is interesting to note that a section of the pavilion was allocated to the elderly men who visited the park and books, newspapers, magazines and board games were provided for their use. In those days, it was not seemly for a woman to be seen on her own in such a setting, but times changed and the kind of facility that was being offered at Inverleith at the turn of the century was an early forerunner of today's day centres. The Ferranti Recreational Club, which welcomes visitors, now fulfils some of that role.

Inverleith pond at the turn of the century was still an attraction for feeding ducks and swans and many people dressed with a nautical flavour to sail their model yachts. The south facing bank of the pond was once used as a drying green and bleaching area. In hard winters, of course, it became a popular skating rink. Inverleith Mains Farmhouse is still there, near

Inverleith park . . . a study in trees along one of the central avenues looking towards the fountain.

Autumn comes to the park . . . the leaves turn to gold on the path above Inverleith Pond.

Look what I've caught . . . on a summer's day at Inverleith Pond.

A place for events . . . including the International Children's Festival.

Model yachting 1960s-style at Inverleith Pond and it remains popular.

what was once the old castle or Fortalice of Inverleith, where archery butts were appropriately in place. At the rear of the farmhouse today is the Council's Inverleith Training Centre as well as a sawmill and the Park Patrol's headquarters. The extensive nursery and hothouse areas were used to supply other parks with trees and plants, although this function has now been centred on the Inch. Inverleith also has the distinction of being home to the highest tree in Edinburgh — a stately elm bred in the Royal Botanic Garden in the 1880s.

The East Gate is a handsome memorial to Alison Hay Dunlop in the form of rusticated piers supporting lions and situated opposite the main entrance to the Botanic Garden.

The North Gate is a pedimental arch opened in 1881 topped by a unicorn with lion shield. Below the archway is the inscription "The gift of Mitchell Thomson, Esq., Councillor for the Ward of St. Bernard's, 1891".

The fountain: when the design of Inverleith Park was completed it had been divided into four sections by two paths. At the intersection of the paths a fountain set in a rough granite obelisk was erected in the memory of John Charles Dunlop, councillor for the St Bernard's Ward, who had been one of the key enthusiasts for the park. He and his sister, Alison, together wrote *"The Book of Old Edinburgh"* along with other books about the city. The fountain is dated 1899.

The Sundial Garden: is a quiet and sheltered bower surrounded by shrubs and trees situated on the site of the old pavilion near the farmhouse. The sundial was presented by Councillor Kinloch Anderson in 1890. It says simply: "So passes time. Alas! How swift". And how true.

Inverleith Pond remains one of the park's pleasures for all ages and, reflecting times past, it is still a favourite centre for the model sailing boat fraternity. Indeed, in 1966 the Inverleith Model Yachting Club was given permission to use the pond one Sunday each month. In September 1981 the first Scottish Model Yacht Racing Championship was held there. At one time the pond presented regular problems with weeds and algae, which was hardly conducive to model yacht racing. Nowadays it is cleared of weeds and rubbish annually and in 1959 a special weed-resistant gravel was introduced.

Facilities: Nine football and four rugby pitches, a cricket square, petanque beds, model yacht sailing, short golf course, bowling green, pavilion, benches, children's play area, toilets. Parking is located near the pavilion and on surrounding streets. Nearest bus routes on Inverleith Row, Raeburn Place and Ferry Road. Access for disabled.

Jewel Park

Situation: Off Duddingston Park South, bordered by the railway line on the south side and Bingham to the north-west. Area: 6 acres (2.43 hectares).

Divided by the Niddrie Burn, Jewel Park falls neatly into a sports section for football and kick-about area next to Duddingston Park South, and a section for strolling and play for younger children. The park has hard paths and lighting and some attractive woodland plantings of birch, ash, rowan, cherry, sorbus and sycamore. There is a small enclosed section for younger children to play football, games or cycle, known by at least some residents as the stockade. The old Southfield park area has been absorbed into it.

Jewel Park, opened by the council in 1959, takes its name from a rich seam of coal that once ran there. It is a valuable green lung between Bingham and Niddrie estates and fulfils the functions of providing open space for youngsters to have freedom to play, yet it is large enough for older people to take a stroll in peace or meet for a chat. It is well used and popular and the carefully-planned shrubberies give it pockets of seclusion.

Facilities: Football, enclosed play area. Off bus route. Access for disabled.

Joppa Quarry Park

Situation: Off Milton Road East, between the railway line, Brunstane Road and Morton Street. Area: 5.85 acres (2.36925 hectares).

This is an unpretentious little park performing an admirable role in the purpose for which it was designed — providing an area for local young people to play and expend energy with a ball, a rough-and-tumble playground for children, an open space where the dog can run or for parents to take toddlers down to a safe play area. It is not a sitting-out park or for contemplative strolls among the roses. The old Joppa

quarry site today is for dedicated play action. But unlike many other utilitarian parks, particularly in other cities, Joppa Quarry Park has a special quality — from its high position above Portobello it looks out across the rooftops to the magnificence of the Forth estuary and its islands, with the Fife hills rising up beyond, and Arthur's Seat lifting its head westwards. Play in such surroundings has additional dimensions. The ground came into Council hands in 1933.

Facilities: One football pitch and play area. Off bus route. Access for disabled.

Keddie Park

Situation: Off South Fort Street, along the lane at the easterly end of Pitt Street and between Largo Place. Area: 1.35 acres (0.55 hectares).

This small green patch, hidden along a narrow walled lane on its western approach off South Fort Street and between the cul-de-sac of Largo Place, is a well-used and much-appreciated neighbourhood park. It has a fine setting above the Water of Leith with its walkway and cycle track and stone steps lead down to what has become a popular strolling area beside a tranquil section of the river as it approaches its estuary below the busy Junction Street bridge. The view southwards from the park is dominated by the northern flank of Arthur's Seat and the cliffs of Salisbury Crags.

Once known as North Leith Public Park and feued from local owner William Calder, with much insistence that no rubbish, workmen's huts or annoyance to the neighbours would be permitted, the park changed its name to Keddie Park in 1927. Nowadays the children's fenced-off safe play area is a popular rendezvous for local parents and their young children, but the surrounding walled square, with its Wheatley elms, whitbeam and new plantings makes a valuable area for older children to play their games, exercise their pets and there is a seat in the sun for those who merely go for the sight of greenery and a chat. Keddie Gardens may be a small, unpretentious open space but, like Edinburgh's other little neighbourly parks set in high-density housing areas, it fulfils an important function for the local community.

Facilities: Safe play area, park benches. Near bus route. Access for disabled.

King George V Park, (Currie)

Situation: Straddling Lanark Road West, Currie. Area: 7 acres (2.835 hectares).

From the Lanark Road King George V Park looks little more than a football pitch with a pavilion surrounded by a grassy area. Yet a step or two beyond the obvious, the ground descends steeply to the banks of the Water of Leith and a delightful path that leads along the riverside. The Lanark Road, heavy with traffic, is 200 yards away, but it is out of sight and out of mind. This is perfect picnic country for families and adventure country, too, with its wild flowers and natural undergrowth, the chance of seeing a rising trout, a bobbing dipper and, occasionally, a darting kingfisher. The other side of the riverbank rises steeply to the Water of Leith Walkway, creating a natural sun trap. It could be the river Amazon for any intrepid eight-year-old explorer. Across the Lanark Road there is another football pitch and a play area with swings and a chute.

There are several King George V parks in Edinburgh. They were named to mark the King's Jubilee in 1936.

Facilities: Football pitches, a pavilion, walks and a play area. On bus route. Access for disabled on to open grass.

King George V Memorial Park, (Eyre Place)

Situation: Off Eyre Place, Canonmills. Area: 2.4 acres (0.972 hectares).

The pleasures of little King George V Park are known mostly to local people in the area and they would probably want to keep it that way. It is delightful on two counts: firstly, as a pleasant park of winding paths, shrubberies, trees and lawns set in an interesting and historic part of the city; secondly, within its grounds is the finest children's playground in Scotland.

As a park, it is a little green oasis set in the densely-populated lower New Town. The

entrance gate bears the legend that at one time it was the site of the royal gymnasium and the home ground of St Bernard's Football Club (1878-1942), once a soccer force which knew the roar of the crowd, but failed to survive the Second World War. A plaque at the gate, erected in 1995, is a reminder of their famous Scottish Cup victory a century earlier.

The park attracts all sections of the community. Some come for a stroll, to walk the dog, for five minutes quiet contemplation, to picnic at lunchtime, to read their newspaper or a book, to catch the sun and the colour of green in a heavily built-up area, and some are just passing through as a shortcut up to Royal Circus and Scotland Street.

The park contains a wide variety of trees and shrubs, including cherry, lime, elm, ash, rowan, elder, willow, sycamore, birch, laburnum, snowberry, varieties of roses, weigelia, bush heather, and potentilla as one section gives way to another. Then a sudden change of pace on entering the great Scotland Yard Adventure Centre area, part of it cut out of the old railway embankment, with its creative and exciting children's play equipment. In 1989 it won the Scottish Playground of the Year Award "for the most outstanding playground in Scotland" and the children pass their own judgement on it daily with their peals of laughter and squeals of delight. It prides itself on its facilities to care for children with special needs like wheel-chair users or the blind.

And in a corner of the garden, slightly sinister-looking, at least for young eyes, is the great, dark entrance of what was the former Scotland Street railway tunnel, now fenced off and overhung with ivy. Here, too, is a gardening interest for the tunnel was once used to grow mushrooms. The park was acquired by the Council in 1948 and developed in the mid 1980s.

Facilities: Paths, benches, large safe play area. On bus route. Access for disabled.

King George V Park, South Queensferry.

Situation: Off Hopetoun Road, on Society Road and Walker Drive. Area: 1.75 acres (0.70875 hectares).

The main feature of this tiny neighbourhood park is the Forth Road Bridge, which dominates the skyline, but the two-way flashing cars and hum of traffic is hardly a distraction. One of the stone pillars at the entrance bears the legend "George V, 1910-1936", with an engraved unicorn and shield. The other post carries the symbols only. This little field, acquired from the Trustees of Sir John-Clark in 1936, is designed nowadays simply for children to play — a set of goalposts for kick-around games and a well-equipped play area. The park is partially walled, but also with a corrugated iron fence. A steep bank of mixed oak, sycamore, hawthorn, elder, ash and dog rose forms a screen on the river side and poplars have been planted beside the road.

Facilities: Set of goal posts and children's play area. Off bus route. Access for disabled.

Lauriston Castle

Situation: Off Cramond Road South with Lauriston Farm Road bordering its southern end. Area: 30 acres (12.15 hectares).

Lauriston Castle, with its 16th-century origins, has two outstanding attractions — its splendid grounds in a wood and parkland setting, with magnificent panoramas across the Firth of Forth, and the Castle for its antiquity and fine collection of antiques.

The grounds are simply splendid — with manicured lawns and sweeping pastures in contrast with woodland walks, displays of daffodils in April, bluebell-carpeted bowers in late May, sudden blazes of azaleas and rhododendrons in June, and winding pathways flanked by some fine beeches, sycamores, sweet chestnut, specimen conifers and even high-reaching monkey puzzles. At under-storey level, there are varieties of holly, lilac, laurel, yew, cotoneaster and wild bramble, with glimpses through the trees of lawns and the ancient grey stone of the castle. The little pond, with its breeding mallards and moorhens at the foot of its island statue, and the rolled croquet lawn, give the castle's surrounds trailing vestiges of an elegant age long gone. Along one of the paths is an ancient well with its date clearly visible — 1672. And among those stately woods are 14 special trees planted in 1984 in memory of the 1st Battalion The Royal Scots Bren Gun Carrier Platoon who were killed or died in the Burma campaign of 1943-45.

The castle had tower house beginnings with major 19th-century additions and was gifted to the nation by its last private owners, Mr and Mrs William Robert Reid, of the once celebrated Edinburgh company of cabinet-makers and house furnishers.

Mr Reid bought Lauriston on his retirement as a suitable foil for his important collection of fine furniture, prints, antiques and objects of art. He and his wife tended his splendid home with loving care, renovated and redecorated it, and rather than see his collections broken up and taken out of context, he presented it as an entity to the nation in 1926. It is now in the safe keeping of the Council.

The Castle has been linked with many notable Scots over the centuries, including the financier John Law, who became a celebrity in the royal court of France. Lauriston and its grounds are now caught forever in a time-warp of Edwardian elegance and refinement that attracts visitors from all over the world. It is the stage for a number of appropriate summer events that range from classic car rallies, classical music recitals, enactments of historical events to family fun days and performances by artists from the Edinburgh International Festival.

Facilities: Tours of the Castle and its contents, car park, woodland walks, croquet, park seats, picnic area and toilets. On bus route. Access for disabled.

Leith Links

Situation: Leith Links is bordered by John's Place on its west side, Seafield Place on the east and dissected mid-way by Links Gardens. Area: 48 acres (19.44 hectares).

The Links of Leith have always been a special place in the story of the Port with historical connections going back to earliest times. The Links once extended as far as Portobello, but that was long before the houses came. The two unusual-looking mounds on an otherwise flat park are old gun positions dating back to the siege of Leith in 1560 when the English army bombarded the French-held citadel. One of the mounds, at the west end of the park, is still called the Giant's Brae, and it was here Somerset's English battery pounded the eastern wall of the old city of Leith. The other mound is known as Lady Fyfe's Brae, where Pelham's battery was positioned.

The Links have been the scene of duels and public executions to the roll of drum, it was where the sick were brought during the great plague of 1645 and the bones of many lie under the green grass. It has been a mustering place for historical meetings through centuries; where

LAURISTON CASTLE . . . the arrival of another spring. The Castle's origins date back to the 16th century.

The grounds
and tree
collection at
Lauriston
Castle are
among the
finest in
Scotland.

LEITH LINKS . . . trees remain one of its features and the park still displays some magnificent elms.

It's Leith Festival time . . . and the Links are turned into a giant party. All are welcome.

Hamilton's Dragoons were encamped before joining General Johnny Cope to be routed by Prince Charlie's Highlanders at Prestonpans; where troops were drilled and where, it is said, Leith was almost "unpeopled" when they turned out to view the presentation of colours in 1797 to the Royal Highland Regiment of Edinburgh Volunteers in which Sir Walter Scott took part on his famous black charger. At one time Leith races attracted thousands to the Links for a "flutter" and the crowds continue to support the Leith Festival, one of the great community events. The Links have been used as bleaching greens, for floggings, the shooting of deserters and the hanging of some pirates (although this duty was normally carried out below the Forth's "flood-mark"). Archery, cockfights, wrestling, performing bears, circuses and fairs have all drawn Leithers to their Links — yet it is probably best known for its connection with the game of golf.

In the 17th and 18th centuries the Links were recognised as Edinburgh's premier place to play golf and the game then, as today, became a preoccupation.

Golf on Leith Links was the great social common denominator because it attracted the cream of society — royalty, nobles and politicians — who were pleased to play alongside those ordinary citizens who had little in common other than a passion for "The Gowff". Montrose played over Leith Links, Charles l heard of the Irish rebellion of 1642 on the Links and it was James Vll's favourite golfing venue. Even the crowds turned out, along with the Duke of Hamilton and the Earl of Morton, to watch the "solemn" match between Captain John Porteous of the City Guard, who is part of Edinburgh's history, and The Hon Alexander Elphinstone for a twenty-guinea stake. The skill of both players was renowned and the match caught the public's imagination. Elphinstone lifted the bet. Many of the city's leading figures built fine houses in Leith close to their favourite pastime as the Port expanded with the help of those old-time golfing fanatics.

No golf is played on the Links nowadays, but it continues to be an important part in the life of Leith and its highly-populated surrounding areas. The Links remain a handsome, large open space with attractive tree-lined avenues and walkways and are much used. Although there are attractive rosebeds and the grass is underplanted with crocus, sponsored by local companies and schools and organised by Leith Community Association, the Links have no pretensions at being anything other than a park to be enjoyed by the whole community. In this respect, it fulfils a need admirably.

Putting and bowling have taken over from the "gowf." It is a great place for walkers, joggers and families, for football, cricket, training, games, picnics, strolls for young and old with handy seats, and there is a well-used children's play area with a separate large climbing rope pyramid. An allotment area is situated on the north side. Horse racing was associated with the Links for many years.

An apocryphal story is told about how the decision was made on where to place the many paths through the Links.

The Provost at the time, goes the story, kept delaying his decision. Weeks dragged into months and all he would say was he would tell the planners where to put the paths when he was ready. Winter arrived and there was still no decision. Then came a fall of snow. The Provost summoned his team to meet on the Links. "Do ye see where a' they footprints are going", he said to his planners. "The heaviest tracks are where the citizens of Leith would like their paths. Build them there".

Nowadays, the sea's tang is still in the winds that cross the Links and the vivid stories of the past are all around. The Links may be smaller than they were a few centuries ago, but with the beauty and dignity of those fine sycamores, lime, ash, flowering cherry, maples, elm, whitebeam, hawthorn, beech and those sweeping green acres they have continued to retain their good looks and sense of importance. In the years ahead they will be further developed to meet the needs of citizens for the next century.

Facilities: Bowling greens, one cricket and three football pitches, putting, tarmacadam walkways, park benches, safe children's play area and allotments. Near bus route. Access for disabled.

Liberton Park

Situation: Off Liberton Gardens, bounded by Liberton Drive and Alnwickhill Road. Area: 11 acres (4.455 hectares).

This little walled park, with its sense of height above the city, was designed essentially to provide a sporting facility, a place for local residents to walk and children to play safely. Situated on the edge of town with the top of Arthur's Seat visible, Liberton Park is well used by families, joggers and dog-walkers. A wooden pavilion provides changing facilities for organised football and the small play area is popular with young children and their mothers. The Alnwickhill Road entrance overlooks green fields and open country out to the Braid and Pentland Hills. Over the next few years its role as a community park will be enhanced.

Facilities: Two football pitches, pavilion and a small play area. On bus route. Access for disabled.

LOCHEND PARK . . . swans and ducks find a home in one of the city's less well-known treasures.

Lochend Park

Situation: Facing the west side of Lochend
Road South and behind Meadowbank Sports
Stadium. Area: 21. 2 acres (8.586 hectares).

Lochend Park was once meadow land belonging to the Earl of Moray, who used the loch for
irrigation. At one time it was a water supply for
Leith, but the Corporation received complaints
that the Earl's irrigation had become a nuisance
and it was stopped. The area was eventually
rented to the old Edinburgh Corporation in
1907 in two parts — the first being the high
ground next to Lochend Road, the second was
the low-lying ground around the loch site where
the Lochend Burn once ran.

The area required much work before it could be
turned into a public park, with drainage and
levelling the top priorities at the time. Today it
is a popular country-style park in a highly-populated area of the city in the shadow of Arthur's
Seat, close enough to hear the roar of the crowd
at Easter Road or Meadowbank, a different kind
of park with all the atmosphere of a rural setting, the cries of the waterfowl, the chuckle of
magpies and garden birds calling from the trees
and the throb of the city a distant heartbeat. The
swampland is a reminder of what parts of

Edinburgh were like before the houses came.

There are two old buildings at the northern end
of the park which attract interest, although their
antecedents seem to be lost in time. One is
called the Doocot and in the long ago was probably used for keeping pigeons for the table as
well as providing a steady supply of eggs. It is
also associated with stories from local residents
that infected clothes were burned there during
epidemics. The other smaller building is a
pump station.

The loch, of course, is a fascination. The south
end is a tangled mass of reeds, alder roots and
bog with only small patches of clear water that
lend it more the appearance of the Everglades
than a small lochan in the centre of a Scottish
city. The clear water at the north end provides
uninterrupted viewing of the large colony of
nesting coots, mallards, herons and swans.
Many of them gather there because they know a
ready food source is available throughout the
day as families with young children appear with
titbits. There are also regular visitors of varieties of duck. The loch is encircled by a path
and made safe by a strong railing. The water
world behind could just as easily be in the
Highlands or on a Border moor.

Lochend is a favourite strolling area for those
seeking tranquillity, but there is also a football

pitch on the Meadowbank end and plenty of scope for children to play their games without interfering with the peaceful setting. It is an ideal site to enhance in the future as an educational and conservation resource.

Facilities: Paths, benches and one football pitch. Near bus route. Access for disabled.

London Road Gardens

Situation: Bounded on the south side by Royal Terrace, with London Road on its north side, and a short section of Easter Road at its westerly extremity. Acres: 10.8 acres (4.374 hectares).

This long narrow strip of mixed country woodland in the heart of town acts as a natural divide between what was the somewhat rarified area of the classical New Town above and the development of the city northwards. Today little has changed — Royal Terrace and Carlton Terrace, with their town houses, fine hotels and embassies, set in Georgian splendour, continue to look down and over the trees to what is one of the busiest exits from the city centre, following the old stage coach route.

But the winding paths through the trees of this strategically-placed rectangle of country woodland continue to give pleasure to residents on both sides of London Road and to the many visitors or city strollers who simply walk on the pavements and enjoy the trees. Known originally as Royal Terrace Gardens, the site was also the property of the George Heriot Trust. It was decided to let the land for garden and nursery use and a gardener's cottage — named Royal Terrace House — was built in 1836. This solitary little lodge in its woodland setting in the centre of the city is still there and remains inhabited to this day. In the early years flower beds made a fine summer show around it and today under-planted bulbs still provide a pleasing woodland scene and a splash of colour in the spring.

The gardens were leased to the Town Council in 1893 and the regulations at the time ensured they would be kept for Edinburgh's future generations, untouched, as the rules said, by so much as a grazing horse, sheep or cow. At one time railings were erected along the top of the gardens, but they went the way of so many other iron ornaments at the outbreak of the Second World War and were removed to help the war effort, although never used. The present dividing hedge has its own attraction, particularly for a variety of garden birds.

Although the London Road Gardens are relatively small they must be viewed as part of that magnificent, green and leafy cover that extends from the top of Calton Hill all the way down to

the boundary of London Road and forms a priceless green oasis at the heart of town.

Facilities: Woodland walks, toilets. On bus route. Access for disabled but steep entrance from Carlton Terrace Brae.

Malleny Park, Balerno

Situation: Behind Balerno High School. Bounded by the Water of Leith on the west and Bavelaw Road to the south. The entrance is beside Currie Rugby Club's clubhouse. Area: 5 acres (2.025 hectares).

Malleny Park is a well-used neighbourhood park, a link with Balerno High School and also home to Currie Rugby Club. The Water of Leith provides the western boundary, with a bridge leading across the river from Balerno High School. There are plans to develop part of the park as an extension of the Water of Leith Walkway, working in close co-operation with all interested parties. To the south, the park is bounded by Bavelaw Road and to the north the rugby ground provides the boundary.

Malleny is a small park for the whole community, a place to stroll, exercise the dog and for children's games. Two football pitches are provided and the rugby club has also two pitches and a small grandstand. Currie Rugby Club is one of the local success stories of the past 20 years, and Scotland's international squad has been known to practise at Malleny before a contest.

Facilities: Two football pitches. On bus route. Access for the disabled.

The Meadows

Situation: To the north side of Melville Drive. Area: 58.4 acres (22.032 hectares).

The Meadows remain one of the most important open spaces in Edinburgh and one of the most popular. In a city built on hills, the flat, wide-open green sward of the Meadows, set in a treescape of more than 1,200 elm, sycamore, maple, ash, lime, beech, cherry, willow, poplar, chestnut, oak and other varieties, the enfolding south side of the city in dramatic skyline silhouette, with sweeping panoramas beyond, conjure sharp and pleasing contrasts — yet it is less than a mile from Princes Street. This was once the site of the wind-swept Borough-Loch, which was part of the historic old Borough Muir, and one of the main water supplies for Edinburgh's Old Town.

As the years passed, the loch took three names: the Borough-Loch; the South Loch to draw the distinction with the North Loch, now occupied by the railway line at the foot of the Castle Rock in Princes Street Gardens; then Straiton's Loch after John Straiton, who unsuccessfully attempted to drain it and the surrounding marshlands in 1658.

In the olden days, the loch was inevitably used for washing, watering animals and, when no one was looking, a depository for rubbish of all kinds, in spite of it being a water supply and dumping strictly forbidden.

In times of drought the quality of the water dropped with the level of the loch and a dyke was built at Lochrin to try to contain and control the water. It is recorded that a vandal of ancient times was jailed for knocking down part of the Lochrin dyke.

In 1722 the Loch was leased to Thomas Hope of Rankeillour for 57 years at the annual rent of £800 Scots. Hope's task was to complete the drainage, create a 24-foot wide walk, enclosed by a hedge and a row of trees on each side; build a 30-foot wide walkway from north to south, lined by a hedge and lime trees, with a narrow canal of nine feet on each side.

The suggested names for the new park were Hope's Park, after the lessee, or The Meadow. Almost three centuries later, both names live on in Hope Park Crescent and Hope Park Terrace and today the Meadows, intersected by Middle Meadow Walk (opened in 1743), Jawbone Walk and Coronation Walk, are properly in the plural.

From the beginning, the Meadows was another Edinburgh delight. Capital citizens came to admire and walk its surrounds of "one mile and a-half and 135 yards English measure".

When Melville Drive was opened in 1859 as part of the South Side development, it brought a further wave of popularity and at weekends, in particular, a steady procession of carriages brought the great and the good of the city to walk or play or picnic as families, parade in the latest fashions or push perambulators to provide Edinburgh's future generations with "the fresh and scented air of The Meadows".

As the city grew, even then threatening precious green places, the far-sighted "environmentalists" of their day saw the need for protection. The Edinburgh Improvement Act of 1827 stipulated that "it should not be competent for the Lord Provost, Magistrates and Council, or any other person, without the sanction of Parliament obtained for the express purpose, at any time thereafter to erect buildings of any kind upon any part of the grounds called the Meadows or Bruntsfield Links so far as the same belong in property to the Lord Provost, Magistrates and Council".

Further later acts reinforced this firm statement and when the Commissioners of Police leased the Meadows for a period of 39 years in 1853, undertaking to keep them as a Public Park but relieving the Corporation of all costs and burdens, it was acknowledged that they had passed into safe keeping.

Over the centuries the Meadows have provided Edinburgh's sports men and women a full range of activities. From football, bowling, tennis, cricket, croquet, quoiting, a strip for toxopholite clubs (as archery was once called) and even target practice for the Royal Company of Archers themselves. Hundreds turned up for the old bandstand concerts, but plans for a Meadows race-course were turned down in 1842. When the great International Exhibition of Industry, Science and Art was held in the West Meadows during the summer 1886, Edinburgh and its Meadows site were given world-wide recognition.

Still in the West Meadows, commemorating the opening of the exhibition, is an interesting and important piece of sculpture. The Prince Albert Sundial is an octagonal pillar with a bronze armillary sphere atop which acts as a sundial. Eight of the 11 stone courses are from a different quarry with varying colours. From the base they are: Moat (red); Corncockle (red); Whitsome Newton (yellow); Cragg (yellow); Myreton (blue); Cocklaw (yellow); Redhall (yellow); Myreton (blue); Ballochmyle (red); Myreton (blue); and Redhall (yellow). At the top of the pillar are shields with the coronet of the Prince, the arms of the Marquis of Lothian, the cipher of the Lord Provost and with the city Arms and the Scottish Arms and the advice: "Tak tent o' time, ere time be tint".

Likewise, at the west end of Melville Drive, the 26-feet high commemorative octagonal stone pillars from a number of quarries were erected by the Master Builders and Operative Masons of Edinburgh to mark the exhibition. They are rendered in different styles and at the top sit 7 ft-high unicorns, while 24 shields present the Arms of Scotland, England and Ireland, coats of arms of 19 Scottish burghs and the crest of the Edinburgh masons. The whale's jawbone arch at the Melville Drive end of Jawbone Walk also celebrates the exhibition and was presented by the Zetland and Fair Isle knitting stand.

Another of those unexpected and fascinating Edinburgh memorials is also situated in the Meadows. Close to the Jawbone is the little fountain dedicated to Helen Acquroff, the blind Edinburgh musician and singer who graced the

THE MEADOWS . . . Middle Meadow Walk under a carpet of fresh snow brings a touch of winter wonderland to the city.

MEADOWFIELD PARK . . . high on the flank of Arthur's Seat it was sensitively fashioned from a wilderness.

ROSEFIELD PARK . . . stands in what were the grounds of the noble 18th-century mansion of Rosefield House. Nowadays the little park is a peaceful corner of Portobello with the Figgate Burn running through it.

city's concert halls and theatres in the second half of the 19th century. During the programme she would compose a verse or two about the guest of honour or dignitaries in the audience and, at the end of the evening, give her special rendering to the delight of everyone.

Helen Acquroff was also a force on the city's temperance platforms, when she adopted the name of Sister Cathedral and it is fittingly reflected in the inscription on the pedestal of her fountain.

Situated just behind Edinburgh Royal Infirmary and close to Edinburgh University, the Meadows remain as popular as ever and continue to be a major attraction for holding all kinds of events from circuses to tented theatre. The role of the Meadows will have to be reconsidered in the future when the old Edinburgh Royal Infirmary is vacated as it moves to a new site and the new Lauriston village is created in its place.

The trees of the Meadows and the adjoining Bruntsfield Links must have the last word. They make a major impact on the city's treescape. Among those not already mentioned are cherry, crab apple, rowan, alder, birch and almond trees. It is interesting to note a third of the trees — more than 400 — are elms. Their vulnerability to the rampant Dutch Elm disease and the future look of the Meadows is obvious.

Facilities: Two bowling greens, two cricket squares, tennis courts, a pavilion, play area, benches, tarmacadamed pathways, toilets. Parking in neighbouring streets. Near bus routes. Access for disabled.

Meadowfield Park

Situation: on the eastern flank of Arthur's Seat, below Dunsapie Loch and above Meadowfield Drive, Willowbrae. Acres: 58 acres (23.49 hectares).

The crater of the extinct volcano of Arthur's Seat is visible only a few hundred yards up the hill in its wild moorland setting of outcropping rock, yellow gorse and tussocky grass. Yet over the wall on the other side of Queen's Drive the contrast in Meadowfield Park could hardly be more sharply drawn. Although it remains the eastern slope of Arthur's Seat, here the grass is finely mown like a golf course fairway, attractive copses of mixed trees soften the bareness of the hillside, create interest and provide shelter. Mature trees — some fine beeches, oaks and sycamores — lend height and a focal point midway along the park's top side set in a natural wilderness area of grass, whin, bramble and dog rose.

The view in every direction from Meadowfield

is riveting. Facing east as it does, the whole of the Forth estuary is visible until it reaches the open water of the North Sea; East Lothian is spread out below all the way down to North Berwick Law; the headland of Fife Ness beyond those East Neuk gems of Crail and Anstruther are on the left and the Moorfoots and Lammermuirs are on the right. Closer to the park, the strategic position of Craigmillar Castle is suddenly clear; Portobello town hall, the wedge of Portobello High School, the Durhams, Musselburgh and Cockenzie are obvious and strollers can almost look down the chimneys along Meadowfield Drive. How fortunate are the pupils of Parsons Green Primary School to have such an attractive green volcano behind them and such a view to the front.

The copses of trees and landscaping deserve special mention. They have been designed and planted with much thought. In the main, they include poplar, whitebeam, silver birch, pine, ash, beech and hawthorn, which create natural suntraps in summer and shelter from a winter wind that rasps the face like sandpaper. They also provide a habitat for birds that normally would not be seen on Arthur's Seat's exposed sides, and children also frequent them to make dens or adventure in their deep and shaded recesses.

Towards the south end of the park a line of hawthorns that were once part of Meadowfield Farm, now invaded by elder, creates the kind of hedgerow scene we used to know and plantings of the next generation of Meadowfield woodland are already in place. Trees were first planted in 1975 and after extensive consultation with local residents the community woodlands were extended in 1995.

The park has a football pitch on a flat area, but Meadowfield essentially is a place to walk and play, picnic and roll Easter eggs, sledge when the snow comes, exercise the dog and admire that magnificent eastern prospect. The ground was acquired from the Abercorn Estates Company in 1952.

Facilities: One football pitch. Off bus route. Access for disabled but this open park has kerb edging.

Morningside Park

Situation: Entrances off Morningside Drive and Balcarres Street. Area: 3 acres (1.215 hectares).

A small, pleasant, elongated park with tennis courts and safe play area make Morningside Park an attraction for children and young people as well as more senior citizens who come for a stroll or watch the activity from a bench. It is one of the city's long-established parks, once part of the old Plewlands Farm, which was a link with olden times. The ruins of Plewlands were still on the site until the 1920s, but the park came into Council control from the Scottish Provident Property Co Ltd in 1913. Surrounded by a wall, the west side of the park is graced by some fine mature silver birch trees, and cherry, holly, yew, rowan and laurel are also present with a frontage of roses at the Balcarres Street entrance with a grove of mature lime trees.

At the Morningside Drive end a number of cedars create impact and interest. The park takes a northern slope, but enough room has been created for a grassed area where older children — and sometimes their parents — can play ball games or merely enjoy a rough and tumble. Both entrances have metal gates and railings and the hard paths through the park have lighting.

Morningside Park has an atmosphere of welcome, it is well used by the whole neighbourhood and will merit improvements in future years.

Facilities: Tennis, grassed play area, separate safe play area for small children and benches. On bus route. Access for disabled.

Murieston Park

Location: Off Dalry Road, bordered by Murieston Crescent, Murieston Road and Muireston Terrace, Dalry. Area: 1.312 acres (0.53136 acres).

Within almost shouting distance of Tynecastle terraces, this little neighbourhood park at Murieston came into the city's hands in 1932. Framed in a square by traditional terraced flats, except at the Murieston Road side where modern flats have been built, this tiny green oasis in a densely-populated part of town is a popular rendezvous for all ages.

Surrounded by a green iron railing and a tarmacadamed path, it is screened by a double width of handsome whitebeam trees with occasional hawthorns. There are plenty of park benches and a children's play area with climbing frames is located in a corner.

In a small park like Murieston, where the whole cross section of the community may meet, ball games have been restricted to under 12-year-olds. Murieston Park provides a focus in the area, a place for quiet chats, a leisurely bench from which to observe the passing scene and where young children can enjoy themselves with grass below their feet rather than the hard pavements.

There is a strong sense of community in the Gorgie/Dalry area and the park is used for a number of community events. It may be a very small park, but it fulfils an important function.

Facilities: Park benches and play area. Near a bus route. Access for disabled.

Muirhouse Park

Situation: Centred in the Muirhouse housing estate, access is by Muirhouse Medway and Muirhouse Park Road. Area: 14 acres (5.67 hectares).

This little community park, in a high-density housing estate, is little more than a closely-cropped field, yet it affords a welcome green open space where children can play, kick a ball or exercise their dogs. A football pitch is laid out during the winter months. The park, which came under Council control in 1947, is in two sections. The lower northern section has a safe play area.

Facilities: One football pitch in season and play area. Near bus route. Access for disabled.

Muirwood Road, Currie

Situation: Bounded by Muirwood Road. Area: 1 acre (0.405 hectares).

No more than an oasis of greenery in the centre of a housing estate, this tiny park is nonetheless a little wonderland to those who know it. The Muirwood Road play area is about 400 yards long and 200 yards deep, but it presents so many imaginative possibilities for those who seek them. An elongated 'S' shaped wood stretches diagonally the full length of the park. Many paths wind through the wood, and children can become hidden among the trees that explode with leaves in summer, but they are never more than a few steps from open space and safety.

In the front of the park there is open grass with climbing frames, roundabouts and swings. At the far end there is a single, vandal-proof metal goal post. Behind the trees there is more grass on a slope which provides just enough gravity to propel a sledge when the snow comes. The Muir Wood once stretched from Gillespie Crossroads to Currie. Little of it remains, but this isolated magical forest, left by Wimpey, is a reminder of what used to be.

Facilities: Woodland walk, play area, benches. Access for disabled. Off bus route.

Newcraighall Park

Situation: Off Newcraighall Road on the south side of Newcraighall village. Area: 9 acres (3.645 hectares).

This attractive little country park, which came into Council ownership in 1922, plays a valuable role in the life of Newcraighall village, now with its own facelift away from the superannuated "miners' raws" image of yesteryear. With open farm fields to the east, its close proximity to the village and local school, Newcraighall Park is well used and popular as a place to play, walk or lounge with the sights and sounds of the countryside all around. Above the park, on its south side, the city bypass speeds the traffic to and from the city, yet below it is a peaceful scene, the most intrusive sounds are the laughter of children playing or the disgruntled notes from small birds in the bordering sycamore trees when a passing kestrel hovers overhead. The motorway embankment has become a tiny wildlife habitat on its own account and a colony of rabbits seem to think they have equal rights of access.

It is a popular football venue, there is a modern safe play area for small children and the park is used as an outdoor focal point for community events. The Musselburgh cycleway runs at the park's south edge.

Facilities: Two football pitches, a pavilion and play area. Off bus route. Access for disabled.

Orchard Brae Park

Location: Split by Queensferry Road and bordered on the north side by Orchard Drive and Orchard Brae. Area: 6 acres (2.43 hectares).

Queensferry Road divides Orchard Brae (or Orchard Gardens as it is shown on some maps)

into two almost semi-circles of greenery, each with a different character and function. The largest section to the north, on the same level as Queensferry Road and divided by a wall from it, is a pleasant grassy area enclosed by trees and a place for children to play, kick a ball or for adults to walk the dog or stroll with a bench handy. The attractive trees along the Queensferry Road side are Wheatley elm. Across the road, the park is laid out more formally as a garden, with a feature of laburnum trees, two beds of red and yellow roses and, at the rear, a shrubbery includes cherry, cotoneaster and laurel. Part of the park was acquired for the city from Sir James Sterling in 1801 and the remainder followed in 1935. Orchard Brae Park will deserve enhancement in the future.

Facilities: Off-street parking and garden seat. On bus route. Access for disabled.

Parkside, Newbridge

Situation: At the entrance to Riverside, off the Old Kirkliston Road. Area: 1 acre (0.405 hectares).

Perhaps it is debatable whether tiny Parkside can be termed a park by definition, but it nonetheless fulfils a role as a place to sit in pleasant surroundings and watch the passing scene. The Council created it from vacant land to improve amenities with a central circular area of rose, birch, oak, rowan and periwinkle, and flanked by two borders containing rosa rugosa, cornus, cotoneaster and privet. Benches offer grandstand viewing of the passing scene. The bowling club is across the Old Kirkliston Road and a safe play area with a kick-around grassy corner is off Riverside leading on to the River Almond.

Facilities: Park benches, bowling and a safe play area. On bus route. Access for disabled.

Patie's Road Recreation Ground

Situation: At the foot of Patie's Road, off Colinton Road. Also accessible from Craiglockhart Drive off Craiglockhart Avenue. Area: 10.9 acres (4.4145 hectares).

PILRIG PARK . . . the ancient Pilrig House dates back to 1638 and has connections with Robert Louis Stevenson.

In this attractive and richly-wooded part of town Patie's Road Recreation Ground holds a prime position facing the full-frontal panorama of the Pentland Hills, which act as a foil for the manicured green expanse of Merchiston Castle School's playing fields, lawns and woodland. At the rear of the little park, the tree-clad bank falls steeply to the Water of Leith and is traversed by some delightful paths through woodland glades. It is like a nature reserve with pigeons cooing on summer evenings, grey squirrels in search of food and the twitter of small birds in the high branches. There are some particularly fine specimens of beech trees at the top of the bank, their pastel grey, smooth bark in contrast to the gnarled textures of surrounding oaks, the dark green of the holly, the sycamores with their broad pointed leaves, tall Scots pines, the handspan-wide blossoms of the elder in June and early July and the tangle below of dog roses and bramble.

Many of the visitors to Patie's Road Recreation Ground come single-mindedly for the sports facilities. There is an excellent railed-off football pitch with a small stand, the home ground for Edinburgh United, but it is also popular for Saturday and Sunday amateur football. The tennis courts are leased to Thistle Tennis Club. The rest of the park is well used by local people as a place to exercise or play, on good days

nearby nursery children involve themselves in games and visitors straying from the Water of Leith Walkway, often suddenly appear out of the woods and wonder where they are.

Facilities: One football pitch, tennis courts, woodland walks and car parking. Near bus route. Difficult for disabled, steps.

Pilrig Park

Situation: Off Pilrig Street with Bonnington Road to the north. Area: 17.3 acres (7.0065 hectares).

This quiet, handsome park was once part of the lands of Pilrig House, built in 1638 by Gilbert Kirkwood and home to some of the city's leading citizens, including the Balfour family, which had strong connections with Robert Louis Stevenson. In earlier times, it was probably a fortalice. It is also where Patrick Moneypenny, an eccentric Laird of Pilrig, lived in the 16th century. Sections of the grounds began to be let out at this time and the Pilrig Rough Haugh became the cause of a celebrated court case, when one David Duff, of Leith, broke the plough of a would-be tenant, threw it into the Water of Leith and threatened to break his head if the assault was ever divulged. Next he went to another tenant, broke his plough and forced him to "work between the shafts till morning". Things have quietened down at Pilrig since those days and the park, which came into city ownership in 1920, now affords much pleasure to local people as a place to walk and play, exercise their dogs in a parkland setting, with trees and bushes and outstanding aspects of Calton Hill and Arthur's Seat in the background. The paths are all tarmacadamed and are well used by old folk and mothers with prams.

Pilrig House has been sensitively restored and sold as private flats and lends the park elegance and a sense of history. A fine central avenue of ash trees, with further species of ash at irregular intervals, seems to lend the park added dimensions of space and a fine, deep woodland of copper beech, sycamore, lime, poplars, oak and birch is as much a joy for children to play in as for the garden birds which make it their home.

Pilrig Park boasts two safe play areas for children at opposite ends and there is also a football pitch. The new Pilrig of flats and bungalows is rising out of this old part of town and this spacious park is not only a link with the old days, but provides an attractive green open space for today's nuclear family.

Facilities: One football pitch, two play areas, hard paths and park benches. Near bus route. Access for disabled.

Portobello Golf Course and public park

Situation: Bordered by Milton Road, Park Avenue, Hope Lane and Stanley Street. Area: 55.244 acres (22.3722 hectares).

This large stretch of parkland on the south side of Portobello, looking across the Forth estuary to Fife, performs the dual purpose of providing a nine-hole golf course and a large play and walking area. Now popular for exercising dogs and playing football, it was acquired by the city in 1898, although golf was played there before this date. The clubhouse was opened in 1911. Play was restricted during World War One, when members of the Ladies' club busied themselves knitting for the troops at the front, and it was suspended entirely in 1940 when the park was ploughed up for agricultural use as part of the war effort. It was 1953 before the club was reopened with a new lay-out to make room for the football pitches at the south side.

Like so many other Edinburgh golf courses and parks it enjoys a fine aspect above the Forth with the broad expanse of Arthur's Seat nosing

above the rooftops and has now been a valuable local asset for more than a century. The golf course is separated from the playing area by strategically-placed young acers and sorbus trees and a mixture of sycamore, ash, oak, elm, Wheatley elm, hawthorn, sorbus and holly lines the edges along with a hawthorn hedge. There is a little garden area at the meeting point of Park Avenue and Stanley Street.

Facilities: Golf and clubhouse, a walking area, pavilion, one soft ball and three football pitches. On bus route. Access for disabled but Milton Road entrances have a step.

Prestonfield Park

Situation: Bordered by Prestonfield Avenue and Prestonfield Road. Area: 3.4 acres (1.377 hectares).

A small intimate park in the shadow of Samson's Ribs on the flank of Arthur's Seat, it is popular with young children and their parents who enjoy the creative safe play area. Their whoops of delight mingle with appreciative claps from the bowling green for particularly fine play. The park is surrounded by a privet hedge, the bowling green bordered by lime trees and a dirt path leads from Prestonfield Avenue to Prestonfield Road. A small kick-around area is popular with older children. The park is much used by local people. It was acquired from J K Dick-Cunnyngham and others in 1926.

Facilities: Bowling, safe play area, park benches. On bus route. Access for disabled.

Princes Street Gardens

Situation: In the valley between the south side of Princes Street, Edinburgh Castle, Castle Hill, Market Street and intersected by the Mound. Area: 37 acres (14.985 hectares). On bus route. Access for disabled to East Princes Street Gardens; King's Stable Road entrance best for disabled to West Princes Street Gardens.

Princes Street Gardens have rightly been called a jewel in Edinburgh's crown. They are an integral part of that dramatic panorama recognised around the world and the first sight of the city for visitors as they emerge from Waverley Station — the ancient Castle on its black rock, the sawblade skyline of the Old Town on its ridge, the towering Scott Monument, the ruined Grecian temple on Calton Hill, the handsome Princes Street, the rose-red endpiece of the Caledonian Hotel, spires and domes — so much to take in at a glance — and the bright green

PRINCES STREET GARDENS . . . from the Scott Monument looking across the Royal Scottish Academy to Edinburgh's West End.

foil of Princes Street Gardens, among the finest in Europe, at the very heart of the city.

Nature may have played the leading role in creating the stage for a garden in the hanging valley below the north side of Edinburgh Castle Rock, but it was the genius of the young Edinburgh planner James Craig, and his associates, who saw the possibilities more than two centuries ago and fashioned the expanding Edinburgh to take full advantage of its hilly, natural contours.

In those days, where the Gardens now stand, the artificial Nor' Loch, part of the city's defences, was at the foot of the Rock and the rest was a marshy valley where in ancient times the Rock dwellers, even before the Romans invaded, would graze their herds and fish in the dark pools and meandering stream that flowed through the reeds and rough grass. There was hardly a roof to be seen, except for St Cuthbert's Church, which had its roots in the 7th century. Princes Street was merely a rocky, wind-swept ridge, where the peeweeps and whaups cried, where Edinburgh folk took their Sabbath stroll, shot hares or admired the crops on Wood's Farm, before retreating back at evening to the safety of their walled city.

King David l of Scotland was first to see the potential of a garden and in 1140 decreed that 15 acres of the marsh should be drained and planted with flowers and bushes. It was known as the "King's Garden". But by the middle of the 18th century Edinburgh had grown to such an extent behind its defensive wall that it was the most overcrowded city in Europe. The city fathers, under the leadership of Lord Provost George Drummond, decided to build a new Edinburgh along the ridge that is now Princes Street, George Street and Queen Street and to their undying credit they undertook to build it in style, a city fit to take its place among the great capitals of Europe. James Craig won the open competition and as part of his grand design, he envisaged gardens, countryside walks and even a canal below his one-sided Princes Street to create space, panoramas and drama at a stroke.

The rubble and unwanted earth dug out for the foundations of the New Town were dumped by horse and cart midway along Princes Street to create an enormous mound 92-feet high — and it has been called the Mound ever since. Immediately the Mound divided the valley into two sections and the gardens were beginning to take shape — East Gardens and West Gardens — and both developed separately.

In those early days, Princes Street was residential and around 1820 the householders between Hanover Street and Hope Street formed themselves into a group known as the Princes Street Proprietors.

They asked leading landscape painter James

Skene to design a countryside garden for their private use in that valley below their homes — and the first step to fashion Princes Street Gardens was underway.

The West Gardens, after a disastrous beginning when most of the trees died, developed into a delightful private promenade area, strictly controlled, mirroring the sophisticated lifestyles of New Town residents and the ambience of their fine homes. No running or jumping, no smoking or shouting were allowed to disturb the tranquillity and appreciation of its wild beauty below the Castle. The cost of a key to enter this private heaven was not inconsiderable.

The East Gardens developed in a quite different manner. In 1761 the Corporation bought the Nor' Loch and the lands known as Bereford's Park from Robert Hepburn. When the fetid Nor' Loch was drained and the North Bridge erected, public access was given to the drained area until the creation of the Mound meant a slow return to bog land. It was then leased to the enterprising Thomas Cleghorn, who carried out further drainage, established a nursery and built gardens to his own design with trees, bushes, flowerbeds and attractive walkways. He granted a key to "persons of respectability", pitched the cost at 10s 6d per year, which neatly undercut the key rate for the Proprietors' West Gardens.

All this time the great railways rush had been moving northwards until only East and West Princes Street Gardens blocked the link-up between Glasgow in the West and the route southwards. The coming of the railway ended Thomas Cleghorn's involvement, but the Town Council then took over, threw the gardens open to Edinburgh citizenry at large — and East Princes Street Gardens are recorded as one of the first truly public parks in Britain.

Pressure immediately mounted on the Princes Street Proprietors to follow. Their first pristine, wild Scottish country garden of tree-lined paths and bushes had given way slowly to a bandstand and eventually even seats were installed. At a time when riots were not uncommon the cautious Proprietors would not permit even sitting on the grass or any activity that could be construed as loitering.

The face of Princes Street was also changing, shops and hotels began to take over and the Proprietors were seen as a waning force. At this time, too, when poor working conditions were the norm with squalor rife among the masses — who were developing their own political power bases — public opinion was against parks and gardens being the prerogative of only those who could afford their pleasures. The Proprietors tried to stand firm, but their time was over. Their rearguard action to prevent the railway crossing their land was viewed as hindering progress and when the first train

Guardian of the city . . . Edinburgh Castle on it's rock overlooking Princes Street Gardens with the Ross Theatre in the centre.

The sun is out . . . and so are the crowds to enjoy the peaceful beauty of Princes Street Gardens at the the heart of the Capital.

Visitors' favourite view . . . looking across Princes Street Gardens to the Castle and the sawblade of the Old Town above.

Valley of flowers and trees . . . with plenty of seats for a rest. Princes Street Gardens looking over to the Old Town on its rocky ridge.

A corner of Princes Street Gardens full of the colour and fragrance of roses . . . looking up to busy Princes Street.

Flower of the night . . . the Gardens during the Edinburgh International Festival with drama from Bank of Scotland's firework display.

trundled through the valley in 1846 the battle was almost over.

It was the Scottish Society for Suppressing Drunkenness that made the first official overture to have the Gardens open to the general public. They believed that if they were at least open on Christmas and New Year's Day the devil's work in the dram dens would be made harder. The Proprietors were forced to agree. Although it took some years, slowly the Proprietors' objections were overcome. With the Edinburgh Improvement Act of 1876, the Town Council took charge of the whole valley.

As the years passed slowly lawns, formal flower beds, specimen trees, shrubs, statues and monuments were introduced, reflecting fashion and fancy and the needs of the people. The classical twin galleries of the Royal Scottish Academy and the National Gallery at the foot of the Mound, separating the two gardens, add further dignity and grandeur to a scene famous around the world.

But it is the combination of that timeless rock with its historic Castle, the sweeping lawns, the fragrance of roses, the whispers of the wind in the trees, the splashed colours of flowers, the fretwork silhouette in grey of the Royal Mile above, the pervading sense of history all around, much of it enacted in Princes Street Gardens, that somehow touches both visitors and local folk alike.

It was here St Cuthbert came to preach more than 1300 years ago, where a tournament of 12 knights was held in 1396 in the reign of King Robert lll, where General Dury placed his cannon during the siege of the Castle in 1545 and a century later it was Cromwell's turn, where witches and warlocks were ducked in the Nor' Loch on their way to the burnings on Castle Hill, where Robert Burns, Walter Scott and Robert Louis Stevenson strolled through the ages with many of the great figures from history books.

It is all these things that make Princes Street Gardens a living, green and special place.

Apart from the activities at the Ross Theatre, increasingly Princes Street Gardens is being used for major events like the Hollywood premier of Rob Roy. The most dramatic event, however, which attracts 250,000 sightseers across the city, is the Bank of Scotland's Edinburgh International Festival fireworks display to music.

 Although the role of the Gardens may be changing, a balance is being struck to ensure they are developed and refurbished with sensitivity.

Today the Gardens have a collection of some of the most fascinating monuments and memorials in the world. The following list gives an indication of their diversity and historic importance.

Monuments and points of interest in East Princes Street Gardens

The **Scott Monument** towers above all else in the Gardens like a giant spaceship pointing skywards. It was built in 1840 to commemorate Sir Walter Scott, one of Scotland's greatest writers. Designed by George Meikle Kemp, it stands 200-feet high and has a double-life-size statue of Sir Walter in Carrara marble by Sir John Steell at its base. The Monument is adorned by 64 statuettes of characters from his works, likenesses of three monarchs and 16 Scottish poets. It has 287 steps to the top balcony and a certificate is available to prove you have climbed to the top.

David Livingstone (1813-73): the statue of the Scottish explorer and missionary is by Mrs D.O. Hill and is found just inside the gate at the Waverley Bridge entrance.

John Wilson (1785-1854): found Edinburgh fame as an Advocate, wit, editor and acerbic writer under the name of Christopher North for the political Blackwood's Magazine. The statue by Sir John Steell faces Princes Street at the Mound Square entrance.

Adam Black (1784-1874): Lord Provost, Edinburgh Liberal MP, publisher of the Encyclopaedia Britannica and the literary journal the Edinburgh Review. The statue by John Hutchison is situated in the shadow of the Scott Monument.

International Brigade Memorial is a rough-hewn stone to honour those volunteers from the Lothians and Fife who fell in the Spanish Civil War (1936-39).

Monuments and points of interest in West Princes Street Gardens

Floral Clock: it is the biggest and oldest floral clock of its kind in the world. In excess of 27,000 plants are used in the design and nowadays it has a pop-out cuckoo. It has a circumference of 10.8m (36 ft) and was unveiled in 1904. It is found just inside the Mound entrance off the stairway.

The **Royal Scots Memorial** is a moving tribute to those of Britain's oldest infantry regiment who fell serving their country in campaigns across the world since the Royal Scots were founded in 1633.

The **Royal Scots Greys Memorial** is located at Princes Street level opposite Frederick Street. It shows an equestrian trooper at the time of the Boer War sculpted by W. Birnie Rhind.

The **Anglo-American War Memorial**: this atmospheric memorial by Robert Tait Mackenzie was erected in 1927 by Scots of

American descent in tribute to the role of Scots in World War One. Known as "The Call", it is located on the main footpath below Princes Street.

The **Falklands' Memorial** is a replica of the garden planted on the same day in the Falkland Islands in memory of the 256 British Servicemen who lost their lives in the 1982 South Atlantic conflict. It is positioned on the south side of "The Call".

The **Gardener's Lodge** was built in 1822 and reworked in 1886. It is one of the West Garden's eyecatchers and, in its picturesque setting with immaculate lawns and flower beds, it is the envy of every gardener in the city. There are plans for it to become an interpretive centre.

The **Peace Trees** near the Gardener's Lodge are known as the Parent and the Daughter in the form of two rare Dawn Redwoods and are situated close to the railway line. They mark the Derry Peace Bus appeal of 1977 and the 1982 Festival of Peace.

The **Parish Church of St. Cuthbert** dates back to the 7th century and is claimed to have been founded by Saint Cuthbert himself. It is highly atmospheric, many famous people are buried there, including Thomas de Quincey and John Napier, the inventor of logarithms, and a gate leads directly to it from the Gardens.

The **Watchtower** is situated on King's Stables Road beside St Cuthbert's Church and was erected in 1827 to stop the body-snatchers robbing the graves for medical research.

St John's Episcopal Chapel is on Princes Street and neighbour to St. Cuthbert's. It was built in 1817 to the design of William Burn and inspired by Windsor's St George's Chapel.

St Margaret's Well is the ruined Wellhouse at the foot of the Castle Rock and dates back to 1362, when it was built by King David ll. Its ruined state was caused by English cannon during the siege of 1545.

The **Norwegian Memorial Stone** is said to be 800 million years old and weighs eight tons. It was presented by the Norwegian Government to mark their appreciation of the kindness shown to their armed forces by Scotland during World War Two. It is positioned beside the lower path next to the railway line.

The **Runic Stone** is situated just below the Castle Esplanade and is probably the oldest memorial in the Gardens, dating back to the Middle Ages. It is Scandinavian and was donated by the Society of Antiquarians at the beginning of the 19th century.

The **Ross Theatre** was originally known as the Ross Bandstand and gifted to the city in 1935. Military band concerts, which began in 1853, were regularly held on the spot. Several upgradings over the years justify its title as theatre and it is a popular attraction in summer.

The **Robert Louis Stevenson Memorial** to RLS, one of Scotland's favourite writers and poets. It consists of a small grove of birch trees and a plaque which simply says: "A Man of Letters — RLS — 1894".

Situated near the Ross Fountain between the lower path and the railway line it is the creation of artist Ian Hamilton Finlay.

The **Ross Fountain** by French sculptor Durenne was in the Paris Exhibition of 1867 and donated to the Gardens in 1869. This beautiful fountain in the shadow of the Castle Rock was originally planned for the West End of Princes Street, but was prudishly condemned at the time as "indecent".

The **Standing Figures** statue by William Brodie of a woman and two children was gifted in 1871 and is said to represent "The Genius of Architecture crowning the Theory and Practice of Art". However, it is also claimed to be a statue symbolising motherhood. It is found on the lower footpath near the Ross Theatre.

Allan Ramsey (1686-1758): Scottish poet, song writer, man of genius, owner of the celebrated bookshop "Hub of the Universe" in the Old Town. Statue by Sir John Steell. He stands close to the Floral Clock opposite the Mound.

Dr Thomas Guthrie (1803-73): one of the leaders of the Free Church after the Disruption, he was one of the great Scottish churchmen and preachers who did much humanitarian work in the city. The statue, by F. W. Pomeroy, was unveiled in 1910 and stands at Princes Street level.

Sir James Young Simpson (1811-70): a great man in world medicine, he was one of the pioneers of modern gynaecology but is perhaps better known for his early experiments with chloroform. His statue, by William Brodie, is found on west Princes Street level.

Dean Edward Ramsay (1793-1872): "The Merry Dean" was head of the Episcopal Church in Scotland, but almost equally well known for his wit and collection of Scottish stories of character and amusement. The tall stone cross at St. John's was erected by "his fellow countrymen".

The **Postern Gate** of Edinburgh Castle is located on the Rock above King's Stables Road and is identified by an iron grill. A plaque marks the place where John Graham of Claverhouse — Bonnie Dundee — held a secret meeting in 1684 with the Duke of Gordon, Governor of the Castle, while the siege was in progress.

The **Zeppelin Raid Plaque** marks the place where a German Zeppelin bombing attack on the Castle took place in 1916. The plaque is not easy to find, but is situated on the cliff face between Johnston Terrace and King's Stables Road.

Trees, flowers and shrubs: The electrification of the railway in 1989 provided the opportunity to begin the refurbishment of plant material in Princes Street Gardens. In conjunction with the Royal Botanic Garden collections of azaleas, lilac and magnolia were planted. The area to the south of the railway line in East Princes Street Gardens, which has been leased to the Council since 1849, was landscaped to emphasise the valley effect. A wide and diverse range of trees, including the dawn redwood, maiden hair fern tree and the southern hemisphere beech have been included. There are now some 2000 trees of around 30 species and replanting continues to ensure a treescape is established for the future.

Shrub borders have been replaced with a view to providing year-round colour and interest and extensive use has been made of a wide range of bulbous plants to provide spring colour.

Facilities: Open-air theatre, cafeteria, refreshment kiosks, putting, children's play area, relief map for the blind on the Mound Square, toilets. On bus routes. Access for the disabled to East Princes Street Gardens; best access for the disabled to West Princes Street Gardens is from King's Stables Road.

Quarryhole Park

Situation: Bordered by Lochend Road, Hawkhill Avenue on the south side and Leith Academy Annexe at the north end. Area: 7 acres (2.835 hectares).

As its names explains, Quarryhole Park was once the site of ancient quarries and a number of large stones have been left as a feature. Out-cropping rock at the southern entrance is also a reminder of its past use. "The Quarry Holes" have frequently been mentioned in Edinburgh's history. It was here, in the 16th century, that the English commander, Sir William Drury, ambassador to Elizabeth 1 of England, treacherously slaughtered a force of Mary, Queen of Scots troops under the Earl of Huntly in what became

known as "Black Saturday"; an attack on Edinburgh from the north by Cromwell was repulsed around the Quarry Holes in 1650; and they were also connected with witchcraft trials back in the reign of James VI.

The elongated Quarryhole Park today is part of a long green arm stretching from Meadowbank, through Lochend Park and almost reaches Leith Links. It is on two levels, a cinder football pitch and kick-about area on the top level, football, rugby pitches and an athletics field in season on the lower level as part of the new Leith Academy. One of the interesting features of the park is the number of sloe trees contained in its shrubberies, along with hawthorn and pink and white roses.

A firm track on the east side leads from Hawkhill Avenue, a name also with roots in the past, down to the Leith Academy Annexe entrance. The park is popular with young folk as a sporting venue, but also fulfils the needs of a neighbourhood park for all. The iron bridge over which Lochend Road is carried still bears a shield dated 1900, built by the Branson Bridge Building Company of Motherwell.

Facilities: Football, rugby pitches and athletics in season. Access for disabled.

Queen Street Gardens

Situation: Bounded by Queen Street on its south side and the elegant Heriot Row on the north side and intersected by Castle Street, Frederick Street and Hanover Street. Area: 28 acres (11.34 hectares).

Edinburgh's first New Town, designed by James Craig, had Queen Street as its northern extremity. But the city looked to the north to expand with the second New Town and William Sibbald —"the Good Town's Superintendent of works" — in conjunction with Robert Reid, submitted a plan that was acceptable to meet the high standards set for them.

Their first decision was to plan a park below Queen Street as a counter balance to Princes Street Gardens on the south side of Craig's "gridiron" plan. The first house of the second New Town was No. 13 Heriot Row overlooking the open wilderness of what was to become Queen Street Gardens.

The new gardens were laid out formally in 1823 as private gardens and maintained as such to this day by the local residents who are key-holders, some of them famous names in the city. It is a pleasure they have shared with their distant, famous cousins of past centuries, and some of their names have been renowned far beyond Edinburgh's bounds. Robert Louis Stevenson, as a child, played in Queen Street

Gardens from his home at No 17 Heriot Row and a framed account of the life of the author of *Kidnapped, Jekyll and Hyde* and *Treasure Island* is placed on the railings opposite his old home. It is said the little pond with its tiny island in the central portion of the Gardens, where RLS played as a child and sailed his toy boats, gave Stevenson the inspiration for *Treasure Island*.

Facilities: Private woodland walks, park benches. Keys may be rented by local residents on application to Aitken Nairn WS, 7 Abercromby Place, Edinburgh, EH36 QF. On bus route. Access for disabled.

Ratho Station

Situation: Off Station Road, at extremity of Hillwood Road. Area: 1.229 acres (0.4941 hectares).

This little park with an open aspect beside the A8 Edinburgh-Glasgow motorway and close to Edinburgh Airport is centred on the Hillwood estate and given over entirely to local use as a playing field with two football pitches. It has a pavilion and a popular safe play area. Acquired in 1962 from the Trustees of the Usher Baronetcy Trust, the park extends into the edge of the estate and provides local people with a place to stroll or watch games. Oak, prunus, silver birch, lime and rowan are found in the park and the hill above the village also provides a backdrop and skyline of trees.

Facilities: Two football pitches, safe play area, car parking. Near bus route. Access for disabled.

Ratho Park

Location: Off Ratho Park Road and bordered by West Croft. Area: 2.74 acres (1.1097 hectares).

Expectedly, Ratho Park has all the look and attractive, intimate character of a village green, with handsome sycamores a striking feature by

the road, but also with a presence of silver birch, ash and rowan along its walled perimeter. In essence, Ratho park is a grassy field with a football pitch, a safe play area and pavilion, but because Ratho is a village the park also has a sense of focal point. It was formerly part of the Ratho House policies. At the bottom end of the park a fence has been erected behind the goal-posts to keep the football out of neighbouring gardens. From its high vantage point, the park's tall sycamores are seen in perspective as part of the pleasant treescapes all around.

Facilities: One football pitch, pavilion, play area, seats and limited parking. Off bus route. Access for disabled.

Ravelston Park and Woodlands

Situation: Off Ravelston Dykes Road and bordered by Craigcrook Road. Park area: 3.9 acres (1.5795 hectares); woodlands: 20.75 acres (8.40 hectares).

Ravelston Park is a little neighbourhood park with a pavilion, a play area and park benches and it has served the local community for almost a century. Originally a field belonging to the Ravelston estate, it has been a traditional venue for the children's Blackhall sports day since around 1909. Over the years this has been a notable local occasion, in the old days with bands and parades, a marquee, pony rides and old-style doorstep sandwiches with tea served in your own tin mug. The Ravelston sports tradition has continued to be handed down through the decades and nowadays it is the local gala run by the Blackhall Association. The park is also used for football, a place to walk the dogs, take a stroll and relax as befits a popular and important community park.

Adjoining Ravelston Park are Ravelston Woods — and they provide an entirely different dimension. In May, with the bluebells in full bloom, they defy description. It is enough to say the Ravelston bluebells are one of the sights of Edinburgh. The woods form a substantial stretch of natural woodland of great beauty, part of the green swathe within the city that includes Corstorphine Hill and Murrayfield Golf Course. Criss-crossed by paths and tracks, through dells and secret bowers, with tall grey-trunked beeches creating space below, then suddenly a bramble thicket or a den of rhododendron, a ferny bank, an outcrop of rock with trailing ivy, the edge of a chasm with the city spread out below.

The cliffs, rock escarpments and the small pond in the woods are reminders of the four stone quarries on the Ravelston estate that in the 1840s provided employment for around 20 per

RAVELSTON WOODS . . . a carpet of bluebells makes spring in this woodland setting one of the sights of Edinburgh.

REDBRAES PARK . . . a tiny neighbourhood park that once was famous. Part of today's cycle track is seen on the left.

cent of Ravelston village menfolk. In their heyday it was a busy scene, winning stone for many Edinburgh building projects and further afield, including St. Giles' Cathedral and Holyrood Palace. But the industry slowly waned in the area and Ravelston quarry did not survive beyond the outbreak of the Second World War.

Ravelston Woods are regenerating with some fine specimens of beech and sycamore, but a wide variety of tree species is found there, including ash, oak, chestnut, sweet chestnut, rowan, silver birch, elder, lime, varieties of holly and along the hard path that leads beside Mary Erskine School playing fields, fringes of laburnum have been planted. The woods are alive with small birds, the cooing of wood pigeons, at night the screech of owls, the rustlings and scratchings of small mammals, squirrels and rabbits and the shadowy, overgrown cover offers perfect hiding places for foxes. High in the trees there are nesting kestrels and sparrowhawks with good hunting ground all around.

Ravelston Woods, which were acquired by the city in 1994, is another fine example of what is almost an Edinburgh phenomenon — a large countryside area, complete with its trees and wildlife, magically beamed down from some remote Highland wilderness into a city where it thrives happily. There are panoramic views of the Pentland Hills to the south, but it is the trees which steal the show. New access to the woodlands from Ravelston Park have now been constructed.

Facilities: Pavilion, play area, woodland walks. On bus route. Access for disabled to park.

Redbraes Park

Situation: Off Broughton Road on a curve of the Water of Leith and opposite Rosebank Cemetery. Area: 2.8 acres (1.134 hectares).

This small park is much appreciated by local people — particularly children and old folk — as a quiet, green place in a built-up area with some light industry. It has a distinguished history because around 200 years ago its grounds were said to be unsurpassed in Scotland and holes were cut in the hedge so that passers-by could catch a glimpse of its charms.

Under the patronage of the Duke and Duchess of Buccleuch, the Countess of Dalkeith, Lady Charlotte Campbell and Mrs Dundas of Arniston, there was an attempt to turn Redbraes House and grounds into a kind of Vauxhall Gardens, then one of London's talking points. A notice appeared in *The Scotsman* to the following effect:

"It has long been observed with surprise that while London boasts of its tea gardens and its Vauxhall Edinburgh, which keeps pace with the 'Sister Metropolis' in every other elegant amusement, has never attempted anything of this kind worthy of notice. In order to accommodate the fashionable world, it is now proposed to convert the beautiful villa of Redbraes with its enchanting pleasure ground, pond and islands, into a place of amusement for a summer season with bards, choirs and soloists. The garden will be elegantly decorated with statues and transparencies brilliantly illuminated. It is hoped the undertaking will call forth the munificent patronage of the nobility and gentry of the higher ranks of taste, fashion and fortune". It is recorded that it was a poor summer in Edinburgh that year, with heavy rain and wind, and perhaps it was the Capital's perfidious climate that put an end to the aspiration. Nothing more was heard of the enterprise.

Redbraes was owned by the Craufurd family, but came into the hands of the Trinity Hospital, who leased it to the Edinburgh Corporation in 1905. It required considerable levelling to create a public park and it never regained its former glory. During World War One, Brown Brothers tested tanks on the slope that existed at that time, but it, too, has gone during subsequent refurbishments and as buildings have encroached over the years.

Today roses remain one of the features of Redbraes with a mixture of shrubs and trees — cherry, ash, hazel, rowan, beech, laburnum — around the park's edge, creating dens and jungles for children. A path leads down to a bend in the Water of Leith. There is a central dirt-track cycle section for older children while toddlers have a separate small play area of their own. It is a place for quiet strolls, chats by local residents on the benches in the sun, exercising of pets and intensive play.

Facilities: Path for walking, cycle area, play area. Near bus routes. Best access for disabled at Redbraes Place entrance.

Redhall Park

Situation: Off Inglis Green Road by Redhall Drive, Slateford. Area: 8.34 acres (3.3777 hectares).

The name Redhall was well enough known in olden times and although Redhall Castle, and Redhall House are located in Craiglockhart Dell, the stone from the ancient Redhall Castle, destroyed by Cromwell in 1650, was used in the making of today's Redhall House which dates back to the 1760s. It remains a pleasant green neighbourhood park for the Slateford residents to walk the bounds, an outlet for youngsters with their games and for parents and grandparents to bring their small charges to the play area. A football pitch with pavilion is also provided. The pavilion and the fenced safe play area are sited at opposite ends.

A gravel path leads around the park and also up to the high ground beside the railway line, virtually hidden by a thick screening of hawthorn, ash, elder, bramble and dog rose. On the other side of the park, below Redhall Drive, there is an attractive mixture of beech, hawthorn, fir, oak, sorbus, with a predominance of black poplar. A line of dark Scots firs and a sweet chestnut near the pavilion provide a strong backdrop and lends the park a sense of enclosure and intimacy.

It is near the old Scots firs, on the brow of the embankment, that the simple Celtic cross of the war memorial is found, erected to those men of Slateford and Longstone who gave their lives in two world wars. It is a supplementary list to the Colinton memorial and the names of those who fell in the 1939-45 conflict begin on a stone parchment at the foot of the memorial and continue round it. Behind those Scots firs a wilderness area creates a habitat for a number of small mammals and insects and the musk of a fox is often on the air. Small garden birds and chattering magpies are seen throughout the park.

Facilities: One football pitch, pavilion, railed safe play area with seating and picnic bench. Bus route to Inglis Green Road. Access for disabled.

Regent Road Park

Situation: Below Regent Road on the south east flank of Calton Hill. Area: 3.4 acres (1.377 hectares).

This narrow, little park affords dramatic views to Holyrood, Arthur's Seat and the Salisbury Crags and continues the cascade of green Edinburgh from the top of the Calton Hill almost into the royal park itself. It was first feued in 1877 from the Governors of George Heriot's Hospital at the cost of £25 per annum on the understanding that "the ground is never to be used or occupied in any other way or manner except as a public park, and shall be put to no other purpose whatsoever, and that no building whatever shall be erected on the grounds in all time coming". It has remained that way ever since, a little, peaceful, green place at the heart of old Edinburgh, a vantage and resting point from which to admire the Capital's southern panorama only a few minutes from the bustle of Princes Street.

In the old days, every 22 years at each Martinmas, the Governors of the George Heriot Hospital were expected to receive a sum of double the feu duty, a practice which continued until some of the Garden was devoured by the development of the North British Railway Company at the handsome cost in 1890 of £2068 under the powers of the Waverley Station Act. The trains still pass below but now, with the passage of time, they glide rather than clank and hiss as Robert Louis Stevenson remembered them from near the same point.

A bowling green still stands on the spot it has occupied for a century, although with the changes in lifestyle of the residents of Abbeyhill and its surrounds, the former children's playground and gymnasium on the site are long gone. Yet some of the modern cousins of those far-away children of the past still find enjoyment in the dens among the bushes and trees in this little park. Regent Road Gardens, which could be enhanced by refurbishment, remains a tiny green gem in the perspective of Regent Terrace's Georgian elegance above and in the shadow of Arthur's Seat.

Facilities: Park benches. On bus route. Limited access for disabled.

River Almond Walkway

Situation: The River Almond Walkway stretches from the village of Cramond by Cramond Bridge, off Queensferry Road and culminates at Cammo Park and the ruined Cammo House. Area: 90 acres (36.45 hectares).

Not so much a park as a nature trail and historical ramble, the River Almond Walkway passes along a clifftop through a mixture of woodlands, marsh, a gorge, beside ponds and meadowland, which support a large diversity of wildlife habitats. It is rich in birdlife, the woodlands are alive with their sound, mallard and moorhen nest on the banks, white-chested dippers bob and dart upstream and the Cramond swans are everyone's favourites at the mouth of the river as they sail majestically around the anchored yachts. There is a wealth of plants and trees — meadow cranesbill, sweet cicely, creeping ivy, ivy-leafed toadflax, butterbur, yellow tansy, oak, beech, sycamore, ash, elm, elder and fungi like lawyer's wig. Generally, the River Almond Walkway is a delight for those with a taste for the countryside.

It is also historic country. In the 2nd century AD, the Romans established their important settlement of Alaterva at the Almond's estuary, part of the Antonine's Wall network of forts. The same safe anchorage at the mouth of a constricted river attracted industrialists in later centuries. Like the Water of Leith, with similar conditions, the River Almond became a centre

RIVER ALMOND WALKWAY . . .   the wild beauty of the River Almond between Cammo and Cramond on the edge of the city.

ROCHEID PATH . . . autumn woodland and the Water of Leith combine to form an idyllic scene behind the Colonies.

of milling, with workers' cottages, and by the end of the 18th century Cockle Mill, Fairafar, Peggy's Mill, Dowie's Mill and Craigie Mill were thriving. But the changes forced by the industrial revolution saw a variety of industries come and go — iron, the manufacture of spades and iron hoops at Dowie's, sawmilling, nails, furniture and even a paper mill and gelatine processing at Peggy's.

Peggy's Mill does not have the expected romantic derivation of being named after some long-forgotten mill owner's wife — it more likely comes from Piggie's or Piga's mill, probably after the "pickieman" or mill servant with responsibility for machinery.

Traces only are left of those earlier activities that once made the River Almond one of the most polluted rivers in Scotland. But the works vanished, the quality of water improved and nature — with the help of the local authority — has begun to reclaim the Almond as her own. Trout, larvae and laceworm are back and with the return of waterlife also some of the birds that feed off it.

Cramond Brig, where the original 15th-century bridge once stood, is also part of the route. Immortality was bestowed upon it by Sir Walter Scott with his description of how Jock Howieson rescued the disguised King James V from a fight and received lands around Braehead for service to his monarch. Braehead House, where Scott's charming young poetic friend "Pet Marjorie" spent her holidays, is still standing along with the alleged remains of Jock Howieson's cottage.

At Grotto Bridge, nearing Cammo, the 18th-century follies created by Robert Adam are visible in Craigiehall land. The project of improvement to this part of the Almond gorge was commissioned by the Hon. Charles Hope Weir in 1752 and included tree planting, building the bridge, the Grotto Bath-house, the Craigie Hall Temple (also known as Lennie Temple) and the Isle of Venus downstream, designed to display classical statues. The River Almond Trail finally leads into Cammo Park by a field gate at Cammo Walk.

Facilities: Parking. Access for disabled but some sections are rough and stairs prevent accessibility for the entire length.

Rocheid Path

Situation: Rocheid Path leads from the top of Arboretum Avenue along the banks of the Water of Leith behind Inverleith Terrace and St Colm's Church to emerge at Inverleith Terrace Lane opposite Howard Place. There is an exit across the river at Bell Place into the Colonies. Area: 3.8 acres (1.539 hectares).

This attractive little path is an unexpected and delightful woodland glade full of the sound of birds and the murmurings of the riverbank. Trout fishers and the occasional blue flash of a kingfisher create the impression that Rocheid is deep in Lothian countryside.

It is named after the haughty but colourful Rochheid family who once owned the property as part of their estates. The name is first mentioned as a merchant and Edinburgh burgess, but the old records show that James Rocheid was Town Clerk in 1680 when, in recognition of certain business in London, the Council granted him "one gratuity of £400 sterling and a piece of plate valued at £50 sterling to be gifted to his lady".

Sir James Rocheid of Inverleith was given permission to "enclose and impark some ground" at Inverleith by an act of 1661. The family became regarded as eccentric and took as its crest a man's head — "rough and hairy" — and the Rocheid coach, emblazoned with heraldic insignia, was a familiar sight in Stockbridge as it plied between the house of Inverleith and business in the city.

It is said pride in family name and status made the Rocheids feel they could ride roughshod over local folk, but a story is told how vanity was punctured at Rocheid Path.

It seems the senior member of the family was riding his horse along the footpath which, of course, was banned to horses, when he met an ordinary-looking elderly gentlemen who refused to give way. The old man politely pointed out that the path was for pedestrians only and horses were expected to take the road. Rocheid was furious and imperiously ordered him to step aside. "Know that I am John Rocheid, Esquire of Inverleith", he shouted. "And I am a trustee of this road. Who are you, fellow?"

"I am George, Duke of Montagu", replied the elderly man. Rocheid made an undignified exit which, it is said, gave locals at the time much pleasure. The Duke was in Scotland visiting his daughter, the Duchess of Buccleuch.

Nonetheless, over almost 200 years the Rocheids did much for Inverleith, one of the family was a distinguished agriculturalist and the houses on Inverleith Row were built on his land.

Rocheid Path leads to the point where the Water of Leith bends alongside Arboretum Avenue and it was here in the old days that the ford was situated where the lairds of Inverleith made their crossing to church or from their return from the taverns to their long-vanished fortalice. Two centuries ago, Gabriel's Road ran from the site of Multrie's Hill, where Register House stands today, down by Broughton and Silvermills and crossed the Water of Leith at the ford. The name of Gabriel's Road survives at the steps on Glenogle Road and took its name from the following incident:

The Laird of Inverleith's son was giving his elderly father a piggy-back across the ford when he stopped half-way. The Laird asked why they were stopping and his offspring explained it would be a grand thing if the old man were to slip off his back into the fast-running water so that he could get his hands on the Lairdship. The old Laird laughed heartily. "Aye, man, Gabbie", he said, "that was the very thocht I once had when I was taking my faither across at your age. And sae ye're just your faither's son, Gabbie!".

Rocheid Path was originally given to the Corporation free of charge by the governors of Fettes Trust to form an access from Bell Place to Arboretum Avenue to be permanently maintained as garden or shrubbery ground. It remains a well-used and favourite walk by locals, giving access to Inverleith Park and a shortcut for The Edinburgh Academy pupils over the bridge from the Colonies as they head for their rugby pitches at New Field off Kinnear Road. Such a secluded vignette of the country so deep in the city, with its high, ivy-clad banks, spring flowers and sense of privacy is another of those special Edinburgh places for those in the know and a delightful surprise for those who walk the path for the first time. Nowadays an extension to the path has been made near the bridge.

Facility: Woodland walk. Access for disabled but rough ground.

Roseburn Park

Situation: Bounded by the Water of Leith, Roseburn Crescent and the northern surrounds of Murrayfield Stadium. Area: 18.1 acres (7.3305 hectares).

Roseburn came into the ownership of Edinburgh Corporation in two parts: the first acquisition of 10.33 acres, part of the lands of Roseburn, was in 1898 from Edward Balfour, Esq., of Balbirnie and others, on the basis that it would be used for all time as a public park. The later purchase of 5.86 acres was from part of the estate of Damhead from Sir Archibald Campbell of Succoth in 1906. During World War Two, air raid shelters were located in the park and part of it was allocated to allotments.

One of Roseburn's attractive features is the Water of Leith running at the back, where mallard feed and rising brown trout dapple the water above the weedbeds as fly-fishers snake out gentle casts to tempt them. Roseburn is another Edinburgh park of character and aspect, with Arthur's Seat, the Pentland Hills and the triple towers of St. Mary's Cathedral part of its setting. The park is in the shadow of Murrayfield's new northern stand and Scotland's rugby fortunes can be followed by the roars of the crowd only a few yards away, but out of sight.

Football and cricket are Roseburn's games, and the cricketers are fortunate enough to have an all-weather wicket to beat the rain. It is the home ground for Murrayfield Cricket Club. Hockey is also sometimes played and local schools, particularly Roseburn Primary, make good use of the park's facilities, including the annual sports day. The walkway through to Saughton along the Water of Leith is as popular as ever.

Flowering cherry, lime, ash, poplars, beech and sycamore trees grace the park during the summer with tall willows overhanging the water beyond the bridge. The elegant stone wall surround is designed to hold back the flood waters when the Water of Leith bursts its banks.

Facilities: One cricket, one hockey and three football pitches, a pavilion, river walk and park benches. Near bus route. Access for disabled.

Rosefield Park

Situation: Bounded by Rosefield Place, Rosefield Lane and Brighton Crescent with the Figgate Burn running at the rear. Area: 3.27 acres (1.32435 hectares).

Rosefield Park is part of the grounds that once belonged to the aristocratic 18th-century mansion of Rosefield House, once the home of William Jameson, the "Father of Portobello". It was acquired for the Council from the trustees of the estate of J. Patterson in 1920. Today it is a delightful park in miniature, on a bend of the Figgate Burn, surrounded by tall hedges and shrubberies with the pleasing feature of stepping across the stream by a little iron bridge to the privacy of a paved seating area. It is well maintained with flowers and rosebeds and the grass is underplanted with spring bulbs. Rosefield is a popular sitting-out park beside the burn, a corner of tranquillity in contrast to the busy Sir Harry Lauder Road and the London trains on the railway line beyond, which are a constant source of diversion for the small children who visit the park.

The whole park and the pleasant fenced-off safe play area is a child's delight in a garden that was first created more than 200 years ago. There is a story how its previous owner, the redoubtable William Jameson, whose ships traded with the Continent and even America, once won a profitable New Town drainage contract when he lived in Roseburn House.

The contract allowed his horses and carts to pass through the Jock's Lodge toll free of charge. The arrangement incensed the toll-keeper, however, who saw his authority flouted and one day stopped the carts from passing unless they paid up. Jameson gave the order: "Coup your cairts at the tollbar", and as the mountain of earth grew to enormous proportions the toll-keeper soon saw the error of his judgement. Some of this material was used in the foundations of Pipe Street, off Portobello High Street, named thus because the pure water of the Figgate Burn was piped there from above Jameson's Rosefield home. The park, which was refurbished in the mid 1980s, has an active local community playing a part in its upkeep and wellbeing.

Facilities: Play area and park seats. On bus route. The best entrance for disabled is at Rosefield Place.

Royal Botanic Garden

Situation: Bordered by Inverleith Row, Inverleith Terrace, Arboretum Place and Inverleith Place. Area: 27 hectares.

The Royal Botanic Garden provides Scotland's capital with two exceptional services. Firstly, it remains an Edinburgh favourite for local people who enjoy strolling its exotic, winding paths, with sight, sound and scent experiences round every corner. Secondly, as a centre for the scientific study and conservation of plants, it brings renown to the city from around the world.

The Royal Botanic Garden is involved at the highest level internationally in important tree and plant studies. This exported expertise may not be visible from a walk around its manicured lawns and sweeping treescapes, but its advice is sought on issues from the conservation of rainforests to global warming or trying to tease-out a more secure living from the parched soil of third-world desert areas.

Mostly unseen by the public are the science laboratories with their latest technology for everything from microscopy to plant DNA studies, a collection of over two million preserved plant specimens and a library and reference facility with over 100,000 books and papers. It makes it one of the leading institutions of its kind in Europe.

The Royal Botanic's links with the city go back to 1761, when the Town Council helped to establish the Chair of Botany at Edinburgh University. The friendly association between "Town and Spade and Gown" has been of considerable benefit to all. After almost 250 years, that bond is as strong as ever, and in recent

times, the Royal Botanic Garden is involved in an initiative in which Council-owned land is utilised to bring improvement in horticultural education and research, which will increase the genetic base of plant life grown in Edinburgh, expand the gene bank and help to save threatened species. Part of that task also highlights the important recreational and educational role of plants to the community.

For most Edinburgh people, however, the "Botanics" remain a leafy wonderland of upwards of 34,000 plants, a large green lung of tree arteries, secret places and sudden surprises of breathtaking beauty; a place for family days out, grandads pushing prams, toddlers feeding squirrels, old folk enjoying the peace (for no one seems to shout in the Botanics), and hushed awe from children as they pass through the exotic jungles of the Glasshouse Experience.

The Royal Botanic Garden began as a Physic Garden in a 40 x 40 feet plot near Holyrood Palace in 1670. By 1676 it occupied an area where the north-east corner of Waverley Station now stands and was known as the Town Garden. It is interesting to note that in Princes Street Gardens some of the descendant rhubarb first introduced to Scotland as seed from Russia in 1763 is still flourishing robustly. The Royal Botanic Garden received a Royal warrant as early as 1699. It has held a number of sites in the city, including a move in 1763 to Haddington Place in the grounds of what was the old Trinity Hospital. Constantly outgrowing its various locations, it finally moved to its present site at Inverleith between 1820 and 1823. Nowadays, apart from its involvement with Edinburgh parks and gardens, it has overflow facilities on three other Scottish garden sites, which provide valuable differences in environment and climatic conditions from Edinburgh's low-lying position only 25 metres above the Forth estuary. The sites are: the Younger Botanic Garden Benmore near Dunoon; Dawyck Botanic Garden in the Borders; and the Logan Botanic Garden near Stranraer.

Points of Special Interest

Arboretum and copse: there are more than 2000 specimen trees in the collection, many in groups and with sharp-contrasting colours, barks, leaf shapes and scents. The copse forms a sheltered area of conifers and hollies with many fine examples of flowering shrubs and rhododendrons.

Herbaceous border and Winter Garden: this 165-metre border is an assault on the senses in summer with its blaze of colours and multi-scents sheltered by a large beech hedge. The Winter Garden in contrast provides interesting colours and textures in the dark end of the year.

Demonstration garden: It is presented as a

themed garden with many examples of herbs, annuals, medicinal plants and is divided by a variety of hedging. Separately on display are different forms of flower and foliage, varieties of seed dispersal mechanisms, as well as fungi, ferns and mosses.

Alpine House and courtyard: It provides sheltered accommodation from the worst privations of an Edinburgh winter to allow an outstanding collection of Alpine plants to flourish.

Rock and heath garden: This is one of the Royal Botanic Garden highlights. It is not only the scale that is impressive, with 5000 Arctic, mountain and Mediterranean plants, but its landscaping of rocks and escarpments and miniature scree runs lend it authenticity and drama. Many of the heathers have been collected from around the world as distant cousins of Scottish heather. There is also an important collection of heaths, some of which provide a flash of winter colour.

Dawson International Chinese Collection: Here is an interesting innovation to place special emphasis on the Garden's fine collection of Chinese plants displayed in miniature in a Chinese landscape.

Woodland and peat garden: Country woodland tracks are the entrances to this peaceful segment of the Garden where groups of shade-loving herbaceous plants have been congregated along with specimen rhododendrons and conifers. The peat garden, raised on terraces, is home to a number of interesting dwarf shrubs and mountain-dwelling plants.

Azalea and pond lawns: May and June are the best months to see the azaleas and smell their sweet scent below Inverleith House, as the hill leads down to the pond. The pond itself is always an attraction, partly for its Monet beauty and filigree trees and moisture-devoted plants, but also because the ducks and other waterfowl are always ready to be fed by visiting children.

The Glasshouse Experience: The famous Royal Botanic Garden's amazing tropical displays are special in the ten computer-controlled giant glasshouses that secure their own particular and exclusive environments. They pass from Amazonian rainforests through desert terrain by tall palms, housed in the tallest greenhouse in Britain, even although it was constructed more than a century ago. Along with other exotic plant life, the largest collection in the world of Vireya rhododendrons is also safely kept behind the Garden's extraordinary glass palaces.

Facilities: Exhibition hall, lecture theatre, guided tours, shop, restaurant, toilets. On bus routes. Access for disabled.

ROYAL BOTANIC GARDEN . . . splashes of colour on the Azalea Lawn in early summer with the Copse in the background.

St. Margaret's Park

Location: Off Corstorphine High Street and Dovecot Road, bordered by Ladywell Avenue and Orchard Field Avenue. Area: 9.0 acres (3.645 hectares).

Here is a delightful and attractive little park with a pleasant atmosphere that entirely fulfils its role as a neighbourhood recreation area. At one side the bowlers are busy beside their neat clubhouse; the tennis courts are active with young people; putting is popular; small boys expend much energy in front of a single set of goal posts; quieter games are played in a grassy section bordered by lime trees; toddlers and small children have the run of a safe, set-aside play area; older people and the dog walkers have the pleasure of strolling the hard, lit paths among attractive trees and shrubberies with handy benches. The park is situated next to the 10th Haymarket Scout Group hut, with Corstorphine Primary School across the road and the children here also put it to good use. St. Margaret's is essentially a local park and much appreciated.

It also has its historical connections. Standing within the grounds is the white-harled building of the restored Corstorphine Dower House, built around 1640 by James, Lord Forrester of Corstorphine. The park was donated and named by American Christopher Douglas-Brown after his wife Margaret. Both their names are engraved on the main gate. The Douglas-Browns, who had Scottish ancestry, owned land in Corstorphine which they gave to Corstorphine Parish Council in 1915 on the understanding that it was entirely for the enjoyment of local people and should not be run as a means of making profit. The park came into the hands of the city in 1923.

Much of the St. Margaret's attraction stems from its established trees and new plantings. Apart from two handsome tree-lined avenues beside the paths, the park includes elm, lime, sycamore, silver birch, conifer, cherry, copper beech, rowan and almond trees, with flower borders and rose beds providing colour in season. There are pleasant outlooks to the Pentland Hills to the south and Corstorphine Hill.

Facilities: Tennis courts, bowling, putting, football posts, benches and safe play area. On bus route. Access for disabled.

St. Mark's Park

Situation: Off Warriston Road, behind Powderhall Stadium and bordered by the Water of Leith on its south and east sides. Area: 10.6 acres (4.293 hectares).

This little park, on a bend of the Water of Leith, built on reclaimed ground, is located in a delightful part of town on the Water of Leith walkway. It enjoys splendid aspects across Edinburgh to the south with many of the Capital's famous towers and spires instantly recognisable: the golden dome of Edinburgh University at Surgeon's Hall, the Nelson Column on the Calton Hill, the Melville Monument in St Andrew Square, St John's Tolbooth on Castle Hill, the ancient slender spire of St. Andrew's and St. George's in George Street, the turrets of Edinburgh Castle, the square tower of St. Stephen's in the New Town and the three tall spires of St. Mary's Cathedral in the west. Arthur's Seat and the Pentland Hills rise in the background to give St. Mark's a splendid prospect of the ancient city. It is appreciated by the local people who go there to stroll. This was once the Warriston estate and St. Mark's came into Council possession in 1905. It is a tree-rich area of the city, a variety of greens, shapes, heights and textures that spreads into the ancient Warriston Cemetery, creating veins of green along the Water of Leith and its various offshoots, melting into a profusion of more contrasting greens and splashes of bright colour where they meet the allotments on both sides of the walkway. St. Mark's has a May fanfare of cherry blossom on its south side, but a natural wildlife habitat next to the railway line provides its own attractions of sycamore, birch, willows, whitebeams, maples, hawthorn, dog rose, elder, sloes, bramble and snow berries in dens and impenetrable thickets. Unusually nowadays there is also a group of intact young elms. It is home for a great many garden birds, foxes have been seen on occasions and an underpass leads on to the Water of Leith weir, where rising brown trout taunt the anglers from the weed beds, white-blossomed in June with trailing flowers.

A floodlighting system has been installed for training beside the pavilion. It is a place for joggers, walkers of Edinburgh's byways, picnics, for older children a place for a kick-around or adventures in the handy jungle and the very young have their own small play area. The Water of Leith Walkway leads from St. Mark's to Victoria Park by Steadfast Gate, opened in 1983 to commemorate the centenary of the

ST MARGARET'S PARK . . . with the Corstorphine Dower House built around 1640 within its grounds.

Boys' Brigade and a walkway and bridge leads to McDonald Road.

Facilities: One football pitch, pavilion, safe play area and park benches. Off bus route. Access for disabled.

Saughton Park

Situation: Bounded by Balgreen Road and Stevenson Drive and the Water of Leith on its south side. Area: 42.5 acres (17.2125 hectares).

Saughton Park remains one of Edinburgh's jewels. Not only does it afford a large tract of well-managed open space with playing fields, a modern sports centre and a creative play area, but over seven acres it also presents a delightful formal garden in classic style, with walls and neatly-clipped yew hedges, flower and heather beds, a sunken Italian garden, specimen trees, a glassed Winter Garden with exotic plants, a garden of sweet fragrances for the blind and a rose garden that has won Saughton fame. When Saughton's 13,000 roses bloom visitors come from far and near to appreciate the sight in the setting and atmosphere of the previous century.

Saughton Park's potential was obvious from the beginning. When the first 98 acres came into the Corporation's hands in 1900, which included the imposing mansion house and Balgreen House, it was quickly realised what a gem had

been acquired for the city. It cost £52,900 from Sir William Baird Tuke and included some fued 36 acres, which became available for purchase a few years later.

The first part of the ground was immediately turned into a nine-hole golf course, the second into a nursery and the laying out of the park followed with a pavilion for golf, football and cricket. The area enclosed by the old garden wall was designed ornamentally to include a rose garden, American garden, rock garden and sweet pea garden.

In 1908 Saughton became the site of the great Scottish National Exhibition, opened by HRH Prince Arthur of Connaught and the streets were lined with cheering crowds as the royal party drove out to Saughton from the old North British Hotel. Public imagination had been caught by both Saughton and the Exhibition, with its domed concert hall, twin-towered industrial hall, an arts centre, bandstand and machine hall.

During the Second World War, the formal gardens were turned into onion beds as Saughton helped to dig for victory. Two tons of onions a year were produced and distributed to Edinburgh hospitals. Land Girls were housed in the Saughtonhall mansion house, which had earlier been turned into an asylum for the mentally ill. It had a sad ending. The stately old house became riddled with dry rot and was reluctantly destroyed in a controlled burning by the fire brigade.

The elegant Italian Garden was created in 1957, with its sunken lawns, natural stone walls and topiary. The original statues had to be removed because in a less-appreciative age they attracted the vandals. Today, however, the Italian Garden remains a delight with an array of seats for those who want to contemplate its beauty.

The Winter Garden was opened by Lord Provost John McKay in 1984 as an Edinburgh District Council initiative in conjunction with the Royal Caledonian Horticultural Society and the help of local businesses. It contains plants to catch the eye in exotic shape and colour, including a Cupressus Cashmeriana from the Himalayas and the strange-shaped cycad with its sprouting leaves like spears and the high-climbing Bougainvillaea. Of course, it is a place of wonder for young children with the pool and goldfish immediately catching their attention at the entrance. Part of the Winter Garden has been turned into a cafe area.

The main gardens have been laid out in four sections on the level: the central formal rose garden with its ancient sundial in the centre; an immaculately-kept lawn area studded with flower beds of changing shapes and bedding plants altering with the seasons — French marigolds, wallflower, tulips, geraniums, begonias, antirrhinums — and many more; the Italian sunken garden; and at the top a heather garden, with various cuppressus of different tones and height, azalea beds and a variety of shrubs, bushes and trees.

The gardens are separated by painstakingly-clipped yew hedges, which act as a dark foil for the large variety of trees and bushes, colours and textures of leaves and barks.

The trees are another of the features of Saughton — acer, birch, sorbus, conifer, a giant and very elderly yew, beech and copper beech and two eye-stopping, delicate green weeping ash trees trail on to the lawns.

The rose garden deserves special mention. It is a showpiece. Set out as a traditional knot garden, each bed outlined by box hedging, it progresses in stately curves and semi-circles outlined by elegant pathways down a central avenue, a different coloured rose in each section with a standard rose as a centrepiece. Along some of the paths are further rose beds rising to a backdrop of bush roses.

The Rose Society use one of the large rose beds as an experimental area to test their rose-rich delicacy against Scotland's fickle weather before they go on to the market. Roses on display, which have already won public approval, enjoy such titles as Queen Elizabeth, Glenfiddich, Ena Harkness and Grandpa Dickson. "Tak tent o' time ere time be tint", says one of the inscriptions on the rose garden's sundial and in such a place the pressures of time in this modern age are somehow placed in clearer perspective.

Facilities: Tearoom, toilets, park benches, sports stadium, football pitches play area. On bus route. Access for the disabled, one wheelchair available for loan.

Sighthill Park

Location: Off Calder Road, bordered by Broomhouse Road and Bankhead Drive, beside Stevenson College and part of the Napier University. Area: 43 acres (17.415 hectares).

This large park of open aspect with a sense of spaciousness is given landscape drama by the giant vertical wedges of the 16-storey tower blocks of Hermiston Court, Weir Court, Glenalmond Court, Broomview House and the giant rectangles of Stevenson College and a section of Napier University.

Beyond the buildings are the constantly-changing light patterns on the Pentland Hills, to the north the wooded Corstorphine Hill and away westwards, passed the Cleish Hills and the unseen River Forth and Stirling, glimpses of the dark blue high tops above Callander are seen some 50 miles away. The views across city and countryside from the flats are stunning and Sighthill Park provides residents with almost their own slice of countryside.

The park is lined by sycamore, lime and cherry trees, across Broomhouse Road there is a concentration of cherry and, on the opposite side of the park, a fine, thick shrubbery of hawthorn, birch, whitebeam, willows, dog roses and snowberry gives shelter for a variety of small birds.

With its activity and wide-open spaces a stroll in the park is a pleasure.

Sighthill Park's flat expanse of grass also makes it an area dedicated to football. Soccer is played at several levels on the seven pitches provided, but there are kick-about games taking place across the park among all ages.

Changing facilities are available in the pavilion on the east side of the park. The tarmacadamed area beside the pavilion is an attraction as a local venue for in-fashion rollerskate hockey by youngsters.

Behind a cowboy-and-Indian wooden stockade small children have their own play area and seats are provided for their watching mothers.

Facilities: Seven football pitches, a pavilion, park benches and a safe play area. On bus route. Access for disabled.

The glory of Saughton

SAUGHTON PARK . . . local people and visitors come from far and near to view the spectacle of the Rose Garden.

Garden of contrasts . . . colour, shape, texture and fragrance change at every turn in Saughton.

A celebration of shapes . . . among Saughton's many attractions the topiary work is always an eye-catcher for visitors.

Year-long colour and a reflection of plants from around the world in Saughton's Winter Garden.

Silverknowes Park

Situation: on the south side of Silverknowes
Golf Course running parallel with Silverknowes
and Muirhouse Parkways. Park area: 12 acres
(4.86 hectares).

What a view! This small rectangular park overlooks Silverknowes Golf Course with a spectacular panorama of the Firth of Forth. There is
much to hold the attention: a grandstand view
of golf in progress on a highly-visual course
featuring trees and woodland; the estuary
beyond with the tankers unloading at Hound
Point, a triangle of the Forth Railway Bridge
rising beyond; Inchkeith, Cramond Island,
Inchmickery, Inchcolm with the Oxcars light
between; Dalgety Bay, Aberdour, Burntisland
and Kinghorn opposite and the Fife coast disap-
pearing into the blue; the distant mountains
around Callander beyond Stirling in the Forth
Valley; at the rear Corstorphine Hill and the
Pentland Hills on the skyline; a sense of space
and distance that incorporates the green sweeps
of the Royal Burgess and Bruntsfield golf
courses and the farmland around Lauriston
Castle to give the north-western tip of the city a
verdant send-off before dipping into the Forth
estuary.

Like the golf course, Silverknowes Park displays some handsome mature trees, in particular sweet chestnut and sycamore. Nearer the
golf clubhouse, the defining line between park
and golf course has been sensitively drawn with
young sycamore, cherry, whitebeam and lime
trees. It also has the feature that it is an open
park with a welcoming access directly off the
main road. The park is home to football in winter, but it is also a joy for those who come to it
to walk, admire the view or run the dog.

*Facilities: Three football pitches in season. On
bus route. Access for disabled on to open park.*

Spylaw Park

Location: Beside the Water of Leith, off Gillespie
Road, West Mill Road and Bridge Road,
Colinton. Area: 8.0 acres (3.24 hectares).

Whichever way this popular riverside park is
approached — down the Water of Leith
Walkway with beech and sycamores almost
trailing the water or off West Mill Road and
through the old railway tunnel with a stately
chestnut tree at the entrance — Spylaw Park is
delightful. Trees are its most attractive feature.
They are many and varied, forming sharp contrasts of colour, shape, form and height: tall
specimen conifers, varieties of holly, towering

beeches, yew, ash, chestnut, hornbeam, copper
beech and even a monkey puzzle create a sense
of enclosed peace.

Spylaw Park was acquired by the Midlothian
County Council in 1911 for use as a public park
and safe playground for local children. In those
early days woe betide those who dared step on
its manicured lawns.

An open-topped charabanc delivered families
with their picnic baskets. Spylaw House, which
dates back to the middle of the 17th century
with major refurbishment in the 18th century,
had a snuff mill below and behind it and the
addiction made James Gillespie, the founder of
the well-known Edinburgh school, a rich man.

Walled along one side, a play area tucked into a
corner, with plenty of seats, this busy park is
popular with families, but remains all-purpose,
a place to stroll, exercise the dog or as a jogger's running track. It has been colonised by
grey squirrels, the movement of birds is everywhere, trees and bushes ring with the songs of
blackbirds, robins, wrens and finches, the tits
chatter and on the mown grass yellow wagtails
feed on insects with a sudden leap and flutter.

Down by the riverside it is a further leafy
delight, the trees again creating dapplings of
light and shade, and sudden shafts and spears of
filtered sunshine, branches almost touching
overhead, with the Water of Leith running clear
and bright.

*Facilities: Play area, benches, access to Water
of Leith Walkway. Off bus route. Access for disabled.*

Starbank Park

Situation: Off Starbank Road, west of
Newhaven Harbour and bordered by
Laverockbank Road. Area: 2.6 acres (1.053
hectares).

Starbank Park commands dramatic panoramas
over the Firth of Forth to Fife and remains a
favourite city viewpoint close enough to hear
the lapping of waves. Originally, Starbank
House and its gardens were the home of the
Rev. Walter M. Goalen, founder and rector of
little Christ Church in Trinity Road, now a private dwelling. In 1889, on the death of the Rev.
Goalen, the old Leith Town Council bought the
classical, two-storied Starbank House and its
grounds, which at that time boasted a fine rose
garden and tennis courts. They were later linked
with the gardens of Laverockbank House and
renamed Starbank Public Park.

The star itself, eight-pointed and with crescent
moons cut into the bank on flanking sides facing out across the Firth, depicts the "Star of the

Spylaw Park . . . a delight of trees beside the Water of Leith below Colinton village.

STARBANK PARK . . . commands a magnificent site looking over the Forth. It retains many sea connections with the old days.

Sea", believed to be symbolic of a ship's compass and harking back to the days when Forth sailormen navigated the oceans by the stars. At one time sailors spread out their sails to dry in the park. In 1920 Starbank House became Leith's own museum but, after the amalgamation with Edinburgh, the Starbank collection was transferred first to the Huntly House Museum in the Canongate in 1932, then across the road to the Tolbooth in 1954. An ornamental circular fountain was erected by Newhaven merchant Thomas L. Devlin in the lower part of Starbank Park in 1910.

An interesting comparison made in the 1930s indicated that the plants at Starbank on the shores of the Firth were about a week ahead of Princes Street Gardens due to Edinburgh's hills and climatic changes. Certainly the top — and level — part of the garden around Starbank House provides enormous pleasure, particularly for some of the area's elderly residents. It is laid out formally with shaped rose beds and a central sun dial, with plenty of park benches, a pleasant small shrubbery, a rich display of spring flowers and ground cover plants.

Starbank is special with its fine views across the estuary and those who take time to watch the passing ships and brightly-coloured yachts know that a century ago, from the same place, others were watching the tall-masted merchantmen beating up river, their sails stretched and booming in the wind.

Facilities: Gardens, park benches, toilets. On bus route. The best entrance for disabled is at Laverockbank Road, other entrances off Starbank Road have steps.

Station Road Park, South Queensferry

Situation: Off Station Road, beside Queensferry Bowling Club by Ravel Bank. Area: 6 acres (2.43 hectares).

This attractive, small and secluded park is positioned above the town, looking between the two great bridges spanning the Forth and close enough to hear the change of note as trains leave the shore and rumble out across the Forth Railway Bridge. Formerly the property of the Earl of Rosebery, the gardens are in two sections of irregular-shaped lawns with surrounding hard paths and a large variety of trees and bushes on both sides, including cherry trees, sycamore, conifer, ash, damson, holly, crab apple, laburnum, fuchsia, dwarf rhododendron, potentilla, hydrangea, cotoneaster, ivy and red and yellow roses.

The trees give the park shelter and a garden seat is appropriately placed to enjoy the tranquillity. The path through the park leads on to the Back Braes and Ferry Glen, a deep cleft formed by the Ice Age, now filled by a dark tangle of fallen trees and thicket through which sycamore, elder, ash and hawthorn have since seeded. It is planned to refurbish this area. The path leads down to an attractive small garden on the Edinburgh Road. Queensferry Bowling Club, founded in 1877, is adjacent to Station Road Park and a popular venue and meeting place.

Facilities: Hard paths, garden seat, bowling. Off bus route. Access for disabled.

VICTORIA PARK . . . a handsome park of contrasts and a junction point for many city walks.

Taylor Gardens

Situation: On the east side of Junction Street near the junction with Ferry Road North and Coburg Street. Area: 0.90 acres (0.28 hectares).

Little Taylor Gardens, acquired by Edinburgh in 1920 under the Edinburgh Boundaries and Tramways Act, has been a Leith meeting point for many years, where local people can relax on a park seat and discuss matters of the day. Visitors to nearby Leith Hospital also find it a welcome green patch and a pleasant place to wait at the busy heart of the Port. The Leith War Memorial, opened by Sir John Gilmour, then Secretary of State for Scotland in 1927, faces the park on the east side and memorial services continue to be held there along with laying of wreath ceremonies. In the park, in front of the war memorial, a collection of peace insignia are displayed.

A fine show of whitebeam is one of the features of the gardens and a hard, circular path leads around it behind railings. There is a small shrubbery and toilet facilities. Taylor Gardens remains a neighbourly place, an area to stretch the legs while exercising the dog, observe the the passing scene or snatch a few minutes of peace for a luncheon sandwich beside trees and green grass in a bustling and heavily built-up area.

Facilities: Hard path, park seats, toilets. On bus route. Access for disabled.

Union Park, Corstorphine

Location: Off Saughton Road North, bordered by Carrick Knowe Parkway and Carrick Knowe

Drive. Area: 10.0 acres (4.05 hectares).

Union Park is the home of Corstorphine Rugby Football Club and Corstorphine Cricket club and therefore hardly surprisingly the park is dedicated to these two sports. A scrummaging machine, cricket practice nets and a cricket square in the middle of the park display the obvious evidence that they are followed with relish. During the summer, the cricket square is caringly attended by groundsmen, while in winter it is roped off to give protection to the wicket from the army of rugby players who train there. Changing facilities and refreshments are provided in a large pavilion.

Acquired for the city in 1924, Union Park is also popular with local people for walking in a fine open setting with Corstorphine Hill dominating the northern skyline. The park is railed off and bordered by a hawthorn hedge and lime trees interspersed with hawthorn. A well-used children's play area also declares that although the park has built a reputation as a sporting venue, it remains essentially a park for everyone.

Facilities: Three rugby pitches, a cricket pitch, cricket nets, pavilion, play area, path and benches. On bus route. Access for disabled.

Victoria Park

Situation: Between Newhaven Road and Craighall Road, off Ferry Road. Area: 18.1 acres (7.3305 hectares).

Victoria Park traces its history through a number of confusing name changes. Towards the end of the 18th century, the little country track of Whiting Road became a carriageway called Bonnington Road, which later changed to Newhaven Road when the present Bonnington Road was built. Bonnington Park stood on Bonnington Road and boasted a fine house within its grounds known as Bonnington Park House. When Victoria Park was created in the name of the monarch in 1919, the house also changed its name to Victoria Park House. Even more confusingly, Victoria Park was known for a time as Raimes Park after the manufacturing chemists Raimes Clark of Smith's Place. The park passed into the hands of the Council in 1920.

Today it is a handsome park of contrasts, a

THE WATER OF LEITH . . . white water at the mill race as it passes through Colinton Dell.

junction for a number of sign-posted city walks along hard pathways, with trees and shrubs — sycamore, ash, chestnut, poplar, cherry, rowan, birch, oak, fir, elder, potentilla, flowering current, roses and an avenue of whitebeam — making attractive features. The extent of the development of new walkways is well appreciated from Victoria Park, the linkage with the Water of Leith system at Steadfast Gate, with its splendid views of the city, makes a delightful traffic-free ramble that is particularly appreciated and now joins up with the main route to Roseburn.

The park is well-used by pupils of Trinity Academy on its north side, by Craighall Education Centre and Holy Cross Primary School and is also a popular rendezvous for local people as a place to meet, jog or take perspective from one of the many park benches. It has a bowling green, a fenced-off miniature football pitch, a safe play area for tots and a separate play area for older children.

Near the bowling green there is a small fountain dated 1899, presented by the Leith Horticultural, Industrial and Sports Society and opposite Summerside Place on Newhaven Road, King Edward Vll in bronze and wearing the robes of the Order of the Thistle, bids a welcome to the park. The statue, erected in 1913, was sculpted by John Stevenson Rhind at the suggestion of merchant Thomas L. Devlin. It bears a one-word legend — "Peace". There are many local residents who visit Victoria Park daily in all weathers simply to experience it.

Facilities: Walks, children's play areas, bowling green, enclosed five-a-side football pitch and park benches. On bus route. Access for disabled.

Water of Leith Walkway

Situation: The valley of the Water of Leith from Balerno to Leith docks.

The Water of Leith may be only a little more than 18 miles long from its source in the Pentland Hills to the harbour in Leith, but for its size it has held an importance and an affection substantially more significant than many much longer Scottish rivers. It passes through some of the finest rural countryside in Lothian,

with vignettes of exquisite beauty, through one-time thriving mill villages, it meanders by sections of Edinburgh's dark old industrial past, vivid parts of the Capital's story have unfolded along its banks and for at least 900 years it has played a key role in the development of Edinburgh and Leith.

Its vast potential for recreational use was first recognised in the Edinburgh plan of 1949, when imaginations were flaring after the war years, but the daunting and painstaking task of its development in the face of so many different owners, was at last taken up by the old Edinburgh Town Council and then the District Council in 1973.

Nowadays the dream of those far-sighted planners has been fulfilled because the Water of Leith Walkway, in the words of that 1949 concept, now "offers one of the finest riverside walks that any citizen could ask for". Apart from its outstanding scenic delights, its industrial and historical heritage, the course of the Water of Leith is rich in wildlife, ancient and modern woodlands and a vast array of plants. It is remarkable that such a full hand of interests and attractions should be associated with such a little river and much of it within the city itself. The Walkway has been divided into six natural segments from the High School in Balerno to the 17th-century Signal Tower in Leith. Some of their points of interest are as follows:

Balerno to Juniper Green: This section includes the 17th-century Malleny House; the ruined Lennox Tower with 15th-century origins; the Waulk Mill of Ballernoch has a varied history as a 13th-century mill and later a distillery; Balerno Paper Mill has roots in the 18th century; Currie Mill had links to the early 16th century; and Currie Kirk (1785) is said to have had a church on the spot for the last thousand years.

Juniper Green to Slateford: Woodhall House is the first point of interest dating to the 16th century; Woodhall Grain Mill is now the only working mill on the river; the Mossy Mill weir is still intact; the village of Colinton had its beginnings in the 11th century; Spylaw House (1650) was the home of snuff merchant James Gillespie, founder of Gillespie's Hospital and James Gillespie's Girls School; Redhall weir once powered Redhall Mill, latterly used to produce wood flour for the plastics industry; Redhall House (1765) was the site of a castle laid waste by Oliver Cromwell in 1650.

Slateford to Roseburn: Slateford's industrial past is remembered in this section by the Slateford Aqueduct (1822) and Viaduct (1847); The Water of Leith Heritage Centre, formerly the village school, retains many of the old records; Stenhouse Castle was one of the names given to the ancient Stenhouse Mill and remains of its dam are still discernible.

Roseburn to Stockbridge: the ruined windmill on the left bank is said to have been a whinmill for grinding gorse to feed horses; the Scottish Gallery of Modern Art, designed by William Burn in 1825, was opened as a gallery in 1984; Well Court (1884) was presented by Mr J. R. Findlay, proprietor of *The Scotsman*, to house workers; the Dean village, was a former centre of milling reaching back to the 12th century; Dean Bridge (1832) was designed by Thomas Telford and makes a spectacular crossing of the river at the Dean gorge; the Doric temple of St. Bernard's Well, designed by Nasmyth after the Sybils' Temple at Tivoli, was once said to have healing waters and is opened by appointment with the Park Patrol; a little to the west St. George's Well, was erected in 1810 over another reputed healing spring.

Stockbridge to Bonnington: The Colonies were built between 1861 and 1911 by the Edinburgh Building Co-operative as one of the first low-cost housing schemes; Canonmills with its 12th-century roots was royal land gifted by David l to the Canons of Holyrood; Puddocky, once a favourite fishing section, lies between Canonmills and Warriston, but it takes its name from the former Paddock Hall and not from Water of Leith puddocks as commonly believed; Warriston Cemetery was once a fashionable burial ground for the rich and it still retains an exceptional number of different tree types; the Steadfast Gate provides a valuable connection with Victoria and St. Mark's parks.

Bonnington to Leith: Parts of the present Junction Bridge date to the original in 1860; Coalie Park is a landscaped part of the bank built from a coal depot; McGregor's Mill was

built around the remains of the Old North Leith Church (1493); Sandport Place Bridge was originally constructed in the 18th century; Lamb's House, now run by Leith Old People's Welfare Centre, remains a striking example of a 17th- century merchant's house; King's Landing was the landing point for the celebrated visit of George lV in 1822; the King's Wark was originally built by James l in 1438; the Signal Tower (1686) once sported a windmill, but it was converted into a signal station for Forth shipping during the Napoleonic Wars.

Facilities: Seats and picnic tables on some stretches. On or close to bus route for entire length. The two most accessible sections of the Walkway for the disabled are from Redhall Park and at Warriston, beside the supermarket.

West Pilton Park

Situation: Off Pennywell Road and bordered by West Pilton Gardens, West Pilton Avenue, West Pilton Grove and West Pilton Park. Area: 15.6 acres (6.318 hectares).

On two levels, West Pilton Gardens have been undergoing a facelift. Laid with hard paths and landscaped with two areas of young hawthorn, birch, rowan, sycamore and alder trees, a circular seating area has been created where paths merge and make a friendly and attractive feature. The fenced-off children's play area on the top level remains busy and popular. The paths are lit and fringed with rowans. The lower section of the path is given over to games and a football pitch.

When completed this little park will be an attractive green place in a densely-populated part of town, with the flats of the new Pilton on the east side looking over it with easy access. There are glimpses of the Fife hills and the Pentlands to the south.

Facilities: Sitting-out area, one football pitch and safe play area for young children. Off bus route. Access for disabled.

White Park

Location: Off Gorgie Road opposite Tynecastle Park, Gorgie. Area: 0.75 acres (0.30375 hectares).

Within earshot of Tynecastle, this tiny park is a welcome respite from the traffic in a busy and densely-populated part of town. More a rest area and children's safe playground than a park, it nonetheless provides an appreciated off-the-pavement oasis with a screen of cherry trees and a splash of colour from rose hedging. The play area is a popular rendezvous for mothers

One of the attractive signposts found along the banks of the Water of Leith Walkway.

and children and the picnic benches and seats are well-frequented by lunch-time workers and shoppers with their sandwiches. The theatre of the Gorgie streets is all around and this park-in-miniature is a handy balcony from which to observe the passing throng from a bench or catch a five-minute break or watch the kids burn off energy. A colony of street pigeons has made White Park their pecking area and they too have become part of the colourful Gorgie stageset.

Facilities: Play area, park benches and picnic benches. On bus route.

Whinhill Park

Location: Off Calder Road, bordered by Saughton Road and Broomhouse Crescent. Area: 11.7 acres (4.7385 hectares).

Surrounded by schools, church, health centre and community centre, Whinhill Park is like Broomhouse's village green and a focal point in the area. As a neighbourhood park, it is much enjoyed by children, but older people also use it for a quiet walk or to exercise their dogs.

Old quarries were once located here, but during the making of the Calder Road's dual carriageway unwanted soil was dumped at Whinhill and grassed over. The park has an open aspect with a fine perspective of Corstorphine Hill, but views of the Pentland Hills to the south are likely to be lost as housing is designated for this southern edge.

A mixture of sycamore, cherry and sorbus trees fringe the park with a single tall black poplar opposite the health centre but further tree-planting to create a sense of woodland is planned. The park offers glimpses of Edinburgh Castle, St. Mary's Cathedral and although the pointed modern spire of St. David's Broomhouse Parish Church is somewhat smaller in scale, it nonetheless is a local landmark. A pedestrians' underpass crosses below Calder Road and Saughton Road.

On the west side of the park there is a large cycle dirt track, full of humps, hairpin bends, graded corners and, in wet weather, mud bath hazards along the route. It is a popular and safe attraction for youngsters to demonstrate their derring-do.

Ball games take place all over the park, but the football pitch on the lower north side is on school ground. The area first came into city ownership in 1934 and the park is now to be enhanced in compensation for a section which is due for development.

Facilities: Cycle track, park benches, paths. On bus route. Access for disabled.   ✿

Along the Water of Leith . . . where trout splash near Canonmills.

. . . and kingfishers are sometimes seen in Craiglockhart Glen.

Colour spectacular . . . among the 13,000 blooms in the Saughton Park Rose Garden the air has the fragrance of perfume.

The flowers of Edinburgh

Along green paths where our contentment lingers,
And flowers and lawns and sweetly-scented banks,
We sense the skill of patient brains and fingers.
And, unseen gardeners, we give you thanks!

A stroll round Edinburgh confirms immediately that the gentle art of horticulture is in robust good health and practised with dedication.

But it is a changing scene. Those meticulously-laid out formal rows of flower pots and shrubs, for example, that a century ago were an admired talking point on Waverley Station roof — even along parts of Princes Street — would be incongruous, dated and dull by today's tastes. As the decades pass, so horticulture in Edinburgh has altered with them, led by innovation, changing fashion, economic pressures, public taste and those necessary pioneering spirits who force change in the search for improvement.

They have influenced almost every aspect of our gardens from choice of plants and shrubs to design and presentation.

One of the early gardening influences on the Edinburgh scene came from the private estates of Dalmeny and Dalkeith Palace back in the late 18th and 19th centuries. Inevitably, the plantings at these two locations were soon simulated across the city. But it was the secretary of the Royal Caledonian Horticultural Society, Dr Patrick Neill, a Town Council member, who was instrumental in giving gardening in the city a major boost by supplying thousands of plants from the Society's experimental garden at Inverleith to the Meadows, Bruntsfield Links and East and West Princes Street Gardens.

They quickly became a talking point and large numbers of Edinburgh folk walked or hired cabs simply to go to admire them. That experimental garden at Inverleith, of course, later grew in size and reputation to become the world-famous Royal Botanic Garden we know today.

The second person who perhaps had even greater influence on New Town gardens was James McNab, who succeeded his father as curator of Edinburgh's Royal Botanic Garden in 1849. McNab prepared comprehensive reports and supervised improvements to a number of gardens such as Queen Street east, St Andrew Square and Charlotte Square. He also advised on the planting at the Meadows, Bruntsfield Links and Princes Street Gardens.

McNab favoured grass areas surrounded by tree belts, which probably prevented wide-spread use of rockeries and annual bedding schemes which were in vogue in the mid 19th century. It is significant that a former curator of the Royal Botanic Garden, Dr Eddie Kemp, a world authority on arboricultural matters, still gives his advice to the city.

Scottish private gardens provided a training ground for horticulturists second to none and indeed many of those who passed through this system found their way to local authorities where their exacting standards influenced parks departments nationwide for many years.

Another major influence in Edinburgh horticulture was the number of nurseries and seed firms located in the Capital. In 1833 there were 25 nurseries in the city, but by 1890 this number had grown to 75. Edinburgh became regarded as a centre of quality for the supply of plants and seeds, not only used extensively within the city, but also despatched throughout the United Kingdom and around the world.

Some of the more notable nurseries at this time were Cunningham's at Comely Bank, where Rhododendron Cunningham's White and Cunningham's Sulphur were bred and are still grown to this day; Lawsons of Goldenacre introduced the Lawson's Cypress to Britain; Grieve's Nursery at St Ronan's Terrace bred the apple cultivar James Grieve; Thomas Cleghorn ran East Princes Street Gardens as a nursery and Eagle and Henderson were in West Princes Street Gardens.

The coming of the railway in the 19th century also gave rise to many horticultural exhibitions in the Capital, where trophies and large cash prizes were awarded and it was not uncommon for a collection of twenty fruits to be displayed by a single exhibitor in George Street's Assembly Rooms.

The Royal Botanic Garden has played an important role in the development of horticulture in Edinburgh. The city and the Royal Botanic Garden, working together as a team formed in 1761, when the Town Council assisted in establishing the first Chair of Botany at Edinburgh University, have formed a valuable partnership in the best interests of green Edinburgh, which has now lasted for almost 250 years.

In the 1850s, for example, when Edinburgh was confronted by such air pollution that it began to disfigure the city — caused by the smoke, grime, soot and fume emitting from factories, steam trains and thousands of coal-burning households — it was the Botanic Garden which again stepped in to help. The title of "Auld Reekie" was not conferred on Edinburgh for nothing as the pollution blackened buildings and blighted trees and plants.

After careful study, the plantsmen at the Botanic Garden began to advise the council on the species of trees, plants and shrubs that would withstand the ash onslaught and they have continued with their advice and two-way friendship ever since.

Edinburgh, 1850

Nursery, Seedsmen, and Florists

Carstairs, Jno, Warriston lodge
Cunningham, Jas. Comely bank.
Dickson and Co. 1 Waterloo pl.
Dickson, J. and Sons, 32 Hanover Street
Downie and Laird, 17 Frederick street
Eagle and Henderson, 81 George street
Kellie, James, Tanfield
Lawson, P and Son, 1 George IV bridge
Macintosh, R. T., 7 North St Andrew street
Methven, Thos, Stanwell lodge
Reid, David and Son, Leith walk
Reid, John, Easter road, Leith
Shanklie, William, Leith walk
Stark, R. M, 1 Hope street
Wright, Sons, and Wright, 1 Greenside place
Wright, Henry, Dean Cottage

Oil Merchants

Craig and Rose, Leith walk
Dawson, Wm. 20 Elbe street

A growing business . . . this entry in the Edinburgh Professions and Trades Directory of 1850 had 16 seedsmen listed. By 1875 the list had risen to 189.

They were also in the forefront in taking advantage of the boom in inexpensive world travel by sea in the latter half of the 19th century. It was then that missionaries, explorers, geographers, prospectors and botanists were transported to the far-flung corners of the globe and among the cornucopia of wondrous items brought back were new and exciting plant species to catch the imagination.

A wave of specialist plant collecting was one of the results, and a horticultural trend was set then that is evident in Edinburgh's gardens to this day. After the long years of green and

Gardening books by Edinburgh nurserymen on sale in the Capital across the centuries

Edinburgh, 1774

James Gordon, nurseryman.

The Planters, florists and gardeners pocket dictionary: being a practical collection from the most approved authors in the English language relating to the above three parts of gardening, founded on experience, worthy of notice, and adapted to the climate of Scotland

Edinburgh, 1775

William Boutcher, nurseryman.

A Treatise on forest-trees: containing not only the best methods of their culture hitherto practised, but a variety of new and useful discoveries, the result of many repeated experiments. Edinburgh, 1775.

Edinburgh, 1825

George Dickson, nurseryman.

Sale of nursery implements, bulbous roots and seeds, drawers, counters, hardware, double desk, iron safe etc to be sold by public auction at the warehouse of the late Mr George Dickson, No 10 St Andrew Street, Edinburgh, on Wednesday the 14th December 1825.

As it was . . . Middle Meadow Walk with the east and west Meadows showing typical iron railings around the turn of the century.

A fine array of bowlers and whiskers as the Council's Parks Committee meet in the East Meadows at the turn of the century.

peaceful landscape gardens of the Georgian era an almost insatiable demand for colour also developed in the mid 19th century as horticulturalists and people at large sought new expression, fresh ideas coupled with a will to experiment to effect a total change of concept from the tranquil Georgian period.

Yet the influence of the Scottish private garden system did not waver as estates were purchased by the council or gifted to the city. The glasshouses and walled gardens of some of these estates — at Gracemount, Saughton, Craigentinny, Redhall and Inch — began to produce plants and shrubs for Edinburgh's parks and gardens. But large scale production gardening is no different to other businesses and subject to the same winds of change.

New methods, new equipment, innovative ideas, greater output required more cheaply is expected nowadays — and in 1982 a decision was taken to bring them all together as one major nursery centred on Inch Park, where this vast plant wonderland now handles all the city's requirements.

It is a remarkable operation. On its nine-and-a-half acre site the Inch nursery produces around a million plants a year. But so thoroughly have they embraced new methods and technology — along with their expertise and efficiency — that the whole enterprise is run by a staff of nine.

It is non-stop. Three-quarters of an acre at Inch is under glass and March is sowing time. It is one of their busiest periods of the year. Assessments are made of how many plants will be needed for Edinburgh's gardens and parks, for civic functions, major occasions that may require floral decorations like the Highland Show, the Military Tattoo, the Edinburgh Festival or other prestigious events — and then the orders roll in by the hundreds of thousands. Twenty-five thousand geraniums for June, please. Fourteen-thousand blue lobelia, 12,000 begonias, 3000 busy lizzies, 2000 pot chrysanthemums. Thank you very much. At least 250,000 bedding plants are on order and bulbs are measured by the ton. Even in the dead of winter orders roll in. Those delightful displays of red poinsettia at Christmas do not appear magically on their own — they have been ordered, potted, nursed, packed and delivered on the precise day looking their best.

After sowing, when the green shoots push upwards irresistibly, they are transferred to the growing area, where they are pricked out from their beds of coir or coconut fibre. By May, depending on the weather vagaries of an Edinburgh spring, they are out to be hardened off.

At any time in the propagation house there are around 5000 plants. In the glasshouse growing area rank upon rank are lined up in order of variety, which produces random mass colour effects beyond description. Thousands upon

A field of Gladioli for flower arrangements.

Red, yellow and pink flames of the celosia.

Concentrated effort in the work area.

Colours beyond description . . . at any time in the propagation house there are up to 5000 plants.

Watering time . . . even with automated ventilation and heating growing is thirsty work for the plants under glass.

thousands. Depending on season, marigolds, alyssum, fuchsias, bellis, polyanthus, begonias, pelargoniums, hydrangea, hypericum, skimmia, senecio, peperomia, cyclamen in purple, white and rose, rubber plants, umbrella plants, indoor conifers, Kentia palms, date palms, weeping figs and ferns. Then with pleasure favourite names are indicated: celosia, the Prince of Wales feathers; coleus, the nettle with the serrated edge in yellow, blue and green; chlorophytum, the spider plant; maranta, the prayer plant, because it curls up at night; pilea, the aluminium plant, reflecting its silver leaf; and the multi-headed chrysanthemums known as pot mums.

Mechanisation has taken over. The long hours in the old days of riddling earth to the right tilth or potting plants with painstaking care have gone. The potting machine handles 600 plants an hour. Ventilation and heating is by time clock and fully automated. The heating of the glasshouse area is by 12 gas-fired boilers. The worst of the back-breaking drudgery has been removed from this kind of large-scale plant production, but perhaps some of the old-timers' skills have been lost along the way. Yet the knowledge remains and the pleasure in watching life grow.

Working with Enable Services, the Inch is also a training centre for those with disabilities and learning difficulties. In the future, with the help of the Council, it is hoped a garden centre and interpretive centre will be established at the Inch in conjunction with them to provide further training facilities.

Twice a year the Inch nursery holds an open day when the public are invited in to look over

The star and the moons shine bright in Starbank Park at Newhaven. The star has a nautical link because it took its name from the Star of the Sea.

it and more are planned. There are demonstrations of potting-up, taking cuttings and, if asked, the staff will even pass on their green-finger secrets.

That old partnership between city and the Royal Botanic Garden has again formed a valuable arrangement in the propagation of plant material for collections within specific parks. There is ongoing joint co-operation to improve horticultural research, widen the genetic base of plant life grown in the city and, not least, to protect some threatened plant species. A further important dual role is to improve educational and horticultural teaching. Hopefully, in time, it will bring increased understanding, knowledge and pleasure. A new course in horticultural plantsmanship will further strengthen this beneficial partnership between the two old friends.

Always there is an impetus to improve, to try new methods, adopt new ideas. For example, although traditional spring and summer bedding displays have long been a feature of our public parks and gardens, there is scope, it is felt, for improvement. Essentially, bedding displays are now seen as an outdated concept, reaching back to Victorian times, but by adopting a policy of naturalisation of bulbs city wide the bright colours of spring can be provided for years to come on a scale and with a drama not previously envisaged. Since 1989 some 750,000 daffodils, narcissus and crocus have been naturalised annually throughout Edinburgh, with displays of spring bedding bulbs reduced accordingly and the Council is determined to see this pioneering work carried through to a conclusion.

The need also arises to examine summer bedding schemes in the same light. By adopting sound ecological principles, and with careful selection, herbaceous plants such as geraniums, agapanthus, kniphofia, and hemerocalis can be combined with selected woody plant material to provide a diversity of colour, texture, form and shape year long. Again with the Royal Botanic Garden, the Council has embarked on changes to summer bedding displays by tapping into the vast wealth of plant resources at the Botanic Garden. Already further new planting is being carried out in East and West Princes Street Gardens, down at Lauriston Castle and at Saughton Gardens.

But one of the most exciting developments in the future is likely to be the introduction of more colour to add floral softness to the Edinburgh cityscape by the use of indigenous flowers and selected perennial herbaceous plants on roadside verges and open spaces in the city. The potential here is enormous to paint Scotland's capital with an even fairer face.

■ Visits to the Inch Nursery can be arranged by telephoning 0131 6644135. ❁

It takes 27,000 plants to create the Floral Clock in Princes Street Gardens with its dramatic displays and intricate designs which
have delighted citizens and visitors since 1903. The design above marks the Bank of Scotland's 300th anniversary in 1995.

The spades are out with the first blackbird's top-branch spring song in Edinburgh allotments. Then the sowing and growing begins. Everything from raspberries to soya beans, mangetout to sweetcorn. Some use their allotment space as private kingdoms, others as personal sanctuaries. They all have one thing in common — a love of gardening and the outdoors. The picture was taken at Inverleith.

Brigade of Greenfingers

AT first glance they are tiny shanty towns, crazy patchworks of greens, browns, greys, exploding rainbows where the flowers grow, in squares and oblongs without apparent pattern or form.

Rising from the confusion are garden sheds that defy description. New ones, old ones, wooden ones, tin ones, tall ones, thin ones, some so long superannuated that patches have been nailed to their patches — and some are still recognisable as former bits of air raid shelters and prefabs. Edinburgh's garden allotments have to be seen to be appreciated and they appear on 22 separate sites.

The allotment community is also remarkable. Rubbing shoulders with each other's cabbage patches are bunnets and bowlers, accents of broadest Leith, lilting Highland and rounded Kent. Among their ranks there is a retired soldier, a city surgeon, a bus driver, a nurse, a postman, a zoologist, a film maker, an ex-policeman, teachers and, in general, a reflection of all of the Capital's citizenry. For all their diversity they have one common link — they enjoy gardening and the outdoors.

There are 1054 plots in Edinburgh, water is laid on and the allotment people appear on their little green patches of heaven with the sound of the first blackbird warbling a spring song. Then the activity begins! Some people dedicate themselves to produce for the table only, inspired by the age of the organic vegetable; some prefer to produce a mixture of everything from raspberries and turnips to mangetout, marrows, tomatoes and cut flowers; others like to experiment with the exotic like soya beans and sweet corn; some dig just for the fun it, for the camaraderie, the exercise and the sheer joy of working outdoors in the heart of the city. Some use their plots as private kingdoms where their rule is law, others as personal sanctuaries, places of peaceful escape where they can be alone.

The allotment movement was born out of adversity. Its roots, so to speak, can be traced back to the 18th century enclosures, but the allotments as we know them today, gathered pace in Edinburgh in the mid-19th century, after the creation of the Capital's New Town left the Old Town on its rocky ridge in a state of decay and impoverishment.

It was at this time, too, a drift of country folk to the city took place, searching for work and hopefully a better life. What they too often found was a miserable, over-crowded existence of privation, destitution, ill health, damp and insanitary living conditions. Some of the temporary encampments that sprang up at this time to cater for the overspill were even worse.

The 1867 Edinburgh Improvement Act brought much needed relief, but reformers believed the diseases that afflicted so many of the poor stemmed from lack of food and nourishment. They demanded plots should be set aside for people to grow their own vegetables.

It is worth noting that the influential landed interests were even then concerned that the development of allotments would be detrimental to their labour market.

A select committee report of 1843 stressed the desirability that profits from allotments should be viewed as assistance and not as a substitute for wages. On no account should allotments be an inducement to neglect paid labour, nor should they be tended during working hours.

The Allotments (Scotland) Act of 1892 empowered local authorities to provide and manage allotments where there was a demand for them. In Edinburgh, of course, there had long existed a well-developed gardening tradition of self-helpers, but the movement generally at this time quickly spread throughout the country.

Allotments in Edinburgh grew out of adversity. When the New Town was created it left the Old Town in a state of decay and the drift of people from the country searching for work brought further privation, ill health and destitution.

The First World War saw a further expansion of allotments as the Government encouraged the production of fruit and vegetables as part of the war effort, like the later "Dig for Victory" theme of World War Two, which had people at all levels cultivating drying greens, railway bankings, hospital grounds, even golf courses and parks like Holyrood and the Meadows in the great grow-your-own campaign that was one of the answers to the U-Boat blockade and helped to win the war. It was during these times of national crisis that the allotment movement developed clearly-defined dimensions far beyond the need to dig to alleviate poverty. Allotments, it was discovered, were a source of fun, good exercise, fresh air and a social pleasure among friends. As the Edinburgh *Evening Dispatch* put it in one of its wartime edition headlines — "Gardening is for everyone".

After the First World War, of course, some of the ground used for allotments had to be returned to the owners and some sites were needed for housing. The price of vegetables rose sharply at this time, returning troops forced jobless figures skywards, confusion reigned as some allotment sites like Holyrood and Saughton were demanded back, but some sensitive authorities were also deeply aware of their obligation to the allotment holders and, where one was lost, attempts were often made to provide another in its place.

The Allotments (Scotland) Act of 1922 confronted some of these problems and set out many of the rules governing the use, size, tenancy and rents that remain the basis for their administration today.

Yet allotment campaigns to ease hardship had to continue for many years. The mass unemployment of the 1930s saw the Scottish National Union of Allotment Holders declare they were "painfully aware . . . of the terrible burden of unemployment . . . when even the very dignity of man is being undermined".

They resolved to try to provide an interest for the jobless as well as the means to produce vegetables for needy families on their own patches. In 1931 a similar government scheme was suspended amid criticism, but a separate organisation, the Society of Friends, who also felt the development of an allotment scheme could help the unemployed, met in Edinburgh. It was decided the two groups would combine their efforts. In 1932 their joint appeal raised £1922. It enabled 2700 garden tools — spades, hoes, rakes and barrows — to be bought along with 17,000 packets of seeds and 30 tons of seed potatoes. They were distributed among 76 associations throughout Scotland. The great allotment boom was underway.

It was never easy. Many landowners turned their faces against the scheme and refused to co-operate, yet within a relatively short period Edinburgh had 350 new plots and by 1938 Scotland could boast that 52,000 jobless men had benefited from the scheme, almost a third of the unemployed total. From those fertile and lovingly-tended little green acres they grew around £180,000 worth of garden produce. By the end of World War Two it was estimated that 10 per cent of all food in Britain was grown in allotments and private gardens.

But since the 1950s the allotments in Edinburgh have had mixed fortunes. For a time social trends were against them as the enormous expansion of private cars brought the countryside closer, shopping easier and the development of convenience food also told against home-grown produce. It was during this period that the Liberton Brae allotments were lost after a spirited rearguard action on their behalf.

Yet as the 20th century closes, allotments are enjoying renewed popularity and staging a comeback. People are taking a keener interest in the environment, and the purity of the food

Creating rock gardens on top of personal air raid shelters was a novel way of selling safety during World War Two.

Growing season . . . the fertile fields in miniature in this allotment patchwork at Midmar Drive are reflected across the city.

they eat, and their own lifestyles have become much more important to them.

The Council encourages their interest and is committed to the upgrading of allotments in conjunction with the Federation of Edinburgh and District Garden and Allotment Associaton as an economic way of producing food as well as a healthy form of outdoor activity. The organic gardening movement is supported generally. In fact, Edinburgh's latest allotment area is at Redhall, the site of a former tree nursery by the Water of Leith. It provides a further 42 plots.

Nowadays allotments are even being hired by groups and the Royal Victoria Hospital, for example, has had much success with its green-fingered members. The development of retirement homes and the increasing numbers of flat-dwellers have also helped to create interest in gardens for the exercise, the fresh air and, not least, the friendship.

The allotment brigade, the Lairds of the Cabbage Patch as they have been called, are likely to ensure that in Edinburgh it is a continuing trend.   ❁

The allotments

Edinburgh's allotments are located throughout the city. They are found at: Balgreen (two fields); Cambridge Avenue; Carrick Knowe; Chesser Crescent; Claremont Park; Craigentinny; Ferry Road; Findlay Avenue/Sleigh Drive; Hawkhill Avenue; Hutchison Loan; Inverleith Park; Lady Road; Leith Links; Midmar (two fields); Pilrig Park; Prospect Bank Place; Redhall; Restalrig; Saughton Mains; Warriston; West Mains.

Where to find information

Plots at the various sites are 60ft by 30ft or 25 ft square. Information about Edinburgh's allotments is available from the Allotments Officer, Recreation Department, 17 Waterloo Place, Edinburgh, EH1 3BG. Telephone 0131 529 7847/7883.

Gardens of the past . . . this old illustrated map of Edinburgh's Canongate by Gordon of Rothiemay shows the ornate elongated gardens that once straddled this section of the Royal Mile. An echo of these days is found in Dunbar's Close Garden, next door to the Canongate Church, which is retained largely in the style of a Royal Mile 17th-century garden. Part of the old city wall is seen at the top of the map and the erection in the middle of the road is the old Canongate Cross.

Rural Edinburgh
. . . the view of the expanding city from the Rest and Be Thankful on Corstorphine Hill in the 19th century. Even the woods here had been largely cleared for industrial and agricultural use by the beginning of the 18th century. The present Corstorphine Hill woods date from plantings in the late 18th and early 19th centuries.

Green fairways

THERE have been few greater contributions to the Edinburgh environment and its greenery than the game of golf. Scotland's capital boasts 28 golf courses and six of those belong to Edinburgh. In comparison to cities of similar size this is a remarkable statistic and their quality is of a high order. It is even claimed the best views of the city are discovered with clubs on shoulder, and there can be little argument with this contention from the yellow whins on the Braid Hills No1 course, with the whole green Edinburgh panorama spread out below.

These well-managed golfing parklands provide a link to other open spaces within the city, elements of that green web stretching from the hills to the sea, which create important habitats for wildlife and help to win Edinburgh's reputa

Braids panorama . . . a game in progress but it is Arthur's Seat and the Firth of Forth beyond that catches the eye.

Lining up a putt in the old days on Leith Links, which was the golfing venue for the top people in Scotland.

From the 'Accounts of the Lord High Treasurer, under James IV', who played over Leith Links.

tion as one of the most attractive and environmentally-friendly cities in Europe.

Golf was first played in Edinburgh in the early 16th century. During the reign of King James VI, club making was a going concern and in a letter from Holyrood Palace, dated April 4, 1603, one William Mayne, burgess of Edinburgh, was "appointed maker of bows, arrows, spears and clubs to the king". The monarchs Charles I, Charles II, James IV, James VI and James VII (James II of the United Kingdom) and the Marquis of Montrose all played over the Links of Leith and in 1744, it is recorded, the city gave a silver club (cost £15) to be played for annually on April 1 by the Edinburgh Company of Golfers, the winner to be named captain for the period.

The other great golfing venue in the old days was the Links at Bruntsfield. The present Ye

Old Golf Tavern on the west side of the park on the little street called Wrights' Houses is the successor of the inn that has stood on the site for at least 200 years with possible antecedents going back to the 15th century.

It was used as a clubhouse by a number of golfing societies and Bruntsfield Links was the club course for such distinguished names as the Royal Burgess Golfing Society (founded in 1735), Royal Bruntsfield (1761), the Thistle (1815), the Honourable Company of Edinburgh (1844), the Allied Golfing Club (1856), St Leonards (1857) and the Warrender (1858).

Another popular Bruntsfield golfing tavern in the early 18th century was Rare Maggy Johnston's, where a particularly potent ale was served. Maggy even had a poem by Allan Ramsay dedicated to her, one verse of which went:

> *When in our poutch we fand some clinks,*
> *And took a turn oe'r Bruntsfield-Links*
> *After at Maggy's at Hy-jinks,*
> *We Guzzled scuds,*
> *Till we could scarce wi' hall our drinks*
> *Cast off our duds . . .*

Bruntsfield Links and Musselburgh were the favourite courses at the end of the 19th century, but the game was also played on the summit of Arthur's Seat. A famous bet in 1798, between a Mr Scales, of Leith, and Mr Smellie, a printer, saw the pair strike six golf balls each over the weathercock of St Giles' Cathedral from the south-east corner of Parliament Square some 161 feet away.

		SCOTCH	ENGLISH
1503, FEBRUARY 3: ITEM, TO THE KING			
TO PLAY AT THE GOLF WITH THE ERLE OF			
BOTHWELL	*XLIJS*	*42 SHILLINGS*	*3/6*
FEBRUARY 4: ITEM, TO GOLF CLUBBES			
AND BALLIS TO THE KING	*IXS*	*9 SHILLINGS*	*9 PENCE*
FEBRUARY 22: ITEM, XIJ GOLF BALLES TO			
THE KING	*IIJS*	*4 SHILLINGS*	*4 PENCE*
1506 ITEM, THE 28TH DAY OF JULII FOR			
IJ GOLF CLUBBES TO THE KING	*IJS*	*2 SHILLINGS*	*2 PENCE*

The great golf surge of building new courses and developing facilities, however, took place after World War One. Many can boast some of the finest clubhouses in the country.

The Council and the Scottish Golf Union are dedicated followers of European green guidelines for golf courses and both have been involved in many tree-planting schemes. Fiercely-contested tournaments, among them handsome works-of-art trophies, strong social bonds and a deep sense of responsibility for the environment make the Edinburgh golfing scene what it is.

The city-owned courses, in the safekeeping of the Council's Recreation Department, are:

Braid Hills No. 1 and 2

Located on the south side of the city off Comiston Road, Morningside. The entrance is from the Braid Hills Approach Road. The Braid Hills also provides facilities for walkers and riders. It has been a public course since 1889. With a wild and craggy aspect high above the city the Braids affords spectacular views.

Length of the Braids No. 1 18-hole course is 5,239 m/5,731 yds. Braids No 2 is also 18 holes, length 4,420 m/4,832 yds. No 1 Par 70; No. 2 Par 67.

Starting early . . . tense moment on Inverleith Park's 9-hole course as the young ones get in on the act.

Club with a view . . . Silverknowes provides enjoyable golf, sweeping views across the Forth and an attractive treescape.

Carrick Knowe

The course is situated on the west side of Edinburgh, with the entrance at the end of Glendevon Park, off Balgreen Road and was acquired from Sir James Baird in 1926. This 18-hole course is on the flat with few hazards except for some strategically-placed groups of trees and offers fine views of Corstorphine Hill. Length: 5,768 m/6299 yds. Par 71.

Craigentinny

On the north-east side of the city, between Leith and Portobello, the entrance is on Fillyside Road off Seafield Road or Craigentinny Road. It is a spacious 18-hole course of gentle slopes with striking views of Arthur's Seat and was acquired by S.R. Christie-Miller and others in 1929. Length: 4,974 m/5418 yds. Par 67.

Portobello

Situated on the east side of Edinburgh the entrance is off Stanley Street and bordered on its south side by Milton Road. It is an uncomplicated 9-hole course on the flat separated from the public park by strategically-placed young trees. Length: 2,196 m/2,405 yds. Par 35.

Silverknowes

Located to the north of the city, the entrance is opposite the roundabout for Lauriston Farm Road, Silverknowes Road and Silverknowes Parkway. In the main it is a flat 18-hole course, fringed with woodland, with a few gentle slopes and commands striking views looking across the Firth of Forth to Fife. It was acquired for the city from Matthew Mather in 1936. Length: 5,684 m/6,214 yds. Par 71.

A choice of Capital courses in profusion

Among the many other golf courses in Edinburgh and its vicinity are: Baberton, Juniper Green, Edinburgh; Bathgate; Broomieknowe, Bonnyrigg; Bruntsfield, Edinburgh; Bo'ness; Carrick Knowe, Edinburgh; Castle Park, Gifford; Craiglockhart, Edinburgh; Craigmillar Park, Edinburgh; Dalmahoy East and Dalmahoy West, by Kirknewton; Deer Park, Livingston; Duddingston, Edinburgh; Dunbar; Dundas Park (9-hole), South Queensferry; Fauldhouse; Gifford (9-hole); Glencorse, Penicuik; Gogarburn (12-hole), Newbridge; Gullane (three courses); Haddington; Harburn, West Calder; Muirfield, Gullane; Kilspindie, Aberlady; Kingsknowe, Edinburgh; Liberton, Edinburgh; Lennie Park, Turnhouse, Edinburgh; Linlithgow; Longniddry; Lothianburn, Edinburgh; Luffness, Aberlady; Monktonhall, Musselburgh; Mortonhall, Edinburgh; Murrayfield, Edinburgh; Musselburgh (9-hole); Newbattle, Dalkeith; Niddrie Castle (9-hole), Edinburgh; North Berwick East and North Berwick West; Prestonfield, Edinburgh; Prestongrange, Prestonpans; Pumpherston (9-hole); Ratho Park, Newbridge; Ravelston, Edinburgh; Royal Burgess, Barnton, Edinburgh; Swanston, Edinburgh; Torphin Hill, Edinburgh; Uphall, West Lothian; West Linton; Winterfield, Dunbar.

On the wildside

THE high perspective of Edinburgh from any of its seven hills declares immediately that the Capital's large swathes of grassland, woods and ribbons of green, the meandering green-fringed blue lines of the Water of Leith, the rivers Almond and Esk, the finer blue traces of burns like Braid and Burdiehouse or the Union Canal, blue pools like the lochs at Blackford, Duddingston and Lochend and the great blue space of the Firth of Forth to the north, studded with its islands, the Firth's rock and sandy shore all make Edinburgh and its surrounds a vast and natural habitat for wildlife — and for birds in particular.

The richness of the city's indigenous birdlife is remarkable. But what also makes it a birdwatcher's delight are the great gatherings of migratory birds that winter or stop over momentarily at Duddingston Loch or the Cramond Foreshore, including the occasional rarity.

Within half-an-hour of the city centre there are also sweeping hill and moorland wildernesses, strings of reservoirs like Threipmuir, Gladhouse, Rosebery, Portmore, Glencorse, Baddinsgill, Harperrig, West Water and this wildlife internet — above, below and on the ground — between town and country has been established for centuries.

Even in Princes Street Gardens, at the very heart of Edinburgh, at least 34 species of birds have been sighted, including sparrowhawks, redwings, spotted flycatchers, gold finches and bullfinches.

The Hermitage of Braid and Blackford Hill have 80 different kinds of birds on their list, which includes the great spotted woodpecker and green woodpecker, siskins, redpolls, pheasants, goldcrests, chiffchaffs, warblers, whitethroats, mallard and tufted duck.

In a city where there are rookeries in the centre of town, the sight of a hovering kestrel is commonplace, owls hoot at night, coots nest on the Figgate Pond within a watery long step from the bank, where traffic stops to allow a troop of ducklings to cross the road, where geese alight to graze on golf courses and even a school playing field, where larks continue to sing from on high at the Braids, where sparrowhawks hunt woodland glades, where anglers land trout from the Water of Leith with a splash, where bats and badgers forage at dusk, where foxes multiply, where a rabbit colony thrives yards from busy Princes Street on Calton Hill and grey squirrels have become one of the visitor attractions in Princes Street Gardens — indeed Edinburgh can say with conviction it is a wildlife-friendly city and it intends to keep it that way.

The Capital has its own wildlife highways in and out of the city, corridors in the air and on the ground where animals and birds live or use as access or as routes to feeding grounds.

The old, disused and overgrown railway lines have become valuable habitats for foxes, rabbits, hedgehogs, small mammals and insect life. They are the equivalent of waterways like the Union Canal and both act as wildlife "motorways" to and from the city, although the combination of parks and open spaces within Edinburgh and a steady food supply of refuse has made the concrete jungle an environment

A nesting swan at Lochend Park.

A greylag visitor to Duddingston Loch finds the weather wintry.

arguably less hostile to foxes, for example, than the open countryside beyond.

There are also time-tested and well-recognised flight paths within the city between roosting and feeding grounds and some birds like herons go the rounds of the Capital's ponds. In an attempt to safeguard the wildlife within Edinburgh's boundaries 31 sites have been identified which require special sensitivity as part of the urban conservation strategy.

The bird sanctuary of Duddingston Loch, at the foot of Arthur's Seat, is important in United Kingdom terms as a Special Scientific Interest site and provides shelter and security for a number of different visiting species, apart from its permanent inhabitants.

The loch and surrounds were gifted to the nation in 1923 by Mr W. H. Askew of Ladykirk and the Duke of Abercorn provided access land. Apart from its easily-recognisable colonies of water hens, coots, mallards and swans, less familiar web-feets are also sighted like pochards, tufted ducks, eider, teal, grebes and greylag geese along with the regular gull overnighters — herring, common and black-headed gulls, lesser-black-backs, sometimes great black-backs — which scour the city during the day and return in the evening for peace and safety. In cold spells, when the water freezes, the birds of Duddingston loch are a sight to behold.

Of course, wildlife and Edinburgh have always

Hovering kestrel . . . in Edinburgh it is a common sight.

been closely linked. It was recorded more than 200 years ago how some Old Town citizens left their walled city to gather peewits' (lapwings) eggs along the grassy ridge that is now Princes Street and George Street.

The labourers who helped to build the New Town regularly had hare soup or rabbit stew simmering on their open fires, freshly poached and potted — along with the occasional partridge — from the Earl of Moray's estate that is now Charlotte Square. Today many of the animals vigorous when Edinburgh was in its infancy are still thriving within the city.

They include: fox, badger, weasel, rabbit, hedgehog, many of the small mammals like mice, moles, voles and shrews, but in those days — and until relatively recent times —it was red and not grey squirrels that played in the trees around Bellevue and Elm Row.

The number and variety of birds found within the city is remarkable. They range from birds of prey to waders, the largest like swans, the widest wing spans like the languid heron to the smallest British birds like goldcrests and wrens; the most colourful like kingfishers and bullfinches; the noisiest like piping oystercatchers to the sweetest like singing blackbirds. The list could go on and on. Some are seldom seen, others are the garden friends we know so well.

The sight and sounds of Edinburgh's birds — above the rumble of traffic or the murmur of the Water of Leith in Colinton Dell or in an almost silent glade on Corstorphine Hill — remains a Capital delight and a note of reassurance about the state of an important part of the city's environment.

But every bird note is also a reminder that Edinburgh must stay vigilant to safeguard this priceless natural heritage. ❀

Serene family . . . swans on the lookout for visitors' scraps at the Figgate Pond with a pair of mallards ready to pick up the crumbs.

Brooding time at Figgate Pond . . . and a coot sits tight on her nest secured by branches a few feet from the bank. Her clutch of eight eggs (right) is clearly visible, but she safely hatched them all.

Visitors' favourite . . . a grey squirrel in Princes Street Gardens.

Cold feet . . . a coot on the ice at Duddingston Loch.

Wildlife Sites

Edinburgh's 31 Urban Wildlife Sites include: The Braid Burn Complex; Braidburn Valley Park; Braid Hills and Mortonhall; Brunstane Burn; Bruntsfield and Royal Burgess Golf Courses; Calton Hill and Regent Gardens; Cramond Foreshore and the coastline; Corstorphine Hill and Ravelston Woods; Craiglockhart Hill; Craigmillar Castle Hill and Hawkhill Wood; The Dells — Colinton, Craiglockhart and Woodhall Mains; the disused railway network; Drum Wood; Duddingston Golf Course; Duddingston Loch and Bawsinch; Edmonstone; Figgate Burn Park; Gogar Burn; Granton Pond; Hermitage of Braid and Blackford Hill; Holyrood Park and Meadowfield Park; Lochend Park; Niddrie Burn Complex; Redford Brae and Laverockdale; River Almond; Royal Botanic Garden; Silverknowes; Straiton Pond; Union Canal; Water of Leith; Warriston Cemetery.

Birds of the Lothians

The list of birdlife in Edinburgh recorded around its boundaries includes: blackcaps, bullfinches, chiffchaffs, chaffinches, eider duck, mallard, tufted duck, pochard, teal, wigeon, greenfinches, goldfinches, goldcrests, grey herons, grey partridge, common gulls, black-headed gulls, lesser black-backed gulls, black-backed gulls, great black-backed gulls, herring gulls, gannets, cormorants, housesparrows, hedge sparrows, linnets, mute swans, moorhens, coots, jackdaws, carrion crows, rooks, magpies, kingfishers, sparrowhawks, kestrels, longtailed tits, blue tits, coal tits, great tits, pheasants, stock doves, wood pigeons, collared doves, tawny owls, swallows, swifts, house martins, green woodpeckers, great spotted woodpeckers, oystercatchers, lapwings, plovers, curlews, sandpipers, snipe, redpolls, siskins, sky larks, spotted flycatchers, starlings, meadow pipits, pied wagtails, grey wagtails, dippers, robins, blackbirds, song thrushes, mistle thrushes, tree creepers, lesser whitethroats, whitethroats, garden warblers, willow warblers, wood warblers, wheatears, woodcock, wrens and yellowhammers.

Contacts for further information

The Countryside Ranger Service, Hermitage of Braid, 69a Braid Road, Edinburgh, EH10 6JF, Tel: 0131 447 7145.
The Scottish Ornithologists' Club, 21 Regent Terrace, Edinburgh EH7 5BT, Tel: 0131 556 6042 also welcome those with an interest in birds.
The Queensferry Museum, District Council Offices, 53 High Street, South Queensferry, EH30 9HP, Tel: 0131 331 5545 provides displays and information about the variety of wildlife along the shoreline of the Forth Estuary at South Queensferry.

A place to play

EDINBURGH'S first parks were not designed with children in mind. Even the so called "pleasure grounds" in 19th century Princes Street Gardens were aimed at keeping children almost on a lead. They must not break into a run, climb a tree, kick a ball or even emit a shout. How different today!

The process of how play has changed through the years is fascinating. It reflects social changes, a growing awareness of the needs of children, an increased appreciation of the environment, sport, popular fads and, as the years passed, even the influence of the silver screen and television.

First there was the street culture play of chasing games, girds (steel hoops) and bools (marbles) for boys and peevers (hopscotch) for girls with their chalked peever beds on pavements. Then came the stotty ba' games to rhymes and rhythms:

The big ship sails roon' the eely ally-o

Eenty teenty number nine dip yer neb in turpentine

Oor wee Jeanie wi' the nice clean peeny — guess what colour it was.

One, two, three a leerie, I saw Wallace Beery, sitting on his bumbaleerie, kissing Shirley Temple.

Better off children took the air in the old days in sedate family outings or with nanny in private parks where the notices of "Keep Off The Grass" were to be obeyed.

Looking back now, some of the park equipment in the early days was almost dangerous: the first clumsy swings on chains that nipped fingers were situated in parks and wasteland. Then there were the heavy roundabouts that turned vicious when a big boy built up speed and a wee boy was hurled off and skint his nose. "Swingboats" that sailed too high, maypoles with ropes that could strangle, three-a-side "horses" that bucked, see-saws with a nasty habit of catching unsuspecting children under the chin when one jumped off, "high up" chutes from which it was all too easy to topple on to

hard ground below were all part of the play furniture of yesteryear.

The biggest change in approach and concept has taken place in the last decade as the value of play has become better understood. Essentially, it is an important part of the learning process and children deserve a serious and a quality approach to their special play areas, which takes full advantage of the new thinking, new building materials available coupled with creative design.

Modern play areas have developed from the ground upwards. In Edinburgh soft landings are guaranteed with impact-absorbing surfaces of bark, sand and synthetic materials. Facilities are no longer aimed at children generally, but at age groups.

Toddlers, for example, have an array of child-development play attractions that make them crawl or swing, climb or jump on safe roundabouts, safe slides down the elephant's trunk and safe swings sitting on the lap of a friendly gorilla.

Highly-creative multi-play units have been developed separately for juniors so that they can scramble on a climbing frame, cross a rope ladder, slide down a fireman's pole or whizz down a giant tunnel in one all-embracing unit. There are a variety of these in different shapes and sizes and names. For example, you will find the "Activator Sigma" at the Meadows or "Activator Delta" out at Dumbiedykes — and the kids love them.

Some of these units have been specially designed and graded for older children, like the Commando "Flying Angels", with their ropes and old car tyres that enable youngsters to pull them into position before making a Tarzan-like descent from one level to another and some of the modern climbing frames would not look out of place on an army assault course.

The emphasis is on fun and creativity and imagination and safety and in recent years they have added a new dimension to children's play areas across the city. ❀

Swing high . . . on the east Meadows at the turn of the century while some fathers enjoy a game of bowls in the background.

Look at me! A high climber on the rope pyramid at Leith Links wonders how he is to return to earth with a safe landing. The frame is typical of the new breed of adventure equipment.

It's got everything . . . a chute, a tunnel, a climb and a castle all in a single piece of equipment in West Princes Street Gardens.

Enter Fort Saughton for fun and adventure . . . behind the wooden stockade Saughton Park's creative play area is in full swing with attractions for children of all ages.

The best in Scotland . . . King George V Park at Eyre Place was voted "Scottish Playground of the Year" in 1989.

Where Edinburgh's play areas are located

Advanced creative play equipment can be found at:

Camus Park

Carlowrie Crescent, Dalmeny

Clermiston Park

Colinton Mains Park

Dalmeny Street

Davidson's Mains Park

Dumbiedykes Road

Dundas Park, South Queensferry

Fort Saughton, Saughton Park

Gracemount Leisure Centre

Inverleith Park

Joppa Quarry park

Keddie Gardens

Kingsknowe

King George V Park, Eyre Place

King George V Park, South Queensferry

Leith Links

Meadows East

Meadows West

Meadows Toddlers

Montgomery Street

Morningside Park

Mount Lodge, Portobello

Northfield Community Centre

Pilrig Park

Pilton Park East

Pilton Park West

Princes Street Gardens West

Ravelston Park

Sighthill Park

Spylaw Park

St Margaret's Park, Corstorphine

Straiton Place, Portobello

Victoria Park

White Park, Gorgie

Across the whole of Edinburgh, in recreation grounds, parks or street open spaces, play areas with imaginative and modern play equipment have been installed. They can be found at:

Barony Place play area

Dumbryden play area

Duff Street play area

Easter Drylaw Drive Recreation Ground

Falcon Gardens play area

Fernieside Recreation Ground

Gilmerton Recreation Ground

Henderson Gardens play area

Keddie Gardens play area

Liberton Recreation Ground

Meadowbank Recreation Ground

Seafield Recreation Ground

Stenhouse Place east play area

Towerbank play area

Pentland View play area, Currie

Muirwood Road play area, Currie

Dolphin Gardens play area, Currie

Craig Park Terrace play area, Ratho

Hillwood Terrace play area,

Ratho Station

Glasgow Road Recreation Ground, Ratho Station

Manse Road play area, Kirkliston

Maitland Hogg Lane play area, Kirkliston

Gateside play area, Kirkliston

Inchcolm Terrace play area, South Queensferry

The Vennel play area, South Queensferry

Having a great time . . . postcards from the past

Calton Hill about 100 years ago.

Scott Monument around 1900.

The Scottish American War Memorial drawn by Andrew Allan.

As it was on Blackford Hill

. . . and as it is today

Then and now . . . the almost treeless entrance to Blackford Hill about 1900 and the same scene today.

Fair city . . . and Edinburgh's objective for the next millennium is to secure its existing natural treasures for citizens and visitors in perpetuity, control change positively and allow the city to flourish as a Capital of green innovation and quality.

Beyond the millennium

THE largest land owners in Scotland's capital are its citizens. This fact is not always appreciated or understood. On their behalf over 4,000 acres of parks and open spaces, including 900 acres of woodland, are in the safe keeping of the Council.

They are precious green acres, but not easy to administer or manage, particularly in difficult financial times. Their wellbeing for the citizens and the city has never been of greater importance as Edinburgh enters the new millennium in what has been a century of change.

At the beginning of the 20th century, an army of gardeners was available for deployment throughout Edinburgh. In 1914 there were 37 public parks, gardens and open spaces listed under the city's charge. Their total annual labour cost was £6,435. By 1933 there were 48 parks with an expenditure of £76,000. Now there are more than 150 listed parks and play areas. The cost approaches £6 million.

The days of cheap labour, unsophisticated management style and crude, inexpensive park equipment have gone for ever at a time when their management has never been more exacting or public expectation more demanding.

Perhaps it is only in recent times a proper perspective of the Edinburgh environment and its future can be taken. It is assessed nowadays in the light of the latest flow of global scientific information filtered by discussion and the increased concern of people world-wide about their local surroundings and quality of life.

Never before have green issues been placed so highly on the public's agenda or taken more seriously by those who can influence direction, including Edinburgh Councillors, the Recreation Department's Parks Division management team and professionals from other Council departments.

In this respect, citizens and the local authority together have helped to make Edinburgh one of the leaders in the green field. Edinburgh is firmly committed to the principles set out in the 1992 Earth Summit in Rio de Janeiro known as "Agenda 21", which is supported by both the British Government and the European Commission.

On this international platform, Edinburgh's objective is to achieve a "sustainable city" — clean, healthy, safe, pleasant, an accessible-to-all-city, giving an improved quality of life, with the ability and courage to take independent decisions locally in Edinburgh's best interests.

The future of Edinburgh's local authority parks, woodlands, wildlife and open spaces is seen as an integral part of that strategy and by persuasion and example less enlightened members of the private sector can also be influenced.

What the future now holds is speculation. For a city of its size — of any size — Scotland's capital, as we have seen, has unique and exceptional open green spaces and wildlife habitats within its boundaries that are not only acclaimed for the beauty of the landscape they form but are also of enormous value to economic development and tourism. Edinburgh's first priority in the new millennium is to secure this existing city treasure as an important resource for both citizens and visitors in perpetuity.

It is with this objective in mind that the city has been seen to hold the line of its Green Belt against a number of commercial predators and, by its declared intentions and actions, no one can therefore be left in doubt about Edinburgh's commitment to the environment. The continuing strategy of the city is to develop and enhance its green legacy for the benefit of all.

Already, in recent years, we have seen how the words have been put into practice. In partnership with Scottish National Heritage and other local councils, ways to improve 40,000 acres of Green Belt, both publicly and privately owned land around the perimeter of the Capital, is being actively pursued by the Edinburgh Green Belt Trust. Important geological sites like

Torphin, Craigleith quarries, Dreghorn Spur and Craigmillar Castle are under protection. Significant wildlife sites like Arthur's Seat, Duddingston Loch, the Forth shoreline, Corstorphine Hill, Cammo, the Braids, Blackford Hill, Seafield, the Meadows Yards and, out of town, by Ratho and Kirkliston, similarly have been given protection and actively promoted with the help of local involvement. Trees remain one of Edinburgh's most attractive features and action has been taken through the Urban Forestry Strategy to ensure they continue to clothe the city delightfully. Yet trees should not be regarded in isolation simply as individual objects, but as part of and representative of a complex eco-system and man's spiritual relationship with his environment. By preservation orders, conservation areas and commemorative tree schemes Edinburgh's woodlands, parks and many of its streets are being put on a secure footing for the future — in spite of the ravages of Dutch Elm Disease.

Wisely, the city has chosen to work in partnerships with other agencies and organisations with similar environmental aspirations.

Valuable joint work has been undertaken with such partners as Scottish Natural Heritage, Lothian and Edinburgh Enterprise Limited, the Scottish Wildlife Trust, the Scottish Countryside Ranger Association, the private sector with particular assistance from Kwik-Fit, the Scottish Conservation Projects Trust, Historic Scotland, the Forestry Authority and local groups like the Cockburn Association, Water of Leith Conservation Trust, the Forth Estuary Forum Management Group or the Lothian Branch of the Farming and Wildlife

Tom Farmer of Kwik-Fit gave valuable service to Princes Street Gardens by paying for the replacement of semi-mature trees after the ravages of Dutch Elm Disease. His act of generosity lessened the visual effect caused by the loss of the elms.

Advisory Group. The Royal Botanic Garden continues as one of the city's most valued and long-standing friends. The involvement with such groups and organisations may be little or large, but their influence and impact can be crucial. For example, Scottish Natural Heritage's support on the Braid Hills area of the city alone has involved work on the bridle path, part-funding of the attractive Braid Hills indicator, 50 per cent funding of the Countryside Ranger Service and Coates Crescent and Atholl Crescent were upgraded in 1992 in conjunction with Lothian and Edinburgh Enterprise Limited.

With Edinburgh's resolve to improve and develop the environment and with such committed partners, the future can begin to take a shape. But entering the new millennium calls for the challenge of new ideas and fresh approaches. Just as that visionary Patrick Geddes beheld the dawn of the 20th century, and met it with new concepts, so must Edinburgh — and the world for that matter — meet the 21st.

It was Geddes who understood that too many city dwellers were becoming remote from the "real" world — of hills, trees, fields, moors and forests and their health and wellbeing, he contended, were fundamentally linked with nature's salve found in the quiet green places where people could breathe and think and relax. In essence it was a vision of taking people back to their roots by providing countryside within a townscape.

Time moves on. Geddes could not have envisaged the ease of access to the Scottish countryside brought by the motor car or the speed of people movement to remote and exotic parts of the world made possible by flight. Yet his concept of a rich green city geared to the needs of all its people remains as relevant as ever — and that remains Edinburgh's policy for the future of the Capital.

So in this light what changes can be expected as Edinburgh approaches the 21st century?

A greater sense of public ownership of Edinburgh's present green spaces — the parks, woodlands, walkways and green corners of the city — will be further encouraged. In this respect, perhaps more public consultation now takes place than ever before. But with a sense of personal ownership acknowledged, hopefully there will also develop more involvement by the public, more inclination to have a say in how the city's countryside within can best be run and tailored to meet the needs and pleasures of Edinburgh's citizens. The excellent work done with schools and children's groups by the Countryside Rangers is one of the foundations for the future.

Hopefully, too, with fingers crossed, it may have a side benefit — some of those who give Edinburgh's green acres such scant regard that they will hack down its trees, destroy its flowers, attack its wildlife and even damage the play

Autumn in Edinburgh . . . in the future trees will be carefully selected to turn the Capital into a city of autumn splendour as a joy for both citizens and visitors.

areas of small children, will be encouraged to be more responsible by their more enlightened peers or parents.

The shape of things to come in Edinburgh, sooner or later, will see a stronger fusion between existing green areas within the city. The grand concept is a great green web between parks and open space, by walkways or cycle-ways, devoid of traffic, among trees or grass-land and wildlife corridors, by burn, riverside or the old railways routes right across the face of Edinburgh, from the Pentland Hills to the sea.

Much of that web is already in place. Although new green linkages would have to be created, a downwards glance from the heights of the Braids confirms the entire feasibility — and its desirability.

As interest in the environment continues to grow, projected as it is in schools and, as we have seen, with the help of the city's own Countryside Ranger Service, so there is likely to be increased demand for more information —about the Edinburgh story, the creation of its landscape by volcanic beginnings, the past events and people who have fashioned the city, its trees and wildlife, mammals and insects, bushes, flowers, plants and their interaction. This kind of information is in demand now and in future it is likely to be met by an increase in

visitor and interpretive centres at strategic sites throughout the city. One of those sites is likely to be at Cramond, where countryside meets the sea, where important Roman and medieval set-tlements were once located, and where wading birds can be studied in their thousands along the Forth shoreline.

Underpasses in the future may link Princes Street Gardens with the National Gallery and the Royal Scottish Academy on the Mound Square as well as with other elements of the green web network.

The crowning glory of the Edinburgh landscape will remain its trees.

Nowhere now in the city is more than a few hundred yards from a tree or a green space. Yet beyond the millennium there will be many, many more trees. Trees everywhere — on streets, in parks, on derelict ground, in odd neuks of the city, the right tree in the right place, trees that can be left to develop naturally, perhaps even a new tree for every citizen. It will create a multi-aged urban forest of diverse species that will be a living asset to the whole community. Chosen carefully, Edinburgh's trees can create a city of dramatic autumn splendour as a foil to the tender pastel greens of late May and June so that people will come from far and near to see Scotland's capital in its crimson and gold glory.

Nowhere in the Capital is more than a few hundred yards from a tree or a green space, but in the future there will be many more trees everywhere, the creation of a new urban forest, perhaps a new tree for every citizen.

Trees will form one of the attractions of the city's Green Belt. A new city forest will appear with woodland walks and picnic areas.

Trees will feature strongly in new country parks centred around Craigmillar Castle and at Burdiehouse, which will be the link between the fringes of city and the open country beyond. The Craigmillar Castle project when completed will focus on one of Scotland's most historic castles, where Mary, Queen of Scots recovered after the horror of witnessing Rizzio's murder at Holyrood. The historic interplay between Craigmillar Castle, Holyrood and Edinburgh Castle is obvious from its sweeping views across the city.

This new park of around 170 acres will mean the creation of an education centre, entertainment facilities, a visitor centre, a cafe and banqueting suite supplying produce grown on a medieval farm and orchard. A market place and shop selling organic produce and crafts will be sited near the castle.

It will be a centre for walking and nature trails and on the cycleway network. It has the potential of being one of the most exciting new country parks in Scotland and it is the shape of things to come.

Of course, new open space within the Capital will also be created, particularly in Edinburgh's inner city estates, where environment has not always been a top priority. It is a failing from the past that has now been well recognised and once again trees will be a feature of a progressive programme already underway.

The Inch complex, that centre of horticultural excellence that feeds the flower and shrub beds of the city, will be given greater public access with educational and interpretive facilities and a focus on training for those with disabilities and learning difficulties.

Sixty years ago wallflowers were used extensively to adorn Edinburgh parks and there was once a plan to clad the Salisbury Crags with them. In the future the addition of flowering plants based on sound ecological principles will make their own colourful impact.

Once again street art will come into its own, spread throughout the city, with murals and sculptures in underpasses and on road roundabouts, embankments and walkways.

As part of that green commitment, with the help of the Royal Botanic Garden, there are proposals to develop a living collection of tree species, indigenous trees and exotics gathered from around the world, as a permanent and important arboretum as another city showpiece for citizens and visitors as well as biologists and scientists. At maturity, well into the next century, another Edinburgh attraction will be in place. The Royal Botanic Garden, of course, is already well known for its research and scientific work around the world, but the Council is also exporting its expertise internationally.

The ongoing assistance given to the Kiev City State administration in developing new skills in the upkeep of their parks, open spaces, nurseries, outdoor recreation, trees and forests has been of major benefit in the wake of the Chernobyl disaster and the changes within their society.

This outstretched hand of friendship, funded by the British Government's Foreign and Commonwealth Office, in what amounts to a technical twinning between Edinburgh and Kiev, has been greatly appreciated and stems directly from the Capital's enviable record in conservation and environmental projects.

It is also a two-way benefit, a forum for discussion and exchanges of ideas, which is part of the Council's policy of innovative twinning around the world. In the future it is a role that can be expanded with its dividends in the medium and long term.

Existing open space within the Capital will come under even closer scrutiny to maximise its potential. It will be carried out with great sensitivity because Edinburgh demands no less. The Calton Hill will be top of the list.

Even when Edinburgh first expanded outside its defensive wall and that extraordinary period when Scottish genius flowered during the "Enlightenment", Calton Hill was singled out as a symbolic site to reflect everything glorious during the city's remarkable classical development in the second half of the 18th century.

This inspirational little hill a few hundred yards from Princes Street, with its dramatic views across the city, with so many historic and spiritual associations with poets, writers, architects, astronomers, visionaries and philosophers, has hardly altered in almost 170 years.

An amphitheatre for the Calton Hill was suggested in development plans of more than a century ago, but nothing came of it for fear of ruining that classical summit. Some will say such inaction is a virtue in Edinburgh terms, but there have been no substantial improvements in all that time or tangible new thinking brought to bear upon what is unquestionably one of the Capital's most prominent and historic landmarks of huge potential — and now Calton Hill is losing its lustre.

It is not a matter of radical change that is required, more a preservation, refurbishment and celebration of what already exists, but a new appraisal of Calton Hill's worth and potential is urgent. It deserves the same focus as Edinburgh Castle or Holyrood House. In the future it will be received.

Princes Street Gardens will change. As the floral fulcrum of the city's green web, it will be redesigned and its use rethought, maybe with the old Nor' Loch or the once-suggested canal returned as a water feature to reflect the Castle above. With modern technology and engineering skills anything is possible. Of course, it will

properly generate much public debate. Already
suggestions have been floated that Princes
Street Gardens be kept largely as city gardens,
or used for an environmental exhibition centre
or an educational resource, an opera house or
amphitheatre for concerts or recitals — or (and
someone sometime is certain to suggest it) turn
Princes Street Gardens into a hyper pleasure
ground like Tivoli Gardens in Copenhagen.
Then the sparks will fly!

The Meadows will also be rethought, almost
certainly with a greater emphasis on its role as a
place for exhibitions, entertainment and passive
recreation in the light of the village development which will eventually be built on the old
Edinburgh Royal Infirmary site.

There will be much new tree planting to replace
the large population of doomed elms that are
still one of the Meadows' pleasures. The
Meadows will emerge with new importance and
status.

The ways in which the city's parks, open spaces
and woodlands are maintained will change.
Traditional environmentally-friendly methods
must be re-learned and re-introduced, coupled
with sound economic commonsense. Not only
will it lead to a reduction in energy use, but
more importantly it will mean maintainance
techniques in the future will be fully in sympa-
thy with the latest environmental and conservation thinking. For example, already a ban on all
pesticides used on city parks is envisaged as
Edinburgh seeks ways to introduce self-sustain-
ing solutions.

The city, of course, is noted for its thriving
wildlife within — foxes, badgers, rabbits,
hawks, owls, a vast variey of ducks, geese and
waders along the Forth. Yet with the continuing
and progressive simulation of countryside conditions throughout the Capital — more trees,
more woodlands, more wilderness areas — the
future can bring untold benefits in the richness
of the city's wildlife and, in turn, a joy for citizens and visitors.

In so many directions there are more changes,
new ideas for improvement, more new developments, more exciting new concepts than at any
time since the New Town was built some 200
years ago. The quality of the ideas and the pur-
suance of them will be judged in the next millennium. That is why Edinburgh will proceed
sensitively, employing full consultation with
citizens, advisory and watchdog organisations
and all interested parties. The sensible way
ahead is to hear all sides — and then act.

Perhaps today we are too rooted in the present
to envisage the Edinburgh of 50 years and more
ahead or the issues that will confront the city
then. Inevitably, Edinburgh will change — and
must change. The city's objective is to control
the change and allow Edinburgh to flourish
with distinction as a Capital of green innovation
and quality.   ✿

Colour . . . new impact from city-wide naturalisation of spring bulbs.

Sculpture . . . street art will once again come into its own.

Calton Hill . . . its lustre will be restored.

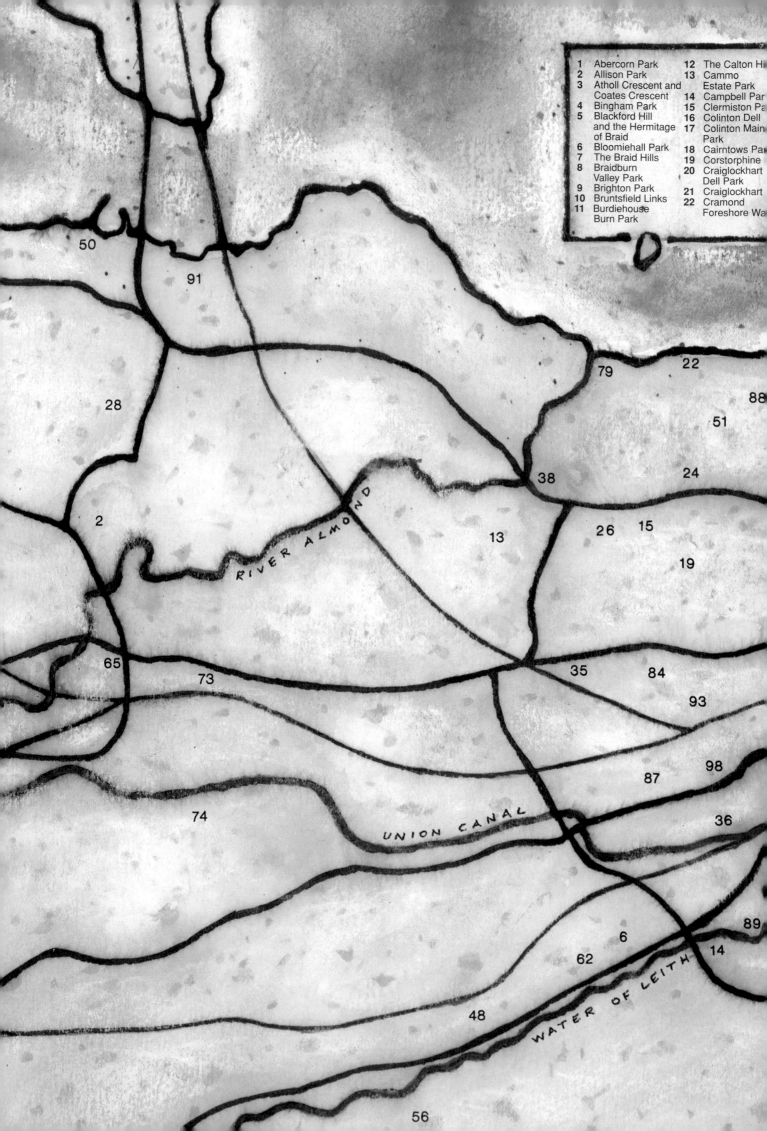

50

91

28

2

RIVER ALMOND

79   22

88

51

38   24

26 15

13

19

65

73

35   84

93

98

87

74

36

UNION CANAL

6

89

62   14

48

WATER OF LEITH

56

Colours of Edinburgh

Above Gorse on the Salisbury Crags

Below Autumn rowans at Jewel Park.

The Council is indebted _____ ____rs for sponsoring the launch of this book